EGO 8

MY BOOKS

★

Novels

RESPONSIBILITY
BLESSED ARE THE RICH
GEMEL IN LONDON

Belles-lettres

L. OF C. (LINES OF COMMUNICATION)
FANTASIES AND IMPROMPTUS
WHITE HORSE AND RED LION
ON AN ENGLISH SCREEN
AGATE'S FOLLY
THE COMMON TOUCH
KINGDOMS FOR HORSES
BAD MANNERS
EXPRESS AND ADMIRABLE
THURSDAYS AND FRIDAYS
NOBLESSE OBLIGE
AROUND CINEMAS

Essays of the Theatre

BUZZ, BUZZ!
ALARUMS AND EXCURSIONS
AT HALF-PAST EIGHT
THE CONTEMPORARY THEATRE, 1923
THE CONTEMPORARY THEATRE, 1924
THE CONTEMPORARY THEATRE, 1925
THE CONTEMPORARY THEATRE, 1926
A SHORT VIEW OF THE ENGLISH STAGE
PLAYGOING
THEIR HOUR UPON THE STAGE
MY THEATRE TALKS
FIRST NIGHTS
MORE FIRST NIGHTS
THE AMAZING THEATRE
THESE WERE ACTORS
BRIEF CHRONICLES
RED-LETTER NIGHTS
IMMOMENT TOYS

Anthologies

THE ENGLISH DRAMATIC CRITICS, 1660–1932
SPEAK FOR ENGLAND
HERE'S RICHNESS!

Biography

RACHEL

Autobiography

EGO
EGO 2
EGO 3
EGO 4
EGO 5
EGO 6
EGO 7

Photo Angus McBean

The Author

Fr.

EGO 8

CONTINUING THE AUTOBIOGRAPHY OF

JAMES AGATE

It is a man's own fault, it is from want of use, if his mind grows torpid in old age.

Dr Johnson

GEORGE G. HARRAP AND COMPANY LTD.
LONDON SYDNEY TORONTO BOMBAY

TO

GEORGE LYTTELTON

First published 1947
by George G. Harrap & Co. Ltd.
182 High Holborn, London, W.C.1

Reprinted 1948

THIS BOOK IS PRODUCED IN
COMPLETE CONFORMITY WITH THE
AUTHORIZED ECONOMY STANDARDS

Composed in Scotch Roman type and printed by Morrison & Gibb, Ltd. London and Edinburgh
Made in Great Britain

ILLUSTRATIONS

1945

Jan. 1 *Monday.* My American friend, Sergeant Thomas Quinn Curtiss, saw the New Year in with me. After which we called on Elliot Mason, who lives above. Jolly party, *and nothing said about the theatre.*

My mail:

Card from Brother Mycroft. This is a reproduction of the seventeenth-century painter Bloemaert's "St John Preaching." Can the twentieth-century artist do as movingly *in his period*? I don't believe it. I am thinking of Stanley Spencer's picture of a doll-like Hitler, with a moustache which has obviously come off one of the spectators' dresses, separating a couple of fighting swans.

New Year cards from George Robey, Gillie Potter, Sid Field, Tod Slaughter, Frances Day, Naughton and Gold.

Diatribe from Spalding, beginning:

> MY DEAR JAMES AGATE,
>
> I have read many articles by you on books, films, and plays. I cannot remember one substantial thing you have ever said, but I can recall many instances when you were guilty of writing the greatest nonsense. I have disliked you fairly intensely for about twelve years—for your well-fed complacency and jangling wit, for the utterly mercenary way in which you have maintained your reputation as a critic, and for your medieval conception of butchers and plumbers concentrating exclusively on plumbing and butchering, and not taking it upon themselves to practise as poets and playwrights. I recently returned from Burma, to find your articles still prominently featured in the *Express*—damn' great headlines vulgar as hell, and nasty little Agatean elves pottering up and down the columns. . . .

A great deal of abuse follows, and suddenly I read:

> Why do you and I love horses? Because their necks are "clothed with thunder," and because the hindquarters of a good-class Hackney are as noble a work of art as anything you will find in the animal or vegetable kingdoms.

Letter from Kensington: "In this war, as in the last, many a man carried Shakespeare in the pocket of his tunic, others perhaps the Bible, and I heard of a case where a man was found in a rubber dinghy with a copy of *Ego* 5. Unfortunately he was dead when found. . . ." Am pondering the implications of this when Jock walks in with a paper-bound, unrevised proof of *Specimens of English Dramatic Criticism: XVIIth–XXth Centuries*, presently to be published by the Oxford University Press in the World's Classics series. He points out that on pages 304 and 306 my article on Edith Evans in *The Way of the World* is attributed to Hubert Griffith! I am getting het-up about this when he tells me he 'phoned the publishers, and was in time.

My one and only New Year resolution: to cultivate equanimity. Rupert Brooke's "And that unhoped serene that men call age" is one thing. Unhoped excitability is a very different thing. I know all about nerves-cum-wind. Nerves-minus-wind is something I don't understand and don't like. To ask the chemist for minestrone when I mean riddobron; to be furious because the horse in Sir George White's statue in Portland Place is looking to his left instead of to his front; to want my own way about everything, and when I don't get it yell like a baby—all this argues either brain-fag or the approach of second childhood. Here, then, is my New Year resolution: TO DO THE WORK OF TWO MEN INSTEAD OF THREE. (Leo insists on typing "the work of two men instead of *one*"!) I am determined that my equableness shall have an active as well as a passive side. Recently I read Cecil Day Lewis's *Poetry for You*, written to explain poetry to boys and girls. In the course of this he praises some lines by Spender:

> More beautiful and soft than any moth
> With burring furred antennæ feeling its huge path
> Through dusk, the air-liner with shut-off engines
> Glides over suburbs . . .

I am determined to go about the flat murmuring this, and to believe that modern youth gets the same thrill that I did when, as a fourteen-year-old, I read how the lover in *Maud*

> . . . arose, and all by myself in my own dark garden ground,
> Listening now to the tide in its broad-flung shipwrecking roar,
> Now to the scream of a madden'd beach dragg'd down by the wave,
> Walk'd in a wintry wind by a ghastly glimmer, and found
> The shining daffodil dead, and Orion low in his grave.

To equanimity and equableness I am resolved to add whatever may be the opposite of umbrage, and to be unpeeved because Richard Church in his broadcast review of the books of 1944 makes no mention of *Ego* 6. Pavia says, "Cheer up, James. Do you suppose that in 1865 Wagner would have heard one word about *Tristan*? Not on your life. Auber, Gounod, Verdi, yes, but . . ."

In the meantime here is No. 1 of my new series, to be entitled *Cocasseries*. (**Cocasse,** *adj., pop.*: Plaisant, ridicule.)

Conversation at the Café Royal:

YOUNG BLOOMSBURYITE. To tell you the truth, I'm blaze about the theatre.

J. A. Come, that's interesting. One of our intellectuals on fire about the theatre. My dear fellow, that's very, very reassuring.

Y. B. (*coldly*). You don't get it. I'm *blaze* about the theatre. Fed-up. French, you know.

Jan. 2 *Tuesday.* Anatole France used to write in ladies' albums: "What is the good of your forgetting me, dear lady, since I shall ever remember you?" How, even if I want, shall I forget Sarah, others ever and ever reminding me? Esmé Percy sends me a *carte postale* of S. as Phèdre addressing a human bundle. On the reverse side I find in Esmé's best French:

Qui est celle à genoux? Est-ce Seylor? Non! Est-ce Dufrène? Non! Non! C'est le théâtre entier à genoux.

ESMÉ

My own view is that it is Œnone, Phèdre's "nourrice et confidente," having the famous "C'est toi qui l'as nommé!" hurled at her.

By the same post arrives this from Maurice Baring:

Beaufort Castle
Beauly
Inverness
29.12.44

DEAR J. A.,

It took me a year to get *Ego* 6, and a little more than a day to read it. It Oliver Twisted me.

P. 125. I am puzzled about *Le Sphinx*. I thought it was one of the plays included in the repertory of the Comédie Française, which the management of the Gaiety Theatre announced in a little pamphlet before the season opened in London in 1879. I possess or used to possess this pamphlet; I think it escaped blitzing and is stored. Some of the "fixtures" were cancelled or altered owing to the furore which Sarah aroused and the temperamental tantrums in which she indulged. But I thought *Le Sphinx* (a play which I never saw, but which I afterwards read) was a drawing-room drama by Octave Feuillet, with some poison in it, in which S. was cast for second fiddle to Croizette and as usual made the second fiddle more important than the first. But I may be mixing it up with another play. I also have a vague recollection of reading that one of the two, S. or C., made a sensation by turning green under the effects of poison in the death scene. This was in Paris. If I am right and the play is by Feuillet it would be frightfully interesting to get hold of the 1882 cast and see which fiddle Sarah chose when she was free of the trammels of the Comédie.

Happy New Year. Good Luck to *Ego* 7.

Yours,
M. BARING

Am replying :

Le Sphinx is by Octave Feuillet, and all I know about it is that the third act takes place in a clearing in a forest. Here is Sarah on another piece by Feuillet produced the previous year. This was called *Dalila.*

" Perrin fit la plus cocasse des distributions : il me donna le rôle de Dalila, la méchante brune et féroce princesse, et donna à Sophie Croizette la blonde et idéale jeune fille mourante.

" La pièce culbuta sous cette étrange distribution. Je forçai ma nature pour paraître l'altière et voluptueuse sirène ; je bourrai mon corsage d'ouate et les hanches de ma jupe avec du crin ; mais je gardai mon petit facies maigre et douloureux.

" Croizette fut obligée de comprimer les avantages de son buste, sous la pression de bandes qui l'oppressaient et l'étouffaient ; mais elle garda sa jolie figure pleine aux jolies fossettes.

" Je fus obligée de grossir ma voix, elle d'éteindre la sienne. Enfin c'était absurde."

Sarah goes on to say how two clans quickly formed themselves—the Croizettistes and the Bernhardtistes. The first was composed of " banquiers et tous les congestionnés." As for the second, S. writes : " J'avais pour moi tous les artistes, les étudiants, les mourants, et les ratés." I don't think S. has ever been given enough credit for her sense of humour.

Jan. 3 *Wednesday.* From a letter :

I am stationed in Uttoxeter. How applicable is the G.I.'s description of Bedford—a cemetery with traffic lights. Except that there are no traffic lights in Uttoxeter ! . . . Your various *Ego's* remind me of a woman I was friendly with some years ago. If I had agreed with her for five consecutive minutes, or if she had done anything expected of her, I should have been bored.

Jan. 4 *Thursday.* Dipping into Emil Ludwig's *Beethoven : the Life of a Conqueror*, I find this on the G major Piano Concerto :

At the beginning the piano emerges gently from dreams ; this is truly Beethoven improvising. Two romantic themes, renunciation and hope, are gradually developed. When, after an orchestral

Sarah in "Phèdre"

> interlude, the piano is heard again solo, it is as if a butterfly rose ecstatically from its cocoon. There are no fortissimos here, and when the call to new adventures sounds, the butterfly sinks back, dreaming. The whole thing is wrapped in dark-red velvet. . . .

And about the C minor Concerto, that it begins with

> stormy scale passages three octaves long, like a roaring lion appearing suddenly with threatening mien in the midst of the orchestra.

I have nothing with all this stuff about cocoons, red velvet, and roaring lions. Presently I read, " Beethoven dedicated his adagios to women." And I say that the man who can read sex into the slow movements of the Hammerklavier Sonata and the Ninth Symphony would believe that Wagner's Venusberg music is a Hymn to Chastity ! Next I read that in the F major Rasoumowsky Quartet " the 'cello continues to exude platonic wisdom." Feeling that this amateur has exuded enough nonsense, I open the window and neatly drop his book on to a passing lorry's tarpaulin'd top.

Jan. 5 *Friday.* In a letter from George Lyttelton :

> I am glad to see you are or have been in *Martin Chuzzlewit*—my favourite of the whole lot. How the Yanks ever forgave it I can't imagine. " When our people's frills is out they're starched up pretty stiff." But I shudder to think what the effect will be " on what we call our feelings " or rather your feelings, when with the most tedious pedantry I take my pen and change " Toopit " in your letter to " Toppit " !

Whereupon I drop everything to write :

*Queen Alexandra Mansions, W.C.*2
January 5*th*, 1945

DEAR GEORGE LYTTELTON,

Have we started something ? You elect for " Toppit." In this you are in agreement with the *Dickens Encyclopædia.* Also with the Everyman edition. On the other hand, the Memorial edition published by Chapman and Hall prefers an extra " t " so that the name becomes " Toppitt." As against these the Imperial Edition published by the Gresham Publishing Company has " Toopit." I am inclined to agree with the last. Miss Codger was the lady who wore on her forehead " a massive cameo, in size and shape like the raspberry tart which is ordinarily sold for a penny, representing on its front the Capitol at Washington." It was Miss Toopit who held that " Mind and matter glide swift into the vortex of immensity." About this lady we are told only that she " wore a brown wig of uncommon size." Isn't it reasonable to suppose a connection between " Toopit " and " toupet " ? Dickens is full of evocative names — Barnacle, Cheeryble, Mutanhed, Snuphanuph, Turveydrop, Veneering, Verisopht. No, if " Toopit " is a printer's error I shall maintain that for once the printer erred on the right side. You might let me know your views.

No more for now.

Ever,
JAMES AGATE

Jan. 6 *Saturday.* A lady has sent me four volumes of *The London Stage*, published in 1824–27 and containing close on two hundred " of the most reputed Tragedies, Comedies, Operas, Melo-Dramas, Farces and Interludes, as performed at the Theatres Royal." A wonderful mine which I have spent most of the day skimming—and that is as good English as some of these old playwrights use. They seem to have had no sense of bathos. Thus, in Arthur Murphy's tragedy, *The Orphan of China*, Etan, entering from the tomb, says :

Each step I move,
A deeper horror sits on all the tombs ;
The shrines look pale around ; each altar shakes,
Conscious of some important crisis.

Infelicities abound, as when, in Southerne's play, Oroonoko says :

I marry'd her : and, though my country's custom
Indulg'd the privilege of many wives,
I swore myself never to know but her.
O, my Imoinda ! *But it could not last.*

Plagiarism, it seems, was rife, even Congreve stooping to it. Almeria, in *The Mourning Bride*, mistaking the body of Zara, who has drunk poison, for that of Alphonso, alias Osmyn, says :

Oh ! noble thirst ! yet greedy, to drink all.

Congreve, of all people, must have known that he was filching Juliet's

O churl ! drunk all, and left no friendly drop
To help me after ?

and ruining it.

Continuing to dip, I discover the original of the two lines quoted by John Thurtell in his speech in his own defence at the end of his trial for the murder of William Weare. *The Newgate Calendar* gives the lines as

The flesh will quiver where the pincers tear,
The blood will follow where the knife is driven.

They are from Edward Young's *The Revenge*, and Thurtell in his agitation got them in the wrong order.

Jan. 7 *Sunday.* Again to G. L.:

*Queen Alexandra Mansions, W.C.*2
January 7th, 1945

DEAR GEORGE LYTTELTON,

Your last letter and a mishap in to-day's *S.T.* have combined to tell me that I am the first sufferer from Agate's disease, or proof-reader's eye. The *S.T.*? Simply that I am made to say: "The real reason I want to see this play [*Venice Preserved*] for myself is that I want to decide whether it is or is not nonsense." You realise that "for myself" should come after the word "decide." The trouble is my old friend Leo, who has developed Pavia's disease, or transpositional mania.

Going back to my own trouble, I sat up late last night reading George Moore's *Impressions and Opinions*. But it teems with errors, apart from the appalling French! I can understand Poor Jo calling Mr Snagsby "Mr Sangsby." But why must Poor George, in a note on Ibsen's *Ghosts*, call Mrs Alving "Mrs Avling" throughout?

To change the subject. Here is a little thing submitted to me last week by a commencing poet:

> When lovely morning lifts her head,
> And laughing flashes on the light,
> We see her rising from the bed
> Of that old blackguard, Night.

My father-in-law used to say, or perhaps quote, about somebody, "Sa rime n'est pas millionnaire," and the same goes for this young man's scansion. But I think the metaphor is fun. It may be that I am prejudiced in his favour since he pays *Ego* 6 the compliment of comparing it to a well-made haystack.

Talking of haystacks, let's have no more beating about the bush. Are you, or are you not, going to let me dedicate *Ego* 8 to you?

Ever,
JAMES AGATE

Jan. 8 *Monday.* Lunch with Hamish Hamilton at the Ivy, the other guests being Malcolm Sargent and Horace Horsnell. What was the best play written since the last war? The talk went something like this:

SARGENT. *St Joan*, of course.

J. A. There's no "of course" about it. We're trying to find the best *play*, and *St Joan* isn't a play, whatever else it may be.

HAMILTON. Well, what do *you* say is the best play, James?

J. A. *Juno and the Paycock*. Shaw's play second.

HORSNELL (*sepulchrally*). Third.

SARGENT. Why third?

HORSNELL. Well, if you put *Juno* first you must put *The Plough and the Stars* second; you can't separate the two.

J. A. I agree.

HAMILTON. What do you say to that, Malcolm ?

J. A. (*before Malcolm can answer*). What is the most perfect opera you've ever heard ?

SARGENT. *Carmen.*

HORSNELL. Attaboy !

J. A. And the second ?

SARGENT. I suppose it would have to be *Meistersinger*. But there's always Mozart, you know !

J. A. (*cold-shouldering Mozart*). Would you consider putting *Rosenkavalier* third ?

SARGENT (*humouring him*). I might consider it.

J. A. Suppose that these are not operas but show-horses, and the class as it stands is headed by *Carmen*, *Meistersinger*, and *Rosenkavalier*. Now tell me. What do you do with that great, hulking, forceful brute now coming into the ring—whose name, by the way, is *The Ring* ?

SARGENT. Well, I've no choice—I should have to put it either first or fourth. Or perhaps not even fourth. There's still Mozart.

J. A. Mozart be blowed !

HORSNELL. Anyhow, Malcolm, you've made James's point and mine. Shaw's play is either first or third ; it can't be second.

SARGENT. What do you say, Hamish ?

HAMILTON. I think we ought to leave it to the dramatic critics.

HORSNELL. It's up to you, James.

J. A. Well, if you want my serious opinion, I should put *Juno* first, *St Joan* second, and *The Plough and the Stars* third.

(*There is a general outcry at this, and a chorus of* " But you agreed . . .")

J. A. I know what I agreed. But I've told *St Joan* to move down to third place, *and she won't budge !*

Jan. 9 *Tuesday.* At supper to-night was introduced to a Trade Union representative and his sailor nephew, a well-spoken boy with one of those homely British ' pans ' that break into an unexpected, heart-warming smile. Very anxious to improve himself, and wanted to know the origin of pantomime, having just come from the Coliseum. Name of Ivan Plowright, an odd combination of Russian and Saxon. Indeed, the boy was so obviously anxious to learn that I was put in mind of my favourite passage in Boswell. He and Johnson had taken a sculler at the Temple Stairs and set out for Greenwich.

" And yet," said I, " people go through the world very well, and carry on the business of life to good advantage, without learning." JOHNSON. " Why, Sir, that may be true in cases where learning cannot possibly be of any use; for instance, this boy rows us as well without learning, as if he could sing the song of Orpheus to the Argonauts, who were the first sailors." He then called to the boy, "What would you give, my lad, to know about the Argonauts?" "Sir," said the boy, "I would give what I have."

Plowright took part in the North African landings, and has got a new ship, which he joins on Friday. Thinks he will be away a year or more, whereupon I undertake to look after his reading. Which means that I spend most of this morning scouring the shops for some Dickens, and find copies of *Pickwick*, *Bleak House*, *Martin Chuzzlewit*, and *A Tale of Two Cities*. To these I add my own *Lorna Doone*, Palgrave's *Golden Treasury*, and Ingpen's abridged *Boswell*.

No. 2 of my *Cocasseries*:

> I'll be thinking of you Easter Sunday
> In every hymn and every prayer.
> The choir will sing, the bells will ring,
> While the scent of Easter lilies fills the air.

Heard on the wireless last night to a maudlin tune subtly combining the atmospheres of cathedral and palais-de-danse.

Jan. 11 *Thursday.* The new edition of *Blessed Are the Rich* was published last week, and *Gemel in London* is out this morning.

Jan. 12 *Friday.* Letter from Jock:

E5 Ward
R.N. Hospital
Haslar, Hants
11*th January*, 1945

DEAR JAMIE,

I have been very peculiarly ill.

> Misérable, et je vis!

Write to me soon.

JOCK

To which I have replied:

Queen Alexandra Mansions, W.C.2
January 12*th*, 1945

MY DEAR JOCK,

Tut-tut! I am miserable, but only at the thought that some day I shan't "vis." In plain English, I have been making my will. Nothing to leave, of course, except gold watch, cuff-links, walking-sticks, etc., but I rather want these to go to the right persons. Even so, there's always income tax, as Van Druten would put it. However, Stanley Rubinstein has insured me for £2000 against loss by

V1 or V2 of life, one or both eyes, and various members. But not against permanent total disablement, as I am sixty-seven and the insurance company's view seems to be that at that age one must expect total disablement from natural causes, never mind Hitler. A cheerful business. Just as I was in full testamentary spate I looked out of window and saw a " corpidge " with four horses. (Do you remember the sailor who always felt jolly whenever he saw what he called a corpidge ? " I'm jolly because it isn't me in the corpidge.") Then to lunch with George Harrap, who gave me three plates by Stephen Gooden—worth £25, it seems—the first of which is entitled " The Rider on the Pale Horse " ! ! But what of it ? We cross our fingers and defy augury.

To hand, this morning, a new highbrow magazine called *Fulcrum*, and promised another called *Dint*. The first is French, and begins with a " Goujaterie Moraliste " whose first word is " Merde." Have also received *Troisième Front*, No. 1 of a series of recent French poetry. The last item in this is a " Petit Poème en Prose," which ends :

> Derrière un arbrisseau, au versant opposé de la montagne, un enfant est assis sur un petit pot et semble souffrir. Personne ne l'aperçoit, à part moi. Je suis saisi d'une immense compassion.

Third, *Message from Nowhere*, with a poem of which the last three lines are

> Et dans ses yeux bataviques
> Brille la provocante splendeur mirabelle plomb fondu
> Des sacrificielles latrines ogivales bombardées.

Last, *Idolatry and Confusion*, a pamphlet with a single illustration. This is a water-closet with a lid shaped like a lyre. Why this universal, ubiquitous interest in coprology ?

No further news, except that I propose to bore you on Saturday in the *D.E.* and dazzle you on Sunday in the *S.T.*

Ever,
JAMIE

Jan. 13 *Saturday.* Jolly meeting at the Ivy with John Sutro, Oliver Messel, and Peter Glenville. This gave me my *Cocasserie* No. 3, Peter telling me that one of his scenes in *The Madonna of the Seven Moons*, the scene in which the wicked Sandro attempts to rape the chaste Angela, had to be shot six times because at the first five shootings he forgot that the Board of Censors will not pass any seduction scene unless the seducer has one foot on the floor.

Cocasseries are coming on apace. Here is No. 4, from the most unexpected source : Lord Dunsany's *Donnellan Lectures* delivered at Trinity College, Dublin, the subjects being prose, poetry, and drama. These contain some exquisite stuff, in the course of which the lecturer quotes Macbeth's "Sleep that knits up the ravelled sleeve [*sic*] of care." Then I read :

> I think I feel sure enough of that simile to say that it must have been written after Shakespeare was married. You see, a simile is merely placing one picture beside another, taking one picture down off the wall and holding it by another one to compare with it. And one asks where was the other picture ; how far did the man have to go to get it ? Sleep of course cures care, but how did a sleeve come into it ? Why a torn sleeve ? It seems to me simple enough : Shakespeare had been having a night out, perhaps with some of those good friends who, because he was such a good fellow, decided that there ought to be some memorial to him and luckily hit on the idea of printing his plays. Well, it had been rather a rowdy night—in fact, very rowdy indeed, so rowdy that he had got his sleeve torn. He remembered that. But the wonderful thing was that when he woke up in the morning the sleeve had been all mended. If that happened the two pictures are side by side and the simile naturally suggests itself. But if it did not happen, then the sleeve seems a very odd thing to have been brought into it, and is in fact inexplicable.

Inexplicable, dear Lord Dunsany ? Only if you confuse "sleeve," that part of the garment which covers the arm, with "sleave," which is the knotted or entangled part of a skein of yarn or thread. And this was said to students ! *Quis custodiet*, etc. But these howlers are easily made. I had been a critic of Shakespeare's acted drama for nearly twenty years before I realised that "When roasted crabs hiss in the bowl" was a reference to crab-apples and not crustaceans.

No. 5 is culled from Paul Tabori's *Two Forests*. The hero of this is a fiddler who, to entice a young girl, goes through the cycles of Schubert's *Die Schöne Müllerin* and *Die Winterreise*, having previously made transcriptions of them for unaccompanied violin. And then the door opens and the girl, who must have been listening for a couple of hours or more, enters. Whereupon the fiddler plays Schubert's *Die Forelle*, *Gretchen am Spinnrad*, *Am Meer*, *An die Musik*, and *Ständchen*, followed by Schumann's *Kinderscenen* and "some of the pieces" in the *Album für die Jugend*, all arranged for unaccompanied violin. We are then told that both performer and listener "forgot everything until Robert knocked at the door and announced that luncheon was waiting." Presuming that the young woman's appetite for food was comparable to her appetite for music, she must have eaten an ox !

No. 6 is from to-day's *News Chronicle*, and is about Michael Tippett's oratorio *A Child of our Time*. Of this the writer remarks:

" It seemed to me to avoid the Scylla and Charybdis of music *about* events. That is, it kept clear both of over-specific literary narrative and of bulbously emotive symbolism."

Jan. 15 *Monday.* George Lyttelton writes to say that my suggestion that I should dedicate my next *Ego* to him

> was so delicate that I did not like, so to speak, to grab at it. I should be *very* proud indeed to be the dedicatee and go down to fame on your shoulders—feeling rather like Leigh Hunt when he wrote about Jenny. The last book dedicated to one of my name was *Tom Jones*. My ancestor was Squire Allworthy, a kindly old fellow, but I suspect a dullish one. He was Chancellor of the Exchequer though, according to Warburton, he never could learn that two and two made four.

Jan. 16 *Tuesday.* In to-day's *Times* Lord Esher and Lord Elton tell me that my " Toopit " theory is " ingenious " and " too ingenious." Both possess the original monthly parts of *Martin Chuzzlewit*, in which the name is spelt " Toppit."

Jan. 17 *Wednesday.* Judging by *The Unquiet Grave*, " Palinurus " would seem to be, at least in part, Gilbert's Bunthorne.

> Angst descends : I wake up in anxiety ; like a fog it overlays all I do, and my days are muffled with anguish. Somewhere in the mind are crossed the wires of fear and lust and all day long nature's burglar-alarm shrills out in confusion. I dread the bell, the post, the telephone, the sight of an acquaintance. Anguish, anxiety, remorse and guilt : TOUT EST DÉGOÛT ET MISÈRE.

And :

> In the small hours when the acrid stench of existence rises like sewer gas from everything created, the emptiness of life seems more terrible than its misery.

Also :

> Morning tears return ; spirits at their lowest ebb. . . . Approaching forty, I am about to heave my carcass of vanity, boredom, guilt and remorse into another decade.

If I knew " Palinurus " I should offer him choice of three remedies. *One.* A box of Bunthorne's colocynth and calomel pills. *Two.* Mrs Crupp's prescription : " You are a young gentleman, Mr Copperfull, and my adwice to you is, to cheer up, sir, to keep a good heart, and to know your own walue. If you was to take to something, sir—if you was to take to skittles, now, which is healthy—you might find it divert your mind, and do you good." *Three.* To stop thinking about "Palinurus," and go and read to blind soldiers, or wheel crippled airmen round the Park. The trouble with these super-clever high-brows—there is some exquisite writing in the book, notably the long passage about lemurs—is that they have no vestige of humour. If "Palinurus" knew what humour is or may be he could not have presented me with *Cocasserie* No. 7 :

> In the jungles of South America grows a trumpet flower fourteen inches deep, and there also is found a moth with a proboscis of the same length, the only creature able to penetrate to the honey and so procure the plant's fertilisation. I, Palinurus, am such an orchid, growing daily more untempting as I await the Visitor who never comes.

Jan. 18 *Thursday.* The capture of Warsaw and the advance of the Russians have put me in mind of something which I am sending to the *S.T.* for its "Famous Retorts" series. This concerns one Népomucène Lemercier, the friend of Legouvé, the part-author of *Adrienne Lecouvreur.* According to Talleyrand, Lemercier was a brilliant chatterbox ; when he was not chattering he exuded tragedies with names like *Agamemnon.* It was Lemercier who, at Malmaison, taught Napoleon the history of France. Later on the two quarrelled, and when Napoleon sent his old friend one of the first Crosses of the Legion of Honour it was returned. In revenge the Emperor forbade the performance of Lemercier's plays ; Népomucène said nothing. Driven from his house, he took refuge in a garret and stopped both chattering and playwriting. And then one day, at the Tuileries, the Emperor perceived his old crony in a corner with other members of the Institute. Waving the crowd aside, Napoleon went up to him and said, "*Eh bien,* Lemercier, when are you going to write a new tragedy ?" "*I am waiting, Sire !*" replied the poet. Surely a magnificent remark to make in 1812 on the eve of the Russian campaign !

Letter from Kandy, in Ceylon, telling me that, as far as the writer can see, "the Bookshops as Bookshops, in this city, is Null an' Void." At the same time he sends me a delightful essay on Amanda Ros by J. O. Bartley, an Ulsterman in Public Relations in New Delhi. This quotes from Amanda's epitaph on an honest critic :

> My ! What a bubbly vapoury box of vanity !
> A litter of worms, a relic of humanity—

"lines which," says the essayist, "in a different context, would not surprise from some of our most esteemed contemporaries." Surely not "contemporaries" but "Elizabethans"—I hate the pernickety

" Jacobeans "—should be the word. I confess I see very little to choose between the quotation from Amanda and Bosola's

> Thou art a box of worm-seed, at best but a salvatory of green mummy. What's this flesh ? A little crudded milk, fantastical puff-paste.

But then Amanda had genius. Consider her verses on visiting Westminster Abbey :

> Holy Moses ! Have a look !
> Flesh decayed in every nook !
> Some rare bits of brain lie here,
> Mortal loads of beef and beer. . .

Nobody but a genius could have written " Some rare bits of brain lie here."

Jan. 19 Letter from Jock :
Friday.

E5 Ward
R.N.H.
18*th January*, 1945

MY DEAR JAMIE,

Thinking on your end you are no more tragic than Falstaff : hoots awa' and havers ! You were making one of your wills away back in October 1926 when I first traversed your doorstep (with Gemel's careful alacrity !).

And I don't seem to remember, then, that you had either a gold watch or cuff-links to leave ! Whence came the watch ? The links I can believe in, because every year the oldest actress still able to hobble on to the stage with two legs and a bad-tempered walking-stick sweetly gives you a pair of elegant cuff-links at the Ivy and promptly dies thereafter. You will receive dozens more of such coy peeping adornments—and rush home each time to write some one's graceful obituary.

Another great man who has been dying these years and years—my dear old James Bone—told me last time I saw him at the Press Club that he used to have a friend who was the prize obituarist of *The Times*, specialising in Church dignitaries. I can't remember his name—let's call him Martin Spade-Prelate. Well, James was telling me how he used to lunch with Spade-Prelate at the Athenæum, and how much he enjoyed his coffee in the smoke-room afterwards because as each pink bishop doddered in with a post-prandial smile he would turn pale to the gills and the gaiter-buttons as soon as he caught sight of Spade-Prelate, knowing his vocation. James chuckled in his Caledonian way at the recollection. And I interrupted his chuckle by saying, " And I'll bet you another whiskey that in due time you wrote Spade-Prelate's obit, yourself ? " " Oh-oh ! " says James. " So I did ! So I did ! "

So you see why I am not unduly grave with sympathy over your wills and testaments (by no means last), your insurances, your omens that come to naught, and your glimpses of Gampish corpidges through glum lawyers' windows. I ache to be back at my job and to be in my dear little *mansarde* again with its balcony, that I used to call a loggia, and something that Sairey somewhere calls " a Parapidge with chimbley-pots to walk on in case of fire." If I were, I'd come round and cheer you up rather more than this scribbled note can do.

Your
JOCK

Jan. 20 *Saturday.* *The Times* devotes its fourth leader to the question of Miss Toppit. Am sending the Editor the following:

SIR,

Miss Toopit retires and leaves the field to Miss Toppit.

I hope you will not think me unduly quarrelsome if I dissent from your dictum in the matter of the evocative case: " Shakespeare, Sheridan, Scott, Dickens, Thackeray, Trollope, du Maurier (who created Sir Gorgius Midas)—they have all done it, all save the ladies, who, following Miss Austen, have refused to demean themselves to these sometimes felicitous antics." But, sir, the ladies have not refused to demean themselves. If we are to hark back to the dramatists Shakespeare and Sheridan we are entitled to go back to the pre-Austen women-playwrights. To Mrs Aphra Behn, who in *The City Heiress* has Sir Timothy Treatall, Dresswell and Foppington, and among the women Mrs Clacket (" a City Bawd and Puritan "), Mrs Closet, and Mrs Sensure. To Mrs Centlivre, whose *A Bold Stroke for a Wife* has characters called Colonel Feignwell, Sir Philip Modelove, Tradelove, Obadiah Prim, and Simon Pure. To Mrs Cowley, with her Lord Sparkle and Lady Bell Bloomer, and Mrs Inchbald, with her Mr Twineall and Mr Meanright.

Again, I find it difficult to accept your leader-writer's statement that in comparison with Thackeray all other practitioners in the evocative are " mere blunderers." *All* others? Did Jonson blunder with Sir Epicure Mammon, Vanbrugh with Sir John Brute, Congreve with Lady Wishfort? If your defence is that your reference is post-Austen, how came you to forget Peacock? Or even Surtees? " Whether in the straightforward Sharp or Newcome, ideal for their respective purposes, or in such a pleasant whimsy as the firm from which Clive bought his paints, Messrs Soap and Isaac, Thackeray was flawless." Even so, where is the flaw in Surtees's smooth toady, Mr Soapey Sponge?

Yours, etc.,
JAMES AGATE

*Holborn, W.C.*2
January 20

Jan. 21 *Sunday.* On my telling my doctor, Norman Newman, yesterday, that I thought a course of something would do me good, he replied, " My dear boy, what you want is a course of nothing." Resolved, therefore, to have a day or two of loafing. Spent it re-conning, or, to be perfectly honest, making acquaintance with the plays of Aphra Behn and Mrs Centlivre. And coming to the conclusion that Aphra was a dull lady-dog and Mrs C. a very considerable wit whose quality still persists. The play of Mrs C. that I chose was *A Bold Stroke for a Wife.* It begins with Freeman telling Colonel Feignwell that Anne Lovely " is the talk and pity of the whole town ; and it is the opinion of the learned, that she must die a maid." Whereupon the Colonel remarks, " That's somewhat odd, in this charitable city." And there is Sir Philip Modelove, who, on being told by the Colonel that a person of his figure would be a vast addition to a coronet, replies, " I must own I had the offer of a barony about five years ago ; but I abhorred the fatigue which must have attended it." In the course of the imbroglio Colonel Feignwell pretends to come from the funeral of his old master. " Pray, sir," says Periwinkle, " what office bore you ? " The Colonel says he was Sir Toby's steward. Periwinkle asks his name, and the Colonel answers, " Pillage, sir." Mrs C. appears to have had fun as well as wit. Feignwell, posing as an Egyptian, produces something which he says " is called poluflosboio." Says Periwinkle, " It has a rumbling sound." To which the Colonel replies, " Right, sir ; it proceeds from a rumbling nature. This water was part of the waves which bore Cleopatra's vessel when she sailed to meet Antony." Yes, I must read more of Mrs C.

Jan. 22 *Monday.* Loafing continues. A nostalgic loafing caused by coming across a phrase in William Gaunt's *The Æsthetic Adventure*—Gautier's definition of himself as " A man for whom the visible world exists." This sent me to my bookshelves and my copy of *Mademoiselle de Maupin,* which I would have said I bought when I was seventeen. But the facts are against me ; I see from the date of the edition that I must have been at least twenty-seven. It is with some confusion, then, that I recall the *Schwärmerei,* excusable in youth, which with me lasted into the thirties. It was on a bicycle ride with one of my younger brothers that I first opened Gautier's book, and I remember the Derbyshire hillside, and the summer's day, and how whichever it was of my brothers went off at my bidding with orders to pick me up in the late afternoon. And how I read for six blessed hours. Later I had the copy bound in an expensive red morocco which has admirably withstood forty years and many moves.

I see that on the first page I pencilled : " For Edward. To mark the beautiful passages is to mark the whole book—he will understand." Nevertheless, I did mark some passages, including one which, slightly shortened, I sometimes feel I should like to print at the top of my *S.T.* articles :

> Many things are boring : it is boring to pay back borrowed money ; it is boring to make love to the woman one kissed yesterday ; it is boring to write a novel and more boring to read one ; it is boring to be a porter ; it is boring to be an emperor ; but what is more boring than anything on earth, in hell or in heaven, is a tragedy—unless it is a drama or a comedy.

Jan. 23 *Tuesday.* " *Du Glückstier !* " cries Leo this morning, bursting into my bedroom and upsetting my fourth, say ten-thirty-ish, cup of tea. " No sooner does one door shut for you than another opens. Exeunt your Swiss Cottage friends ; enter Mr Hatch. Look at this ! " And hands me the following letter, with the postmark " Chiswick W.4 " :

London
January 22*nd*, 1945

DEAR MR AGATE,

I am twenty-six years of age. I am of independent means, that is to say I have an annuity of £3 17*s.* 10*d.* per week, which enables me to live in a quiet, if not luxurious, fashion. I have not taken any active part in the present war for the reason that my health did and does not permit of my exerting myself in other than intellectual ways. I have many certificates to this effect. Harley Street testifies to a chronic lesion of the cavorta ; Wimpole Street is witness to the syphonic degeneration of my bladder ; Welbeck Street pronounces my liver to be statomichic, my kidneys katomichic, and my spleen to be in that rare state known as hypertricomastia. So much for my health, which, however, has permitted me to contribute three articles to *Offing* and *The Young Politician* under the pseudonym of Tintin Nabulate.

As you see, I give no address. The reason for this is the following :

I am writing a novel, to be called *The Trials of Saccharissa.* This is a protest against the vapidity of latter-day fiction. A novel dealing with contemporary life and thought. A novel by an intellectual, about intellectuals, for intellectuals. A novel of massive ideas, complex emotions, superb talk.

The matter is what the unintelligentsia would call " clean." You know as well as I do that all that scabrous rubbish of the early forties, dealing with such ephemera as socratism, lesbianism, sadism, masochism, coprophilism, necrophilism and all the other " isms," are not only *vieux jeu* but, from a cultural standpoint, as dead as the Æsthetic Movement itself. If they are alluded to it is only to point a moral or moralise a point. My novel avoids such *non sequiturs*.

I have written the first chapters, of which I shall shortly send you some extracts. You will see from these, which are intended merely to whet your appetite, that my book is a work of genius replete with every quality that I have always admired in my favourite authors. Amongst these I give first place to George Meredith. At the age of eight I was enthralled by his later novels, and at my preparatory school would take my fellow-pupils on long walks. Then, in the middle of some ploughed field, I would read them the opening chapters of *One of Our Conquerors*, that masterpiece among masterpieces. *Eheu! fugaces* . . . Yes, dear Mr Agate, the classical side of my education has not been neglected.

This morning I decided to dedicate my book to the memory of that great epigrammatist whose wit was ever translucency's self. I do not believe that you have forgotten "The figure with the helmet of the Owl-Goddess and the trident of the Earth-shaker, seated on a wheel, at the back of the penny-pieces; in whom you see neither the beauty of nakedness nor the charm of drapery; not the helmet's dignity or the trident's power; but she has patently that which stops the wheel; and posing for representative of an imperial nation, she helps to pass a penny." Or that you do not recite in your bath: "Mr Durance said that a blow now and then was wholesome for us all. He recommended a monthly private whipping for old gentlemen who decline the use of the gloves, to disperse their humours; not excluding judges and magistrates. He said, that old gentlemen were bottled vapours, and it was good for them to uncork them periodically. He said, they should be excused half the strokes if they danced nightly—they resented motion." Who except the Master could have presented so succinctly the case against sparing the rod and spoiling the old gentleman? Finally, I am teaching my landlady's little daughter to lisp, "The remainder of life is in the activity of my diseases." The dedication will run:

TO

COLNEY DURANCE

ARISTOPHANIC CREATION

OF

THE GREATEST OF MODERN NOVELISTS

THIS EPIGONIC TRIBUTE

You will ask why I give no address. The reason is to prevent your writing to me and saying you do not wish to receive further letters from me. I shall write no further letters. I shall send you a synopsis of each half-dozen chapters as I finish them, together with extracts from the chapters themselves. Don't make the point that my plot is not my own, that I have gone to the most familiar sources. Of course I have. Deliberately. I regard plot merely as a peg for the book's decorations, an easel on which to place my canvas.

I shall go on sending you these extracts until you are completely captivated. Mr Agate, I intend to be ONE OF YOUR CONQUERORS !

For the time being, I use a name not my own.

DURANCE HATCH

Jan. 24 *Wednesday.* Letter from Jock :

Staff Quarters
R.N. Hospital
Haslar, Hants
21*st January,* 1945

DEAR JAMIE,

Strictly I ought to send you a serious letter *in re* The Richardson Nose. You and Ivor cannot *both* be right this morning. Your article seems to me a superb and characteristic expression of a quite crassly idiosyncratic point of view. It is just untrue to say (if you don't say it you imply it) that this actor cannot move us because he has a funny round nose. He moved lots of people (certainly including *me* and, I seem to remember, *you*) in, amongst other things, Maugham's *For Services Rendered* (as an axed naval officer who was driven to suicide) and Priestley's *Cornelius* (as the eponymous business-man who couldn't make good at the end of the last war). You are on very much firmer ground if you make out that his nose prevents him from excelling in romantic or classical serious parts as distinct from modern ditto ditto. (Surely he'd make an admirable Helmer, Dr Stockmann, or even Solness ?) The Nose, I do agree with you, was a considerable handicap in the matter of his Othello, his Iago, his Henry V, and that silly Silent Knight of Humbert Wolfe's. But his very bluntness *helped* to make his Kent, his Enobarbus, and his Faulconbridge. I saw the last, but don't think that you did, or know that he had played it. Clever of you, therefore, to mention its possibility this morning. It is one of the six best Shakespearean performances I have ever witnessed. The other five, by the way, were John Gielgud's present exquisite Hamlet, Henry Ainley's Benedick (in 1926), Laurence Olivier's Coriolanus, Leon Quartermaine's Banquo, and Robert Atkins's Caliban.

Ever thy,
JOCK

My reply :

*Queen Alexandra Mansions, W.C.*2
January 24*th*, 1945

DEAR JOCK,

I am surprised that you should quote any practising dramatic critic against me. How many more times must I tell you that not one of you has ever seen a great actor or actress, with the possible exception of Mrs Pat *en décadence* ? Not one of you ever saw Irving, or Forbes-Robertson, or Charles Hawtrey, or Ellen Terry, or Mrs Kendal, or Janet Achurch. Not one of you ever saw Coquelin, the elder Guitry, Baron, Brasseur, Galipaux, Sarah, Bartet, Réjane, or Granier. And very few of you, even if you had seen them, would have understood a word they said. Ivor is an easy prey to anybody who sits in a corner and mopes : he calls this "quietism." You fall for some nice, sturdy, straightforward player who obviously isn't going to make off with the night's takings. You call that a "natural" actor, and I say : Yes, he is natural. But according to whose nature ? You insist that I admire Richardson's Kent and Enobarbus : I have paid tribute to both performances in the *Sunday Times* and in book form. But don't you realise that both parts are serving-men and can be played *without elevation*, which is why R. was so good as Bottom, an Athenian working man ? You ask me whether he was not moving as Cornelius. But if I remember aright, C. was a broker who went broke, and about this play's ending I find that I dictated and you took down : "Mr Richardson is too genial and too chubby to make a purely philosophical exit, and too English and phlegmatic to make a theatrical one." About R.'s performance in *For Services Rendered* I remember that he played the part of an ex-Commander turned garage-proprietor who issued dud cheques and then committed suicide ; I thought him excellent as a stupid fellow as much at sea in a garage as anywhere else. And now, me bucko, as Mrs Madigan would say, let me remind you of R.'s performance in *Too True to be Good.* Again I dictated, and you took down :

"The piece was run away with, in vulgar parlance, by Mr Ralph Richardson, who spoke the long speech of the sergeant with a medieval forthrightness and a controlled passion beyond all praise ; the actor, taking his time from Bunyan, affected us like a soldier coming into church from the open field."

Does the word Bunyan suggest nothing to you ? You with your quick brain will say at once : What, is there no elevation in Bunyan ? And I say : Yes, but not the kind of elevation I am talking about. You ask me whether R. would not be admirable as Helmer, Stockmann, or Solness. I give you that dull fellow Stockmann, astonished that the shareholders in the Baths aren't delighted to be told the water stinks. But not Helmer, who is an exquisite in his way, as you would know if you had seen Courtenay Thorpe play the part. And certainly not Solness, who is as mad as a hatter, whereas R. is as sane as all the hatters in London put together. To be quite frank, Richardson has never moved me *as an actor* ; he could play Charles I and have his head chopped off in sixteen different positions without beginning to worry me. Whereas Irving. . . . But then you never saw Irving, and therefore cannot know what pathos is. On the other hand, let's give R.

the quality of his defects. He would be my first choice for Mr Valiant-for-Truth—one would believe in those trumpets. He would be my last choice for Antony; riot just doesn't go with that sturdy British countenance and that smug, self-satisfied vocal intonation. I feel about R. exactly what Lewes felt about Charles Kean:

"He has the power of coarse painting, of impressive representation when the image to be presented is a simple one; but he has no subtlety of sympathy, no nicety of observation, no variety of expression. He is peculiarly rigid—this is his force and his weakness: 'he moveth altogether if he move at all.' His face is utterly without physiognomical play; one stolid expression, immovable as an ancient mask, is worn throughout a scene which demands fluctuating variety."

I said all I have to say about R. when he played the Apprentice in *The Knight of the Burning Pestle*:

"But surely Mr Richardson is miscast? His stolid, inexpressive mien, altogether admirable in Bottom and in all delineations of the downright, and his general suggestion of the tongue-tied do not belong to the volatile, mercurial Apprentice who has been an amateur actor and spills the loquacity of which he is full. Histrionics should tumble out of Ralph because he cannot help it, and to invite Mr Richardson to do this is like asking a stonewaller to play one of Macartney's innings."

The trouble is that R. has neither vivacity nor melancholy. If he must play Tchehov let it be Lopakhin in *The Cherry Orchard*; as that highly unimaginative if speculative builder and ex-serf he would be excellent. No, Ralph is an admirable actor as long as he keeps within his limitations, which, of course, applies to all actors. Irving? I can think of only three instances in which the Old Man miscast himself—Romeo, which he couldn't look; Lear, which he couldn't speak; and the mesmerist and lion-tamer, to give him Shaw's title, in *The Medicine Man.* (This was the play which brought Shaw to bed; his Saturday article on it appeared on May 7, 1898, followed by "G. B. S. Vivisected" on May 14, and "Valedictory" on May 21.) On all other occasions there was a facet of H. I. to correspond with the part, and since he played rôles as different as Lesurques and Dubosc, Charles I and Louis XI, Dr Primrose and Cardinal Wolsey, there must have been an immense number of facets. (D'you remember Max's "multi-radiant"?) But Ralph has only one facet, something between Joe Gargery and Joe Bagstock, a solid, impermeable compound of *bonhomie* and *Gemütlichkeit.* (Why can't I learn to write English? I asked Leo about the spelling of the German word. He said they don't use the old "th" nowadays, and I said I didn't think they had any further use for the word!) To go back to R., I think he is an excellent actor in his vein, and that Vanya is outside it.

Yours ever,

JAMIE

Jan. 25 *Thursday.* A plague on these revivals of the *Dream* with Somebody Else's music! With the exception of Shaw, dramatic critics have been a notoriously unmusical lot. I don't believe that either Archer or Walkley would have known the Overture to this play from the Overture to *Ruy Blas*, the Nocturne from "O Rest in the Lord," and the Scherzo from the last movement of the Violin Concerto. But has the fact that a dramatic critic cannot distinguish between the Trio in *Rosenkavalier* and "Three Little Maids from School" ever prevented him from having views on what music should or should not be used for Shakespeare's fairy play? No. He will hold that one should use "the music of the period," by which he generally means Purcell, ignoring the fact that that composer is first heard of in Pepys's *Diary* some forty-five years after Shakespeare's death. To those who are not tone-deaf the argument that music vaguely of the period *must* express that period is unsound. Unsound because we are not listening with the ears of that period. I hold that Richard Strauss gives to modern ears a better notion of the daughter of Clytemnestra and Agamemnon than any concatenation of conch, ram's horn, harp, pipe, lute, theorbo, shawm, sackbut, psaltery, tabor, and cymbals that Euripides could have heard.

Jan. 26 *Friday.* "Must a man sit esurient at his own table?" asked Lamb. Must I keep silent about my latest *Cocasserie* because I play a leading part in it? At the Café Royal to-night Dicky Holmes, whom I used to meet at Monty Shearman's, leans across from the next table and says, "May I introduce Mrs Procter? You probably know the name." Whereupon J. A., who is all in after four days of loafing but remembers E. V. Lucas's dictum that a gent never shows he is tired, capers into the conversation like some sprightly elephant. No, he doesn't what you might call *know* the name. He remembers being at school with a jolly boy called Proctor—all smile and freckles? At any rate, he spelt his name with an "o." He knows a bore of that name, and will ask the bore the next time he meets the bore which boring vowel he affects. Then wasn't there once an Adelaide Anne P. who wrote *The Lost Chord* and other of what Millamant would have called filthy verses? And that's all the Procters he knows; except, vaguely, something about a Mrs Dod P. who used to paint nudes made of pewter lying on beds made of zinc. Whereupon the lady smiles and says, "I gave up painting like that twelve years ago." At this J. A. makes a lumbering attempt at recovery and says he thinks women should give up all forms of painting except perhaps a little dabbling in water-colour. The lady says she gave that up even earlier, having found it too difficult. Has Mr Agate any other interesting views about painting ? J. A. " Only that the art stopped with Renoir." The lady then asks J. A. what, since he is so fond of horses, are his views on Munnings ? J. A. " He doesn't paint them as well as Stubbs." THE LADY. " Oh, but Munnings gives them such beautiful, glossy coats. Which is naughty of me, because I'm very fond of Munnings. Besides, he's a very good painter." J. A. " Madam, Whistler was a very good painter, and the polish on his piano is perfect." And so the game goes on for half an hour with Dicky sitting there, umpiring as it were. Presently they get up to go, and J. A. finds himself telling D. P. that she is a very witty and charming woman. Yes, I think my *gaffe* is entitled to rank as No. 8 in my *Cocasseries*.

Jan. 27 *Saturday.* An unknown friend from Bristol sends me what I take to be an exquisite little poem :

SNOW ON MY SEVEN DAYS

English snow from a heavy English sky,
Quietly greeting me, drifting incessantly, slow.
Strange I should find it enchanting—I who have cursed,
Stumbling blinded and chilled, hating the snow.

Snow on my seven days' leave. How they will laugh !
How to explain the peace and the silence it brings ?
Mine to recall it, swirling and dancing a welcome ;
Laughing it smothers me, laughing it settles and clings.

Home and the faces, rosy with happiness, waiting ;
The kiss and the long, long gaze into eyes that burn . . .
And the friendly snow crowning the blessed moment ;
Mine to remember, to live on when I return.

E.P.B.

Jan. 30 *Tuesday.* Propinquity ! I spent the first hour of to-night's play, Daphne du Maurier's *The Years Between*, wondering what service Humpty Dumpty would have imposed on that word. The drama now unfolding was all about Diana, an English war widow (Nora Swinburne) whose husband, Colonel Wentworth, M.P. (Clive Brook), had crashed off the coast of Greece. But I had just come from a film about an American war widow whose husband had been reported missing in the Philippines, and I found myself asking whether to tackle the make-believe of the theatre so soon after the actualities of the film was quite fair. Some years ago I was told by a chauffeur that he preferred the pictures to the theatre " because they are so much more real." Was the young man setting up a case for celluloid as more life-like than flesh-and-blood ? No, what he was stressing without knowing it was the difference between a photograph of, say, an express train speeding through steam and rain and Turner's painting of the same thing. At the cinema I am, like that chauffeur, completely illuded. I had no doubt this morning that the American film company had paid some world-famous star a hundred thousand dollars to be unseen as the husband and do a thinking part away from the set. Indeed, I shouldn't have been surprised to hear that they had given him another hundred thousand dollars to go to the Philippines, crawl about, and pretend to be missing. I *felt* that the fellow was alive somewhere, tucked away, out of sight. I believed in him though I never saw him. But then I utterly believe in the cinema unless, of course, it is behaving cinematographically. When some highbrow director shows me a guttering candle and tells me it is Colonel Newcome rehearsing his " Adsum " I just say, " No, it isn't; it's a guttering candle." And when he shows me a view of a beach at low water and claims that it is Barkis going out with the tide I say, " No, it isn't; it's a bit of Ilfracombe." But otherwise I am completely deceived. As a filmgoer I have not been taught to pretend; whoever alludes to a rogue elephant or to a volcano in eruption must show it to me, and will. Whereas the whole art of playgoing is concerned with pretence. And alas, I cannot believe in to-night's colonel, in spite of the fact that he is tremendously in evidence.

The author doesn't help by starting off with a whopper. Or rather, three whoppers. First, we are to believe that Colonel Wentworth didn't really crash but only pretended to, so that nobody would suspect him of being chief organiser of the underground movement in Europe. Second, we are to believe that Diana is not allowed to know any of this because she is Ibsen's Nora all over again, a tweeting song-bird who is to chirrup all over the house except when her lord and master is at his desk writing his books and speeches. Third, we are to believe that, his mission concluded and the war ended, the Colonel returns to find the canary turned bird of wisdom and representing the constituency in his stead! Well, I don't think the du Maurier can have it all three ways any more than I believe that a heroine wearing three rows of whacking great pearls cares twopence whether working-class houses are provided with baths or not. The truest thing in the play is the Colonel's insistence that the soldier doesn't want to come back to an unrecognisable world, a world with hot and cold laid on everywhere, a world in which chamber music and poetry readings in saloon bars interfere with the proper business of drinking. (Has the Colonel been reading *Ego* 7, pages 178, 179?) He wants the world he knew, improved, if you must, but *along his lines* and not what the Pardiggles think ought to be his lines. A world of better and stronger beer; of higher wages and shorter hours; of more dependable horses and more reliable greyhounds ; of larger and more palatial dance-halls. A world in which a wife stops at home and wipes her kiddies' noses instead of gadding about Westminster trying to catch the Speaker's eye. Right or wrong, this new argument, very forcefully put by the Colonel, seems to me to be of greater interest than that stale romantic stuff about the lover who goes out of a woman's life. But then I had spent the morning weeping over one abnegatory fellow, and two in one day is too much. Propinquity again.

Feb. 1 *Thursday.* Until this morning I thought I knew most of the minor annoyances of existence. But I must go back a little.

For some months, and in order to give me a modicum of time in which to attend to my own work, Leo has had instructions to write to the senders of MSS. telling them that my fee for an opinion is ten pounds, payable in advance. Alas, one or two tenners started coming in, which meant that I had to put up the price to twenty pounds. Arrives, the other day, from South Wales, the MS. of a 150,000-word novel. The usual letter is dispatched, back comes the reply saying the author can't afford twenty pounds, whereupon I spend half an hour making a neat parcel of his unshapely mess, taking it to the post in the midst of a snowstorm, and standing in a queue to register it to the address on the MS. and his two letters. All this was over a week ago. This morning the parcel comes back marked " Not Known " ! !

Feb. 3 *Saturday.* Letter from the gentleman in South Wales, saying that unless he receives his MS. by return he will put the matter in the hands of his solicitors.

Feb. 4 *Sunday.* To a lady :

*Queen Alexandra Mansions, W.C.*2
February 4*th*, 1945

MADAM,

You are worried because nobody will take a short story about a charming girl who adores Siamese cats and cold-bloodedly destroys them in turn as the first kitten is born, because kittens are more attractive. I can only suggest that you haven't hit on the right ending. Why not give the girl a fiancé who keeps putting off the wedding-day, and when reproached for not coming up to the scratch, replies, " Look here, sweetheart, I have a complex too. Only in my case it's babies instead of kittens ! "

Yours sincerely,
JAMES AGATE

Feb. 5 In a letter from New Zealand :
Monday.

I have a cobber who says you are all wrong about Rachel and Sarah. Their biographical notes (he says) should be : Sisters. Born Kansas City. Worked in Hiram P. Sloshky's dry-goods and drug store. Joined Warner Bros. as crooners, tap-dancers, and hot mommas. At present working on the film *The Private Lives of James Agate.*

Cocasseries, No. 9 :

Shakespeare's play, *The Tempest*, is a " musical," according to the U.S. Federation of Musicians, whose ruling compels sponsors of the current Broadway production of the classic to employ sixteen rather than the scheduled twelve-piece orchestra and pay the musicians £7 a week more each. In reply to the producer's contention that it is Shakespeare's play with incidental music, not a musical with book and lyrics by Shakespeare, Mr Jack Rosenberg, chief of the Federation, said, " We don't care if it's by William Shakespeare or Joe Doakes. If the producers don't abide by our ruling we'll close the show."—*Reuter.*

Evening paper

Feb. 6 Hatch is as good as his word. To-day I receive this :
Tuesday.

THE TRIALS OF SACCHARISSA

CHAPTERS 1–6

(*With apologies to Goldsmith's Olivia*)

SYNOPSIS

Saccharissa, beautiful daughter of the vicar of Daydream, is pursued by a handsome country gentleman of loose morals. In due course Squire Maybrow lures the unsuspecting girl from the paternal roof and seduces her. Abandoned in the middle of Virginia Water, she hails a friendly Spitfire and returns to the forgiving arms of her father, Dr Daffodil.

EXTRACTS

Chloe thought the two would come to blows. Hypius glared at Sapor, Sapor clenched his fists as if to strike his friend. Chloe had one of her inspirations. " *Escuchar, mis amigos !* " she cried. " Matteo Grigoroso may or may not be a master of cloristic rhythm —but this is the point—every one, every painter who is also a critic and vice versa, admits that Florio da Melacrino was the greater virtuoso in sheer *line.* This isn't merely my idea ; ask

Pierre." Pierre Langouste, true son of the South, who was sketching an apple-tree growing in the lake, turned round and said, "*Mais oui. Je comprends. C'est la vie !*" After Elfrida had translated this to the others peace was restored.

. . . .

Millamant Foss, sprucer than ever in her soya stockings, is the first to turn on him. "So," she cries, but not without a slight grating of the œsophagus, "you come here, Valentine, just to tell us that, in your view, Leonardo could paint. But *could* he? He could draw. He could design. He could invent. But *paint*? Not what *we* call paint. Not as the Cerisians, or the Neo-Cobaltists, or even the Ultra-Gambogists paint—and they are the only authorities on the really modern use of colour. Painting, *qua* painting, must be three-dimensional, ilistic, biometrical if necessary—every child learns that at school. It must be peristeal as well; or, if you are so pedantic, the more vernacular peristheal." "Enough!" cries Valentine, protecting himself with his parasol. "I am converted. Let us call painting a peristheal symbosis. Does that satisfy you?" Millamant, good-natured as ever, smiles: "For the moment, yes. But later we'll ask St John Pushcart—he's more authentically definitional."

. . . .

Cleverly reaching the summit of Gwrngwrn, Hilda stopped and said in her most thrilling tones, "Philosophical pictures should never be in a major key. Enharmonics, yes. But plastic planes cannot enter into the sphere of chromatic energism. There is always a tinge of the pseudo-heterogeneous, a whiff of what dear old Beagle Blossom used to call spiritual Woggery." Hilary Ellis interrupted to lead them to his studio, situated plumb in the middle of Salisbury Plain, and measuring 120 yards by 90. They were all struck by the new sketches in gouache, a little derivative, Julia thought, of post-Eleutheristic symbolism. Lady Carstairs sniffed audibly. "Really, Mr Ellis," she protested. "I find these figures a little sub-dimensional! Think of Mantegna." "Madam," returned the painter, "you should remember the old tag—*Tempora mutantur, et nos mutamur in Ellis*!" Hilary realised that it was the quip of his life.

. . . .

Raoul Figtree was reading part of his essay on the Geometrics of Design. He ended: "Is this a lacheitis, or merely the old, old *bépouperie*? Not for me to answer. Thousands have asked the same question. Sailors huddled in their fo'c'sles, soldiers bumping in their tanks, airmen nonchalant in the midst of flak. The best I can do is to quote my favourite author, Teneber Mastix: 'Lacheitic can never be lacheitistic. A rhombus can never be a rhomboid.' In other words, the manubial can never be the manubrial." Looking round, Raoul was surprised to find Messalina Oldcock in tears.

Feb. 7 Wednesday. Depressed at the thought of having to sit through *Emma*, at the St James's to-night. Jane's " two inches of ivory " has never deceived me. She was a whale for length. It would take a hoarding twelve feet by six to hold the four hundred and forty-four small-print pages of my edition of *Emma* ; no Janeite would find it extraordinary that the public should be driven into the roadway to enable him to peruse, without interruption, on step-ladders and through magnifying glasses, this opuscule in all but length, having for a centre a work-basket and for circumference the wall of a gentleman's park. To the Janeite there is no world outside Jane, and he insists that you swallow her whole. Now there is no " balzacien déterminé," in Paul Bourget's phrase, who will not grant out of the two thousand five hundred characters in the *Comédie Humaine* at least two hundred unreadables, whereas the Janeite *enragé* insists upon perfection everywhere. Leo tells me he heard E. V. Lucas maintain that the three sentences in which Emma accepts Mr Knightley's proposal are among the greatest in the English language ! Walkley endorsed Miss Thackeray's statement that " Jane's very bores are enchanting." I disagree. I hold that Miss Bates is as boring to read about as to live with.

> " Indeed they are very delightful apples, and Mrs Wallace does them full justice, only we do not have them baked more than twice, and Mr Woodhouse made us promise to have them done three times. . . . The apples themselves are the very finest sort for baking, beyond a doubt ; all from Donwell—some of Mr Knightley's most liberal supply. He sends us a sack every year ; and certainly there never was such a keeping apple anywhere. . . ."

Is this anything except wildly dull ? Compare :

> " In Italy is she really with the grapes and figs growing everywhere and lava necklaces and bracelets too that land of poetry with burning mountains picturesque beyond belief though if the organ-boys come away from the neighbourhood not to be scorched nobody can wonder being so young and bringing their white mice with them most humane. . . . Venice Preserved too I think you have been there is it well or ill preserved for people differ so . . . you are acquainted Arthur I believe with Mantua what *has* it got to do with Mantua-making for I never have been able to conceive."

Thus Flora Finching. The truth is, I suppose, that Dickens's gusto and Jane's fastidiousness are as oil and vinegar—the difference between a gormandiser and a governess. Walkley went on to splutter : " The fact is, people who are bored by Jane Austen's bores are probably bored by Jane herself." But that cock won't fight. I am not bored by Jane's bores *en masse.* I dote, for example, on Mr Collins. But then Collins is a bore of relish, whereas Miss Bates is a bore of realism.

Feb. 8 *Thursday.* " Why, Sir, if you were to read Richardson for the story, your impatience would be so much fretted that you would hang yourself." *Emma* was even more tedious than I expected. If the evening was saved at all it was saved by Miss Bates, turned by Gillian Lind into Miss Tox with the addition of St Vitus's dance plus a turban straight out of *Chu Chin Chow.* Good support by Ambrosine Phillpotts, who, as Mrs Elton, stormed that drawing-room at Hartfield House very much as Miss Snevellicci might have stormed the Dedlocks' drawing-room at Chesney Wold. (Yes, I know I am telescoping two books.) The walking, stalking, talking gentlemen walked and stalked and talked, and Neagle's Emma wanted the camera. And, of course, it was unending. Why did Gordon Glennon, who adapted, keep us in the theatre long after all pretence at interest had evaporated ? Was he fired by recollection of that Henry James story of which Chesterton said that " the excitement becomes tense, thrilling, and almost intolerable in all the half-hours during which nothing is said or done " ? As we came out I heard Flora Finching whisper over my shoulder, " Macaroni if they really eat it like the conjurers James why don't they cut it shorter ? "

Feb. 9 *Friday.* Sat up late to-night reading Lord Moran's *Anatomy of Courage.* " Courage is a moral quality ; it is not a chance gift of nature like an aptitude for games. It is a cold choice between two alternatives, the fixed resolve not to quit ; an act of renunciation which must be made not once but many times by the power of the will. Courage is will power." But courage and cowardice are relative to the things about which a man is afraid. During the last war I had no compunction in walking down the dubious back streets of Marseilles at two in the morning. Whereas I would not, and could not at any time, walk a mile of English country road at midnight, any more than I could spend a night alone in a haunted house. (I don't believe in ghosts, but I'm afraid of them !) Last week a friend of mine who wears the ribbons of the D.F.M. and the D.S.C. was spending an evening at my flat. I asked him to fetch a syphon from the kitchen, and he at once refused. " I couldn't," he said : " there's a cat in there." I said, " I think you'll manage it," and went on smoking. He did manage it, but it took him twenty minutes !

Feb. 10 *Saturday.* " May I ask whether these pleasing attentions proceed from the impulse of the moment, or are the result of previous study ? " said Mr Bennet. Change a word, and the same might be asked of my outpourings. Take this week's article on *Emma.* I made a first draft of this on Wednesday night after seeing the play—say, three hours. Spent the whole of Thursday licking it into shape—say, a further eight hours. Should have continued longer except that George Blake, an old friend of mine and a captain in the Merchant Service, blew in. It seems that one night during the January gales his ship's anchors wouldn't hold, the engines refused to work, and he was washed overboard, but, seeing that nobody paid any attention, he climbed back again. Burly people never look under the weather, but I thought he could do with cheering up, and hauled him off to see *Three's a Family.* Vera Pearce was in magnificent form, and the only remark George made was to ask whether she was married. No, I don't think that as a novel *Three's a Family* would bear comparison with *Emma*, but I found it ten times more amusing than Wednesday night's play. Spent all yesterday, Friday, revising my notice of *Emma*, sent it down to the *S.T.*, and received the proof at five-thirty the same night. Worked on it till eight-thirty, or thereabouts, handed it in, then to cinema and supper, in the middle of which I realise that to talk about " railings " to a gentleman's park is pure Cockney and that the word should be " wall." Finish supper hastily, get a car, and retrieve proof. And once having started tinkering, tinker till 3 A.M.—another five hours. By this time my brain is in a whirl, and to quieten it I absorb quantities of whiskey, sleeping tablets, and Chesterton on Dickens. Bed about four. All told, I must have worked some twenty-two hours on this notice, and even now I think that " deceived " should be " hoodwinked." But since this is getting brainsickly, I decide to-day, Saturday, to go to the concert at the Albert Hall, for which Ernest Helme has sent me two seats. Somebody is going to conduct the *Symphonie Fantastique*, and I have arranged with George Mathew to come and drag me to it. As I write, the telephone rings. It is the *S.T.* printers, to tell me that my title of " Miss Austen's Thin Gruel " won't fit, being a letter too long. Do I mind if they change " Miss Austen " to " Jane " ? No, I don't mind. Leo says the above should be called "Symphonie Typographique: Épisode de la Vie d'un Journaliste."

Alas, we didn't get to the concert after all. On the way I called in Fleet Street for a final glance at my proof, and found that somebody, possibly I myself, had miscalculated, and will I cut sixteen lines, please ? Now I know how a painter feels when the frame-maker

Photo Felix H. Man

Morning's at Seven

says, " This canvas won't fit—will you cut two inches off the foreground, please ? Unless, of course, you prefer the sky ? " Messing with the stuff takes me an hour, which means either concert and no lunch, or lunch and no concert. Choose the second. After which to Grape Street, and savagely tear 14,000 words, say forty pages, out of *Ego* 7 !

Feb. 11 *Sunday.* The *Observer* prints this exquisite poem. It was written in the spring of 1944 ; the author died of wounds in Normandy last June, aged twenty-two.

A WISH

Let me not see old age: let me not hear
The proffered help, the mumbled sympathy,
The well-meant tactful sophistries that mock
Pathetic husks, who once were strong and free,
And in youth's fickle triumph laughed and sang,
Loved, and were foolish : and at the close have seen
The fruits of folly garnered, and that love,
Tamed and encaged, stale into grey routine.
Let me not see old age: I am content
With my few crowded years : laughter and strength
And song have lit the beacon of my life,
Let me not see it fade, but when the long
September shadows steal across the square,
Grant me this wish : they may not find me there.

D. R. Geraint Jones

Feb. 12 *Monday.* The surgeon who removes a carcinoma on Wednesday has lost interest in Tuesday's appendicectomy and forgotten all about Monday's vesical calculus. The layman can never understand this. Similarly he can never understand that when a dramatic critic has dotted the last " i " and crossed the last " t " in his notice he has had enough of both notice and subject. This morning I am deluged with letters about Mendelssohn and the *Dream*, the writers not realising that I put paid to that a fortnight ago. Since then I have finished with *Emma*, and am now tangled up in Wolfit's *Macbeth*, with which I shall be wholly preoccupied until, on Sunday morning, the notice goes into my cutting-book. After which, just as the surgeon is going to forget Thursday's gall-stones in Friday's short-circuit, so next week I shall have forgotten *Macbeth* in some other play.

Feb. 13 *Tuesday.* Sup with Tom Curtiss, who has unexpectedly returned from Paris. He tells me that while there is plenty to drink in that once gay but now embittered city, there is nothing to eat—" eating is virtually against the law." The French are bitter because they have not been invited to the Crimea conference. France has been liberated, it seems, by the French themselves ;

at least, the Americans and the English are never mentioned. Tom brought me a bottle of cognac, a new book about the Goncourts by Pierre Descaves, and a copy of *Le Figaro*, a small single sheet sixteen inches by eleven. It appears that the theatres are full and offer a programme which should make us blush, the plays ranging from *Antigone* to *Volpone*, and, amongst the moderns, Barrie, D'Annunzio, and Armand Salacrou. The Comédie Française has had to close owing to lack of heating facilities, Wolfit had a great success in two of Shakespeare's comedies, but Katherine Cornell in *The Barretts of Wimpole Street* just didn't go.

Feb. 14 *Wednesday.* The new Deanna Durbin film at the Leicester Square is entitled *Can't Help Singing*. By my calculation she has seven songs. Allowing three minutes for each makes a total of twenty-one minutes, and the film runs for ninety. Subtract twenty-one from ninety, and the result is sixty-nine minutes of the most appalling, flat twaddle I have ever endured. All round me this morning were a number of Negro airmen, who, being children of the South, and therefore easily entertained, should surely have responded. They were not amused. On the other hand, the whites laughed a great deal, and it cannot be assumed that they were all nursemaids and pantry-boys. There was a time when D. D. used to keep still while singing ; now she wanders through bog, through bush, through brake, through briar—indeed, she falls into the first of these—down staircases, behind columns and fountains spouting some nauseating cherry-coloured liquid. And she sings and she sings, always with the same vocal intonation. Always, too, with the same facial inexpressiveness, rendered by Technicolor in terms of lightly baked gingerbread. And, of course, always the same melodic line meandering level, whatever Macaulay may say, with Jerome Kern's commonplace fount. In my view D. D. would be well advised to stop trafficking with Red Indians in the neighbourhood of the Grand Canyon and get back to that story of the Voice which, discovered one fine afternoon by a millionaire connoisseur, appears on the following evening at the Metropolitan Opera House as the Queen of Night, exercising such magic upon her audience that she is able to marry the second flautist.

Feb. 15 *Thursday.* The fact that Wolfit cannot play Macbeth is neither here nor there, since many great actors have failed in the part. If Lear is often regarded as unactable it is because it is held that an actor's momentum *in a single direction* cannot be as great as Shakespeare's. If Macbeth is unactable it is on the more reasonable supposition that it is not given to a player to be in the maximum degree and simultaneously extrovert and introvert. (I have seen one first-class Macbeth and one only—Benson. Benson was a superb Henry V and an exquisite Richard II, and his Thane was the result of adding the two together.) Wolfit's Macbeth fails because the character doesn't lie in the actor's personality. Because no actor can be Macbeth who deprives him of his poetry, introspection, vacillation, remorse. " Be bloody, bold, and resolute ! " enjoins the Apparition. But then Wolfit is already bloody, bold, and resolute, and has been so from the beginning. The character goes wrong from the start, from the words: "Duncan comes here to-night," followed by Lady Macbeth's " And when goes hence ? " This is the first in a long time (" What beast was't *then*," etc.) that murder has been mentioned between them, and now the impetus comes from the lady, who in her immediately preceding speech has already settled the business in her own mind. (" Papa is in the study praying for guidance ; Mamma is upstairs packing.") Murder is as yet only at the back of Macbeth's mind (" My thought, whose murder yet is but fantastical "), which means that there should be no more than the glimmer of an idea behind the words : " To-morrow, *as he purposes*." But this is not D. W.'s notion. At his wife's question he disengages himself, steps back a pace, goes through prodigies of winking and nodding, and ruins Lady Macbeth's " O, never shall sun that morrow see ! " To reduce this from the instigatory to the corroborative is to trump the actress's best trick. In the scene which immediately follows—the colloquy between Lady M. and Duncan—I can find no justification for Macbeth being present, veiling his face with his arm. The Thane of Cawdor is a First Murderer, not a Second ! In short, D. W. turns the whole play into a ranting, roaring, Saturday-night melodrama, full of very capable sound and fury but signifying nothing of the play's pity and melancholy. G. H. Lewes said of Macready's Macbeth that he " stole into the sleeping-chamber of Duncan like a man going to purloin a purse, not like a warrior going to snatch a crown." Wolfit's Macbeth comes out of that chamber like a furniture remover weighed down by an invisible wardrobe ! Only the most complete insensitivity could condone that jolly little march-tune which heralds the fatal entrance of Duncan under the battlements, and suggests that the play to follow is something about *Merrie Scotland* !

Feb. 16 *Friday.* Bored by *Laura*, at the St Martin's to-night. Does a would-be murderer shoot somebody without making sure that he has got hold of the right person ? Does a young woman whose fiancé has a mistress lend her apartment to her rival and then disappear ? Does a "womanthrope," to use Miss Prism's convenient neologism, commit murder because one of the sex to which he is allergic won't have him ? Do American detectives investigate a crime by making love to the suspected criminal over her coffee and cookies ? As a plain dramatic critic I just wouldn't know the answers. What I do know is that it was a pity to omit some of the original novel's dialogue. "The magnificence of my skeleton is hidden by the weight of my flesh." "I leaped like a mother leopard." "Aunt Susan once sang in musical comedy. Then she became a widow. The hyphen of marriage is best forgotten." The acting was probably very good. Raymond Lovell, trying hard to believe in his rôle, scattered tenth-rate epigrams with gusto. As the incredible Laura, a writer of advertising slogans with a passion for hot jazz and a knack equal to Helen's for turning men's heads, Sonia Dresdel swept the stage in blood-red négligés and the eager vivacity of a leading actress "resting." But then, this is the theatre whose audiences expect acting, and not the cinema where to look on catastrophe sympathetically, glamorously, and with the sweet simplicity of a boiled haddock is the most that is demanded by Streatham, Finchley, and what is known as "practically Ealing." Later I take up the paper and I read about Miss Baba la Bilbo, or some such name, that she is "the greatest screen find of the war, and a national sensation in the U.S.A. She's twenty years of age, and was an usherette and cover girl. She is like slow electricity and has the smoky and disillusioned voice of Garbo, her mystery and careless grace, but her personality and torrid magnetism are all her own. London will have to wait till the summer to see her." Madam, I can wait.

Feb. 17 *Saturday.* There is nothing like finishing a job properly. Having proof-read Cardus's *Ten Composers*, the next thing was to review it. But how ? *Express* readers are not supposed to be interested in classical music. But where there's a will there's a way, and I think I get round it with the following :

> I am emboldened to put Mr Neville Cardus's *Ten Composers* at the top of my column this week because of Dr Malcolm Sargent's story of the labourer who said after a recent symphony concert, "'Itler's done one thing—turned me inter a blinkin' 'ighbrow ! "
>
> Now the labourer in question might well have heard a symphony by Schubert, Brahms, Sibelius, or he might have heard the Elgar *Enigma* Variations, or even that superb picture of London life called *Cockaigne.*
>
> The concert might have opened with the Prelude to Wagner's *The Mastersingers*, marvellous tribute to that sanity and generosity

of mind which Nazi Germany has discarded. This music-lover has certainly, like Delius, heard a cuckoo in spring, and probably, like Debussy, thrown his full length upon the grass and dreamed. If Dr Sargent's friend was listening to his radio set last Sunday he must have heard Richard Strauss's *Don Juan*, and would have known that to the musically-minded there is an intenser thrill than anything imparted by Clark Gable or Gary Cooper to the nitwit screen-gazer. Those are eight of Mr Cardus's composers. The other two are Mahler and César Franck, and if our friend thinks these composers are trying him a bit high I shan't quarrel.

Cardus is that rare thing among musical critics: he is a critic who is musical and who likes music. And then there is another matter. Cardus is not one-sided. I like to know that an art critic understands something about boxing and a dramatic critic something about pedigree cattle. I mistrust the musical critic who is bounded by oboe and clarinet, piccolo and bassoon, and outside that windy frame knows nothing of the world.

One of the reasons that Cardus is one of the best living musical critics is that he is the best writer on cricket. This book will tell Dr Sargent's friend all about ten famous wickets and what those were like who batted on them.

Feb. 18 *Sunday.* Yesterday Jock, on leave, took me out to lunch, and I was delighted to find him in much better form and almost his old self. Told me that to criticise *Emma*, or anything else that Jane wrote and which will, could, or might be adapted from her books, is to behave like a navvy who, offered a glass of vintage claret, spits, throws it on the floor, and says, "B—— this muck; let's 'ave some bloody wallop!" As I was turning this over Jock told me that he had made the acquaintance of a French-Canadian called—Jock swore he hadn't invented it—Fidèle Galant. I told him that this must be a character straight out of Maurice Hewlett. Anyhow, the name was so beautiful that on the strength of it I proposed to buy Jock some brandy, at which he demurred. I said, "I have more money than you have." He said darkly, "That's as may be." Now I had often wondered how he could retain his flat in King Street on the pay of an ordinary seaman, and it suddenly dawned on me that he must have made a small fortune out of the *Henry V* film. Mollified by the brandy, Jock conceded that if he were on a desert island and given the choice of one author it would not be either Jane or Proust, but Charles Dickens. I said, "If it comes to that, any sane castaway would rather have a hogshead of wallop than a bottle of Mouton Rothschild." After this went home and worked. Then to supper with Tom Curtiss. Tiny club at the top of five or six flights of stairs, lift into which four people can squeeze, and in the corner of the men's lavatory a door with a wee notice: "Fire Exit." There may be other exits and notices. I didn't see them. Extremely good food, excellent drink, a dance-floor some twelve feet square, and a band with a loud-speaker! This rendered all talk impossible, and finally I made my apologies, and went and sat in blessed silence in the street until the car arrived.

To bed early and sleep well, with no nightmare to speak of. Spend the morning in bed, perusing the Sunday papers with, as Amanda Ros would have said, my accustomed grace. Ernest Newman very good on the vanity of conductors, though he will never better the reply of my friend Alec Whittaker (the oboe-player) to my question about who had conducted that afternoon's concert: "Sorry, James, I forgot to look." Spend four or five hours correcting the proofs of *Ego* 7, which have just started coming in. Then ponder my reply to a communication received during the week from two young ladies in Birmingham calling themselves Barbara Siggs and Hazel Young. Here is part of an enchanting letter:

> Is Mr Pavia still helping you? If not, here is a list of things we can't do:
>
> (1) Our typing is slightly hesitant (British genius for understatement).
> (2) We don't know shorthand. (Jock couldn't do shorthand, could he?)
>
> On the other hand:
>
> (3) We don't wear jewellery, and we can both manage without hairpins.
> (4) We do *not* use scent.
> (5) We would endure draughts gladly.
> (6) We would be prepared to cope with allusions to almost anything from Herodotus to Popocatepetl.
> (7) We're awfully good at looking happily vacant!
> (8) We will dress exclusively in brown velvet (in fact, it would suit us)—or has your taste changed?

In reply sent this duplicate letter:

> DEAR BARBARA AND HAZEL,
>
> Normally—and I think that perhaps I allude to this somewhere in my *Ego* books—I answer letters like yours with something Pooh-Bah says in *The Mikado*: "Go away, little girls. Can't talk to little girls like you. Go away, there's dears." The difficulty is that I find I somehow can't bring myself to say this to you.
>
> So let me tell you a true story. Years ago there lived somebody called Horace Walpole, who was one of the nicest, nastiest, wittiest, and spitefullest old gentlemen the world has ever seen. He flourished—and what an epistolary flourish, seeing he was the best

of letter-writers !—when George III was King, in a delightful house near Twickenham called Strawberry Hill. He knew every one, including Kitty Clive, the great actress and friend of Garrick, and died a few years after the French Revolution.

Now one day, when he had become an extremely old and highly curmudgeonly old gentleman, Horace met two young women called Mary and Agnes Berry, who were about the age of his great-nieces. They had come to live with their widowed father near Strawberry Hill, and presently Walpole invited them to view his private printing-press. Although he was fifty years older than they were, the two girls conceived an affection for him which lasted until his death. After which they "cherished and embellished" his memory until they died, both in 1852.

But there is this difference between Walpole and me. In his will he left the young ladies £4000 apiece: I shall not be able to leave you anything. I should require more cherishing and embellishing than he did. He wanted to marry Mary Berry; I don't want to marry either of you.

However, I am persuaded that you are charming children. Write to me from time to time (but not too often), and I promise to read your letters, even if it is Mr Pavia who answers them. The present admirable example of the epistolary art is, however, entirely authentic, put together without any help from anybody.

Now run along, there's dears.

Your sincere friend,
POOH-BAH AGATE

Feb. 19 *Monday.* Tom Curtiss left for Paris last night, this time more or less for good.

Lunch with Eunice Frost, a bright, intelligent creature and London representative of Penguin Books, to whom I sell the first thing I ever published, my war book, *L. of C.* We are going to drop this title and call it *Lines of Communication.* Am told that owing to the paper restrictions they cannot promise an initial printing of more than 60,000 copies. Since there is no money to speak of in it, in view of tax, etc., why reprint the old book ? Because I hold that all wars are the same, and that there is no difference, except in inessentials, between Agincourt and Waterloo or between the First and Second World War. Unless I very much mistake, to-day's civilian turned soldier must be feeling very much what I felt in 1915, and might like to see his feelings put into words.

Feb. 20 *Tuesday.* It was really very naughty of Studio One to put *L'Homme Qui Cherche la Vérité* in the same programme as the revival of *The Man in Grey*, one of those pieces of Regency twaddle in which the British film shows itself at its worst. Male film stars in this country are film stars not because they can act but because they have nice long noses or sleek foreheads or something of the sort. There are one or two exceptions, of course. But the fact remains that if a young man has a good photogenic profile one picture will make him a star even if he hasn't enough acting talent to carry in the tea-things in a play at Kew. As for the young women —always with one or two exceptions—the British director seems to have taken as his slogan :

> So dumb but so beautiful,
> So dumb that it hurts,
> And I don't care how dumb you are,
> So long as you're beautiful. . . .

I didn't believe to-night in a single thing that any man, woman, child, horse, or dog did or thought or said or neighed or barked in the absurd Regency story. Whereas I passionately believed in all the actors in the French film. Think of the principals : Raimu, Alerme, Gabrielle Dorziat, Jacqueline Delubac. But then one expects these people to act. Raimu, for example, is a great comedian in the country which gave the world Coquelin. Also, it's the smaller fry who are such good actors. Are they supposed to be cashiers, or croupiers, or cab-drivers ? Very well, they *are* cashiers and croupiers and cab-drivers. You accept them. They are so good that you never dream of thinking how good they are. Whereas about your English film actor you say to yourself, " Isn't that Monty Mumble—such a clever young man. Let me see now, what did I see him in last ? Was it *Topsy Turns Turtle* or *Bob's Your Uncle* ? I remember he was awfully good as a ship's steward—I had no idea he could play a reception-clerk." The mere fact that you notice how good an actor is is clear proof that he's no good at all *in the French sense*.

The film itself is a charming little piece of malice about an elderly banker who, by the simple device of pretending to be deaf, discovers that his employees detest him, that his family loathes him, and that his mistress is deceiving him with his godson. The only flaw in an otherwise perfect little picture is that the banker appears never to have seen a play with the elder Guitry in it, because if he had he must have known that every elderly Frenchman expects his mistress to deceive him and counts himself lucky if the young man is as respectable as a banker's godson is likely to be. In fact, I remember a comedy in which Guitry insisted that he should approve his mistress's choice. But then the whole matter was thoroughly explored long before Guitry—actually by Balzac, who divulged to the world the name given by mistress and her young man to any elderly protector : *le singe*. Apart from this wee flaw the picture is witty and delightful.

And no wonder, seeing that it is by that witty and delightful writer, Pierre Wolff.

Feb. 21 *Wednesday.* Jock calls and tells me that the entire cast of the film of *Cæsar and Cleopatra* is going to Egypt for three months, except, of course, Cleopatra ! And I tell him about a well-known actor who, taking the drama to the troops in France, said as the curtain fell on Christmas Eve, " And I look forward to being with you all again next Christmas " ! Jock spends the next three hours or so over the proofs of *Ego* 7, and then says, " Man, do ye no' wish you had a wee bit genius instead of a' this talent ! "

Cocasseries, No. 10 :

> When Collette Lyons stuck two fingers in her mouth and whistled for a cab in front of a Los Angeles theatre she whistled herself into a film career. . . . Her labial dexterity was not the only factor that opened the Hollywood gates to her.
>
> General Film Distributors Ltd., *Film News*

Feb. 22 *Thursday.* Not even Gorky at his gloomiest ever made me believe that all Russians are miserable all of the time. And no English novelist is going to persuade me that the whole of the East End is vicious. In *It Always Rains on Sunday* I read :

> Blissfully unaware that a police car had just pulled up outside his house, Mr Sandigate was in the public bar of " The Two Compasses," getting slowly but surely intoxicated. His daughter Vi was sitting on a divan bedstead three floors above Lisle Street. Slopey Collins was clinging to the railing of Coronet Grove, Tommy Swann was running breathlessly down an alleyway that led to Coronet Square. Whitey Williams chewed the damp end of a Woodbine as he came out of " The Duke of Teck," a raw whiskey burning pleasantly inside him as he went forth to " do " Mr Caleb Beasley—to " do him good and proper." Morry Higham was driving down to Brighton. His wife, Sadie, sat on a bedside trying to console her youngest baby.

The implication is that all fathers of East End families get fuddled every Sunday evening, that one daughter in each family is a prostitute, that anybody in a hurry is an escaped convict, that whoever is seen idling is waiting for a chance to bash somebody, and that all flash-looking young men are faithless husbands totally indifferent to their offspring. The blurb to this book says, " This is the real East End—flashy, lusty, and full of unconquerable vitality. You can forget the war when you read this book, for here described is the life that goes on in war and peace." This is just not true. This is NOT the real East End. This is NOT the life that goes on in war and peace. It is a lie to suggest that if in peace-time you take six houses in a row you will find them occupied by six different kinds of criminal. As for war-time, will the author maintain that all the East End lads who have joined Army, Navy, Merchant Navy, and Air Force are actual or potential criminals ? The author, who is a Mr La Bern, should go and have a look at the East End, and at the same time get somebody to explain to him the difference between rule and exception.

Feb. 24
Saturday.

A great struggle to get into fewer than nine hundred words all I want to say about the nature of comedy and farce, and also tell readers what the new Drayton-Hare play is about, and how it is acted, and whether they should book seats for it. The last is the first and only thing looked for in a dramatic critic's notice by 999 out of 1000 people, blast them ! Here is part of what I ultimately evolved :

> Farce is not comedy produced to absurdity in the Euclidean sense, any more than man is an extension of monkey in what the layman takes to be the Darwinian sense. As I understand it, both humans and simians stem out from the same tree but on different sides of it, and possibly the first is a little higher up the trunk than the second. Wherefore production, while it may mean sillier and sillier men and wiser and wiser monkeys, can never fuse the two. The same with comedy and farce. May I say that I have invented a rule which works for me, though I can find no authority for it and claim none ? Set down in simple terms, the rule is : Comedy treats of unreal persons in real situations ; farce deals with real persons in unreal situations. Never was any real-life old gentleman so testy as Sir Peter Teazle, uncle so benevolent as Sir Oliver, scapegrace so heart-warming as Charles Surface, hypocrite so plausible as Joseph. Immerse these in a plot, and the enjoyment of the spectator comes from the deployment of character. In farce it works the other way. The finest example in the English language —and but for Wilde's literary snobbery, according with his astrakhan collar and that ubiquitous silk hat without which he was never photographed, this masterpiece would have been labelled a farce instead of a comedy—is *The Importance of Being Earnest*, which shows how perfectly normal people behave when confronted with handbags stuffed with babies. Wherefore two things follow. The richer the comedy the more flamboyant the playing can afford to be ; the richer the farce the more solemn must be its enacting. Every character in Sheridan's masterpiece must abound in its sense of itself, revel in its own gusto, and show that it is revelling ; let Lady Bracknell betray consciousness of her absurdity by so much

as the flutter of an eyelid, and that gorgeous vessel founders. There are, of course, an enormous number of so-called farces having to do with the behaviour of unreal persons in unreal situations. These, being mere concatenations of buffoonery and conglomerations of horse-play, are not matter for critical consideration.

Feb. 25 *Sunday.* Spent the greater part of last night and the whole of to-day looking through the proofs of May's *Madame Sarah.* To my great astonishment I found the chapters on the "mute e" as exciting as a detective story. May has succeeded, by some means which I cannot identify, in putting the whole thing back in time so that we see Sarah through May's eyes as a young girl—a feat which Henry James and Proust would have done consciously, but which with her must have been subconscious. I was particularly interested in this passage:

> The most versatile member of Madame Sarah's company was Madame Boulanger, to whom fell all the character and comic women—a lovely Prudence in *La Dame*—a face like a cockatoo and very stout. A brilliant natural actress with no traditional nonsense about her, but whose Œnone in *Phèdre* was a really fine performance. Her features could assume a tragic cast, and she was a master of make-up. Barbara Gott always recalled her to my mind.

This confirms Maurice Baring's view, and mine, that the photograph of Sarah sent me by Esmé Percy shows her saying to Œnone: "C'est toi qui l'as nommé!"

Feb. 26 *Monday.* A film parable. There was once a talent-spotter who was paid £10,000 a year to spot talent. For eleven months he kept his eyes open without encountering so much as a ha'p'orth of aptitude. At the beginning of the twelfth month he decided that what couldn't be spotted must be invented. So he hied him to a suburb full of ordinary-looking girls, stationed himself opposite a fish queue, and watched the young women file past. Presently he noticed one of the queue-ers whose eyes had the dreamy look of a codfish. She had no hair to speak of, her complexion was muddy, her back humped, and when she asked for a pound of plaice her voice reeked of commonness. Questioned, she said she had acted quite a bit; once as an Indian maiden in *Hiawatha* at the Albert Hall, and once as a banana-seller in an amateur production of *Chu Chin Chow.* Whereupon she was carted off to the studio at Greensleeves on the Medway and given the once-over by a casting director in receipt of £20,000 a year, but who had yet to cast somebody. "O.K.," said this gentleman. The human codfish was then put in a crate and despatched to one of the more celluloid reaches of the Thames, where she was kept in plaster of Paris for six months to straighten her back, during which time the manes of horses were grafted on to her head, and interior and exterior decorators messed about with her complexion. Her throat was hourly sprayed with a mixture of coal-tar and fish-glue, after which cohorts of camera-men shoved her about, and out of some thousands of shots enough were selected to make a two-minute sequence. This being shown, the Biggest Noise of All said, " Hell, bung that lollipop back where she came from ! " Is there any more to this story ? Yes. The talent-spotter's salary was doubled, the casting director's trebled, and the B. N. of A. gave himself a bonus of £100,000 for Having Made a Decision. End of parable.

Feb. 27 *Tuesday.* Two ways of saying the same thing :

> I am dying, Egypt, dying ; only
> I here importune death awhile, until
> Of many thousand kisses the poor last
> I lay upon thy lips.
>
> SHAKESPEARE, *Antony and Cleopatra*

Jean Gabin as the deserter in *Quai des Brumes* shot by bandits and saying to his sweetheart : " Embrasse-moi. Vite. On est pressé ! "

Feb. 28 *Wednesday.* James Bridie has a genius for going off at a tangent, but his inconsequences, like the boomerang, mostly come home to roost. His fun is the reverse of Bunthorne's, for the reason that there is more calculated malice in it than the casual spectator might imagine. In short, this descendant of Puck and Queen Mab is a joy. But why, in his new book of essays, *Tedious and Brief*, does he make the statement : " The animating motive of most critics is to make the artist look like a fool " ? Surely this is to confuse criticism with fault-finding ? My dictionary has the following :

> CRITICISM. 1. The art of judging with knowledge and propriety of the beauties and faults of a literary performance, or of a production in the fine arts ; as, *dramatic criticism.* 2. Animadversion, censure.

Every serious critic takes this order for granted ; whoever reverses it is none.

March 1 *Thursday.* I first saw *Les Trois Valses* as a film and was enchanted. Because of that French genius for making something out of nothing, an entrée out of a potato-peeling, a confection out of a handful of rags. Because of the lightness of touch.

Because of the charm. I next saw the film as a musical play at the Marigny Theatre with those exquisite players, Pierre Fresnay and Yvonne Printemps, and I remember thinking that of light comedy the same thing might be said that the French philosopher held about pleasure in general : " Le plaisir est comme la glace ; n'appuyez-pas, glissez toujours." This skimming quality was entirely lost in to-night's transfer to London and Daly's Theatre in the days of George Edwardes. Everybody worked hard, perhaps too hard. When Printemps warbled she piped but as the linnets sing, whereas with Evelyn Laye vocalising is a very strenuous and highly organised affair. " If I had learnt music," said Lady Catherine de Bourgh, " I should have been a great proficient." Now Laye has learnt music, and her desire to exhibit proficiency is wholly laudable. It is not, however, linnet-like. Her acting ? I remember an American critic writing of an American film star that " while she's having a soul, she's also got a mass of draperies ; watching them sort of hypnotises people, and keeps their minds off the spiritual things she says." Laye in this piece wears a great many elaborate frocks, and wears them so naturally and prettily that one is absolved from paying attention to the conflict of art and heart. Esmond Knight plays the three lovers, and it is not his fault that Latin sentiment doesn't go, in the arithmetical sense, into English forthrightness and pluck. The settings ? Mostly less than enchanting. Oscar Straus's music ? " Hélas," as the French critic wrote of Beethoven's share in the Paris production of *Egmont*, " pourquoi y en a-t-il si peu ? "

March 2 *Friday.* Three letters. The first is from my old and still unknown friend. The school at Broadstairs was, of course, a girls' school.

Tuesday 27.2.45

MISTER AYE-GATE, SIR,

A LARGE piece of paper as you will see, because it's no use using a weeny piece to you, knowing how I shall ramble on and on. Isn't my writing shaky ? Am very tired. I shall die in one of these tirednesses, and not a bad way either.

First of all and oh boy, oh boy—I have—yesterday (before I knew it)—eaten a piece of pudding made with raisins sent from America by guess whom ? Lloyd Osbourne !

I spent 22*s*. on Mr Wolfit, not counting coffees and programmes. Took two six-shilling tickets for *Macbeth* for a nice little woman I work with and her Wren daughter who " wants to go on the stage " ! This woman is a descendant, of some kind, of Mrs Siddons. A nice original mind, very bright dark eyes though she looks seventy, and nice eye-sockets. Her son is a fighter pilot in Holland and was a test pilot until lately. He has a wonderful Highland name that I can never remember so cannot tell you. This old-looking lady thinks nothing of going to Inverness for two days, the last time in the middle of that awful blizzard.

Your "Word to Mr Wolfit" was fine. I went to see his *Much Ado*, it is such a merry little play (I always don't really notice Hero, and wait for her to finish) and liked it, he's a lovable creature (per Willyam S.)—hope he doesn't get any heavier in his mannerisms. What a *nice* person Benedick is. One treat about Mr W. is that I hear every syllable of everything he says. Hope I never see *Lear* again, I cannot stand the blinding of Gloucester; and Lear's making *such* a fuss—even a beautiful fuss—over his hundred knights when an immeasurable tragedy is riding out invisibly overhead. Last year when I saw *Lear* bombers were streaming over the theatre, heavy laden; this year they streamed over still, over the Winter Garden. What is all Shakespeare's Lear compared with that throb of a bomber procession? The curtain speech wasn't bad, for once, though intoned. Didn't drop any bricks much. The first act is always unearthly familiar to me, I was cast for Lear when I was ten at Broadstairs.

And this:

438 *Belchers Lane*
Little Bromwich
Birmingham

10 *Longmore Street*
Balsall Heath
Birmingham 12

March 1*st*, 1945

OUR ECSTATICALLY DEAR JAMES AGATE,

! !

Our usually so fluent pens are frozen by your so great kindness that we can only say, simply and very sincerely, "Thank you."

Our reactions to your letter were varied. Barbara rushed from room to room in a state of wild excitement (comparable only to the Polovtsian Dances from *Prince Igor*). Hazel, who received her letter in the early morning and was thus still in bed, bounced up and down so much that she broke a spring (comparable only to Donald Wolfit in *Volpone*).

We are prepared to "cherish and embellish" you as and when required. Perhaps, by riveting, when we are thirty-five ("the ideal age for a woman") we will have amassed about £4000 apiece and we will be able to start a fund for "The Cherishing and Embellishing of the Works and Person of Mr James Agate."

We had had the temerity to think of adopting you as an honorary uncle—or great-uncle (shade of our now-even-more-beloved Horace Walpole!). May we now have that very great honour? (N.B. This should be read in a very deep voice—like the Rev. Chasuble—and if this reads like Stephen Leacock we can't help it.) We hope that you will excuse our "forwardness," and may we as dutiful "great-nieces" inquire solicitously about your health? We have been wanting to do this before, but we did not know whether it was "quite nice." We fear that we might have committed a breach of etiquette in referring to Mr Pavia as "Leo Pavia," but having referred to him as "Leo Pavia" for so long between ourselves we can't lose the habit!—and anyhow the mere thought of calling Jock "Mr Dent" reduces us to helpless laughter! (If ever we did meet Jock would he expect us to call him "Mr Dent"? Actually if we did meet any of you great people we would probably stand gaping and tongue-tied, looking like soulful plaice!)

By the way, it was a great effort to restrain ourselves from writing to you straight away, but you did say "not too often," and your slightest wish is our command.

We think that's all for now.

Au revoir,

Your affectionate "great-nieces"
(by adoption—on our part, anyhow),

BARBARA SIGGS
and HAZEL YOUNG

P.S. Riveting is one of our proposed methods of obtaining a lot of money quickly. If we start riveting when we're eighteen, by the time we're twenty-six, by spending money only on bare necessities, and receiving £6 per week, we will have saved £3200 between us. *Q.E.F.* Other proposed methods of getting money are: being chauffeuses, being shop assistants; being theatre-cleaners or programme-sellers (this is pleasure as well!); usherettes; factory hands, etc. B. S. & H. Y.

P.P.S. It *was* sweet of you to remember to send us a letter each. Thank you. B. S. & H. Y.

P.P.P.S. { Pray send our kind regards to Mr Dent.
Give our love to Jock. }

B. S. & H. Y.

Also this:

Kildarroch
Milner Road
Heswall
Cheshire

26 *Feb.* 1945

DEAR SIR,

I don't want the following incident to die with me, so I pass it on to you. It shows that in the Carlyle family Thomas was not the only "thrawn" member.

About forty years ago an old watchmaker told me that he was sent out from Ecclefechan to the farm of a brother of Thomas Carlyle, as a boy, to bring back a clock to be repaired. (I was told the Christian name of the brother, but I forget it.) The farmer was away for the day, and the men on the farm, having finished their tasks, came to the farmer's wife to know what they should do.

There were some palings in the yard, and she knew where her husband wanted them to be erected, so she told the men to put them up. My friend was there when Thomas Carlyle's brother came home. When he saw the erected fence, and his wife had explained what she had done, he turned to the men and said, "Pull them all down, I'll be ruled by no woman." And they were pulled down.

Yours sincerely,
R. J. WALLACE

March 4 *Sunday.* Took an hour off in the middle of the afternoon to listen in with Leo and a friend to the Henry Wood Memorial Concert. Ida Haendel had not played two bars of the Mendelssohn Violin Concerto before three voices sang out: "Too fast!" The nostalgic second subject might have been from *Merrie England,* while the last movement was a scramble. By which I don't mean that Haendel couldn't play the notes, or that the orchestra couldn't keep up with her, but that the pace turned the thing into a frolic in which the gunpowder ran out at the heels of everybody's boots, including the conductor's.

March 5 *Monday.* Letter from Jock:

Staff Quarters
R.N. Hospital
Haslar
4th March, 1945

DEAR JAMIE,

I wait and wait and wait to hear about my destiny—impatiently.

Meanwhile I take what is, I hope, a final survey of my fellow S.B.A.'s. "I wish I liked the human race: I wish I liked its silly face!" said Professor Raleigh. It's not its silly face so much as its mindlessness that I find so mislikeable—when the war obliges me to mix with it, gregariously.

I can perfectly understand my colleagues finding difficulty with the Group Quizzes (a form of my own invention—example enclosed) with which I daily bombard them. This I do (*a*) out of sheer intellectual snobbery, and (*b*) to keep up my reputation, which—at least among the younger sort—is that of a mixture of Joad, Datas, and God.

But when, yesterday, I set an intelligence test of what you must grant to be absolutely general knowledge, I must say that I (even I who expect so little) was rather shaken by the extensiveness and peculiarity of the universal ignorance. Who was Mrs Siddons? How far away is the moon? Who is Somerset Maugham? Who was Lord Lister? What instrument does Artie Shaw play? And Benny Goodman? Who was Plato? And who is James Agate?

For Sarah I got a series of " Don't knows," and three of them called her " a murderess " ! (Probably associative idea with Seddon the murderer.) The distance of the moon, which as every schoolboy should know is only 240,000 miles away, varied between " several billions of miles," " millions and millions of miles," and " two light-years." Most of them, oddly enough, knew Maugham as a " writer " ; and all of them, maddeningly enough, knew you ! Lister, whom they *ought* to know as S.B.A.'s, drew an almost complete blank, though one said he invented chloroform and another got near enough by saying " he discovered sterility under Queen Victoria " ! A mildly witty chap said of Plato that he " invented an unexciting form of love," but none of the rest knew that he was either a Greek or a philosopher ; one, mistaking the name for " Pluto," called him " that screen dog." Can you crown it ?

As ever,
JOCK

March 6 *Tuesday.* Hundreds of thousands of young men and women all over the country are trying to write poetry without having grasped anything at all about scansion or rhyme. Hundreds of thousands of young people who would see nothing wrong in :

Mary had a little lamb,
Its fleece was whiter than snow ;
And wherever Mary ran
Her pet lamb was sure to follow.

Every day, by every post, some of their efforts arrive. Half-sheets of creased and dirty notepaper with scrubby little poems on them. Will I tell the authors what I think ? What I am beginning to think is that all elementary schools should have a poetry class in which some notion of the rudimentary principles of verse, including punctuation, should be got into the child-brain. Here are extracts from two poems received this morning. The first is called " The Tramp " :

Maybe, he is, a forgotten hero of Mons
Just like the rest, of, our English sons
Maybe he fought, for, that freedom, you got
But, now, to be a tramp, is his lot.

The second is from something in the nature of an " Ode to Winston " :

We quote all England's battles, from Hastings to the Marne,
Saying, in these wonderful events, the English stood by, calm.

My invariable answer is to tell these poor devils that their stuff is not poetry, and to advise them to go on writing it if writing gives them any solace. And then I cross out " solace," and put " comfort." Wonder 'tis how little mirth, or poetry, or doggerel, or anything else " keeps the bones of man from lying On the bed of earth."

March 7 *Wednesday.* Again two ways of saying the same thing :

For myself I confess to have the smallest possible pleasure in a French actor when he is " profond et rêveur."

G. H. LEWES, *On Actors and the Art of Acting*

Furthermore, the guy seems to be improving right along, and gets so he can box fairly well and punch the bag, and all this and that, but he always has that far-away look in his eyes, and personally I do not care for fighters with far-away looks.

DAMON RUNYON, *Bred for Battle*

March 8 *Thursday.* I cannot any longer disguise the fact that I am almost completely allergic to Shaw as playwright. Not entirely, but almost, since I can always see the whole of *The Devil's Disciple* and *Androcles and the Lion* and four-fifths of *The Doctor's Dilemma.* The rest of the time the plays either bore or antagonise me. To have to sit through *Man and Superman, Pygmalion, Heartbreak House, Back to Methuselah,* and even that masterpiece, *St Joan,* is to me the very ecstasy of theatrical boredom. I am prepared to admit that Shaw is the greatest brain the theatre has known since Shakespeare, but it is a brain put not, so to speak, to the service of the theatre, but using the theatre for its own purposes. Add that Shaw's world is one I don't want to live in, a joyless, arid world in which sex is merely an instrument of the Life Force to be brought into play at the bidding of the Female. In his preface to *The Six of Calais* Shaw is scornful of Congreve, who thought that " cuckoldry and concupiscent old women are things to be laughed at." Well, aren't they ? I shall stop laughing at Lady Wishfort the moment one of Shaw's hard-bitten females makes me smile. And then I don't trust Shaw. I feel he will pull a fast one on me if he can. Take his anti-vaccination remarks in the preface to *The Simpleton of the Unexpected Isles,* in which he talks about the " overwhelming evidence that vaccination has killed thousands of children in a quite horrible way, whereas no child has ever been a penny the worse for baptism since John the Baptist recommended it." The implication is that deaths from vaccination are still going on. If this is not the implication, then the statement is like arguing that because on battlefields and warships men have lost their lives through having their arms and legs cut off by hurried and ill-equipped surgeons, amputation under modern conditions should not be allowed. I imagine that what is at the back of Shaw's mind runs like this, though he may not know it : Slums are an evil. Overcrowding encourages smallpox. Vaccination discourages smallpox. But doing away with smallpox removes one of the incentives for doing away with slums. Therefore let us have epidemics of smallpox, which will frighten the wealthy classes into bettering the conditions of the poor. Away, therefore, with vaccination. I go to a Shaw play, then, knowing that I must for three hours be in contact with a way of thinking with which I am not in sympathy, nine-tenths of it expressed in a footling idiom which Shaw thinks is wit, and I find exasperating. And knowing, too, that at any moment he is likely to break out with something which might be Isaiah or Blake, so that I dare not go to sleep. The concernancy of all this ? Simply that I spent the whole of yesterday reading *The Simpleton*, extracting and getting on to paper what it is essentially about. In the evening I went to the play knowing that I should hate every moment of it—which I did. Then home and re-wrote my article in the light of the piece as acted. Bed at three and up again soon after eight, when I tackled the thing for the third time. Worked all day, and finally turned in the article on my way to *Gay Rosalinda*, at the Palace. This turned out to be a Gargantuanised version of *Fledermaus*. Reinhardt plus Korngold. Three and a half hours. Bandbox into pantechnicon. Cohorts of flunkeys immersing bevies of sylphides in Blue Danube. Cast rather less Viennese than Oxford Street.

March 10 *Saturday.* Again from Jock :

9th March, 1945

Postscript. My point—and writing in a hurry I forgot to make it—is that almost every one of these likeable ignoramuses knew that the instrument bewhored and bestrumpeted by Artie Shaw and Benny Goodman is the clarinet.

And then there's another thing. The whole mess (when I brought the morning papers in this breakfast-time) was far more interested in the reprieve of Mrs Jones (of " Cleft Chin " murder fame) than in the capture of Cologne. I suppose you'll call this healthy and right-minded and just as it should be ? Or do you ?

JOCK

Am replying :

*Queen Alexandra Mansions, W.C.*2
March 10*th*, 1945

DEAR JOCK,

I respectfully submit that you've got the wrong angle on culture and the working classes. One of the questions in the Group Quiz which you sent me asks : What is common to *Macbeth, Hero's Life, Don Quixote, Till Eulenspiegel, Thus Spake Zarathustra* ? But do you really think that a man makes a better sailor through knowing about Richard Strauss ? Ropes and knots are his job, not strings and chords. I don't expect a taxi-driver to know his way about the Restoration dramatists ; what I want him to know is his way about London. Why should I complain because a bricklayer doesn't know about Mrs Siddons ? I can't build a wall ! Would you trust an engine-driver with his head in Shelley's clouds ? Seeing that until you told me I had no notion what instrument is associated with Artie Shaw, why should I expect these boys to know what Goossens plays ? I am not in the least surprised that they were more interested in the reprieve of Mrs Jones than in the capture of Cologne. Come now. Putting aside the question of the bringing nearer of your release from the Navy, would not you be more excited by the discovery of, say, a last movement to the Unfinished Symphony than by the fall of Berlin ?

No time for more, the last galleys of *Ego* 7 having arrived.

Ever,

JAMIE

March 13 *Tuesday.* Hatch again :

THE TRIALS OF SACCHARISSA

CHAPTERS 7–12

(*With apologies to Becky Sharp*)

SYNOPSIS

Saccharissa answers an advertisement for a governess in a baronet's family at Wapping. There she meets Croydon Rawley of the Pinks, to whom she becomes affianced. Seduced by the wealthy Lord Pavilion, she is surprised by her fiancé as she is playing a Sibelius symphony to the old rake. Rawley strikes the nobleman and wounds him in the forehead. Saccharissa pleads misunderstanding, but the flower of the regiment stalks away after returning the gold cigarette-lighter which was Saccharissa's engagement gift.

EXTRACT

Whether it was the lure of Camille's excellent coffee or just because of the news that Roddy Rankin's book of verse had been accepted by Plummer and Pish, the whole gang appeared after lunch. The Spanish girl flourished her latest nosegay, Gilbert Flossey produced a sheaf of MSS., the others bulged at every angle. Camille, though just as excited as others, held up her hand for silence. " Children," she cried. " One at a time. Yesterday four of you read your poems all speaking together—I couldn't get the proper hang of any of them. I shall stage-manage this afternoon. First the Narcissans. Who speaks first ? " Walt Willow held up two tobacco-stained fingers. After much fumbling he found what he was looking for. " This poem is horizontal," he explained, " Any fool can do the perpendicular stuff." Camille, fearing that this might be a hit at Roddy, quickly interposed : " Read it to us, darling." Walt intoned :

Succour

" The mirror of your gaze reflects,
Avows itself that not
Where vine asserts and swells to grape
Such Be that ruminates the all-abating plot."

Opinions differed. Roddy, pontifical, was heard to grunt through the haze of his hookah : " Not altogether bad, but too limpidic. Not opaque enough." Camille raised a different point, asking, " Isn't it a little *artificial* ? I mean, those tropes sound a bit *redundant*." But Gilbert would have none of this. " As clear as day," he insisted. " Too clear, if anything." Walt smirked at such unwonted praise and lurched over to the decanter. But others had been before him. All this time Gilbert had been lying in wait, and when Camille said, " And now for the Post-Prillians," he began to chant his

Lines for a Child

" Drooping aphasically
the pheasant dreams
of the lilyness of skies
in the vast, euphorionistic
camel-trace. Now can
he flint, glint, mint
the solid æons of his turbid peace. . . ."

Every one liked this, and Noble Newpin, *gauche* as always, said, " A hint of Keats somewhere, don't you think ? " Gilbert was livid. " You lumber-headed son of a keg ! " he shouted. " D'you compare *me* with that demoded little Cockney chemist ! " Camille, tactful as ever, smoothed matters over by saying, " What Noble means, Gilbert darling, is that if Keats had had *your* genius. . . ." " Which he decidedly hadn't," simpered Barbara. The discussion was interrupted by Lucifer Lux saying, " All my poems consist of one word. But it is for me to decide whether it is to be a long word or a short one. Sometimes I stretch the word to two lines, in a few cases even to three. It all depends on the mood. I call this the egocentric approach—Anatole Lessonier, you know." Whereat Netta kissed him. " Marvellous ! " she gurgled. " Darling," laughed Camille, seeing them so close together, " yours is the *real* egocentric approach, my sweet ! "

March 17 *Saturday.* Letter from Clifford Bax :

*D*2 *Albany*
London, W.1
March the 16*th*, 1945

Amiable and peaceful James,

Don't you think that we might begin the most amusing of post-war parlour-games, to be called " Obituaries " ? What fun if you and I were to exchange obituary notices of one another. . . . Yes ?

After all, everybody grieves that he will never see his obituaries: and I, certainly, would like to see what you will write about me. Have you no curiosity at all to read what *I* shall send to *The Times* when you have wings and a harp?

Yours goutily,
CLIFFORD BAX

Am replying:

*Queen Alexandra Mansions, W.C.*2
March 17*th*, 1945

DEAR CLIFFORD,

"Do not speak like a death's head; do not bid me remember mine end." Besides, I shouldn't know what to say about you except that you had been a man composed in equal parts of wit, charm, and genius; that you looked like Shakespeare, Charles I, and Beecham; that you wrote an exquisite fist; and that at the age of ninety or so you crept, not into Abraham's bosom, but into Buddha's navel.

Ever,
JAMES AGATE

March 20 *Tuesday.* Advance copies of *Immoment Toys* arrive. To take a leaf out of Swift: "Good God! What a genius I had when I wrote those early articles!"

March 22 *Thursday.* There is one talent for writing and another for proof-correcting. Judging from *Close of an Era*, Percy Colson is woefully lacking in the second. Queen Charlotte was the consort of George III, not of George IV. The author of *History of Sir Richard Calmady* was Lucas Malet and not Mrs Humphry Ward. H. W. spelt her hero's name "Elsmere" and not "Ellsmere." There is no English poet called Grey. Oscar Wilde did not say, "I feel like a lion in a den of Daniels." There would have been no point in it. The quip belongs to the disfrocked (after a libel action) Horne Tooke. Nobody ever called Henry Irving "Harry." The book is peppered with wrong French accents, and in one place bad punctuation makes Sudermann's Magda a character out of Stephen Phillips's *Paolo and Francesca.* It is news to me that Congreve and Sheridan only wrote one first-rate play, and I don't think that Shaw would relish being told that his *St Joan* is likely to rank with *The Importance of Being Earnest.* To say that *The Second Mrs Tanqueray* was "a rather silly melodramatic play" is adding insult to the injury of misquoting Paula. But the book warms my mind because I am a Victorian. Everybody of my generation must know the remark in the old melodrama: "O God, put back Thy universe, and give me yesterday!"

(Borrowed from Shakespeare's "O, call back yesterday, bid time return.") I know none of my age who would not willingly put back the clock, and this Colson does very vividly. I like his "If Queen Victoria had ruled in Florence in the fifteenth century she would have nipped the Renaissance in the bud." And I will forgive all this book's slipshoddery for the delightful remark of Professor Jowett, who, on hearing that a junior play-producing don had cut some lines about the Athenian code of morals, sent for him and said, "I hear you have been making cuts in a Greek play. Aristophanes wrote it. Who are you?"

Cocasseries, *No.* 11:

At an evening party. Young Lady (*rushing up to pianist*). "Roger darling, do be a lamb and play that exquisite little thing by Delius. It isn't Delius really—the thing I mean is Delius, arranged Chopin."

March 23 *Friday.* Some time last autumn I reviewed John O'Hara's *Appointment in Samarra* on its re-issue in Penguin Books. I said:

O'Hara's novel is an exemplification of the old truth: that those who live by the sword shall perish by the sword. Except that, in the case of Julian English, for "sword" we must read "materialistic outlook and commonness of mind." There is nothing whatever to distinguish Julian from the beasts of the field except that his appetites are more complicated. His outlook is entirely dominated by high-powered motor-cars, highballs, light women, and dance bands. That there can be such things in the world as intellectual interest, art, sociology, or anything except that which satisfies his immediate physical needs never occurs to him. . . .

Within two days dozens of mothers of fifteen-year-old daughters bombarded the editor with letters calling his attention to a passage in the book in which Julian's wife, anxious to make up a quarrel, starts fiddling with his braces and suggests that they should go to bed. Now this makes reviewing very difficult. To-day Leo begs me to review a book by a young friend of his, saying, "You'll probably hate it, but it's your duty to review it." So I read it. It turns out to be a study of the day-and-night dreams of a boy of fifteen, and the pleasure he gets when a refined seventeen-year-old ties him up and whips him. And I say, "Yes, Leo, I agree that it's very well done. But what about mothers proposing to send their kids to a public school?"

March 24 *Saturday.* Fairly large and highly attentive and appreciative audience at to-day's meeting of the Henry Wood Proms Circle. The routine is as follows. Lunch with Stanley Rubinstein, then repair to Columbia Studios in the Abbey Road, where some two hundred people are gathered together to listen for three hours to the chairman and a gramophone. 33⅓ Mercury and 66⅔ Apollo. I think I was mercurial enough to-day.

"Let me say straight away that I have one piece of good news for you. This is that throughout the afternoon you will not hear a single note of British music. Speaking strictly as a layman, I permit myself to say that there are only three British composers of whom I ever wish to hear another note. These are Purcell—I include him merely to save my face, since with the exception of an odd song or two he bores me stiff—Sullivan, and Elgar. Do I hear somebody say Delius ? My dear friends, Delius is not a composer ; he is a monodist, a meanderer ! You will remember how Macaulay, in his analysis of Robert Montgomery's poem, quotes the couplet :

"The soul, aspiring, pants its source to mount,
As streams meander level with their fount.

And how he goes on to say, 'We take this to be, on the whole, the worst similitude in the world. No stream meanders, or can possibly meander, level with its fount.' But then Macaulay had never heard any of Delius's music, or he would have known of one fount which never does anything else."

On the subject of British music generally I quoted something a distinguished conductor said to me when I told him what I was proposing to say this afternoon : "The reason modern British composers don't write tunes is not that they can't but that they won't. Tunes are no longer their concern ; what they're after is something that will look well on paper. You won't be very far wrong in saying there hasn't been anything to hum since Elgar. I conduct a lot of the modern stuff, and I know."

The usual practice is to play eight or nine short records in the first half and a big work in the second. Here is what I gave them :

HANDEL. *The Origin of Design* : Musette, Battle, and Finale.
GIORDANO. *Caro Mio Ben.* (Marian Anderson.)
WOLF-FERRARI. Overture, *The Secret of Susannah.*
VERDI-LISZT. Rigoletto Paraphrase. (Alexis Kligerman.)
DUPARC. *Phydilé.* (Maggie Teyte.)
SCHUMANN. Symphony No. 2 : Adagio.
STRAVINSKY. *Baiser de la Fée.*
MAHLER. Symphony No. 5 : Adagietto.
MACEBEN. Strauss-Parodie.

In the second half I played Richard Strauss's *Also Sprach Zarathustra*, preluding this by saying :

> " Let me draw your attention to the fact that musical sound has nothing to do with non-musical sense. You all know that a great actor reciting the multiplication table is more moving than a bad actor messing about with Shakespeare. The sun shines equally on the just and the unjust, and great music is indifferent whether it transfigures sense or nonsense. The fact that Nietzsche was an ass—an ass of brain but an ass—detracts nothing from the fire and passion of Strauss's music. Don't listen to this music with your eyes ; use your ears. Don't worry what sort of pattern it makes in black and white. Strauss didn't ; why should you ? "

March 25 *Sunday.* Musical comedy is something I do not wish any part of in any manner, way, shape, or form. To-day's article has to be about the revival of *Irene*, and this is the way I get out of it :

IREEN AND MELPOMEEN

Henry James recounts how at a dinner-party he heard Tennyson say to a young lady, " Miss de Sade ? The name sounds familiar. Ought I not to know something about an uncle of yours ? " The answer is that he ought, and then again that he ought not ; since even for Poets Laureate a little learning is a dangerous thing. Certainly it was a snag in the path of that promising author who in a recent novel quoted " Gilles de Rais' well-known account of the Marquis de Sade " ! The centuries may " kiss and commingle," but hardly to the extent of three of them.

Considering the programme at His Majesty's and reading " Book by James Montgomery," I caught myself wondering whether I didn't ought to know. . . . Yes, reader, I have descended to the idiom of " Ireen " and her friends. And what fun one could have with this idiom ! Little rhymes about

> Calling Persephone
> On the telephone. . . .

Now where was I ? Oh yes, that other and earlier Montgomery (Robert). He was the author of

> And thou, vast Ocean, on whose awful face
> Time's iron feet can print no ruin-trace.

Which couplet, said Macaulay, was an unabashed theft from Byron's

> Time writes no wrinkle on thine azure brow.

What, then, had Time done to Ireen and her friends ? Nothing. One cannot injure nothing. Since the play inflicted on me what the poet Cowper calls " the indolent vacuity of thought," I took refuge in my own reflections. I contemplated a letter to the Muse of Tragedy based on the story of the minister at the Dissenting chapel who prayed, " O Lord, Thou knowest that we are gathered together for worship in an edifice known for its architectural qualities throughout the whole of the North of England." I would write, " O Melpomeen, art thou or art thou not aware that in the noblest modern theatre in the South of England we are gathered together to-night in admiration of a piece of witlessness hankered after for twenty-five years to the point of revival ? " And I went on to construct the lady's reply. (Note that she ignores the affront to her own name.) " Hail, Agathon ! Not I, but my sister Thalia—whom I beg you not to rhyme with dahlia—is in charge of the risibilities. She would probably remind you of a line in the prologue to a better-bred play :

" Unmov'd tho' witlings sneer and rivals rail ;

and go on to tell you that Montgomery the Younger would be justified in remaining unmov'd by aught you may say or write in your Sunday paper. That he has been

" Studious to please, yet not ashamed to fail.

And that in her opinion he has not failed. Agathon, farewell ! "

That, dear Melpomeen, is O.K. by me. I declare the intrigue in this old musical comedy to be more subtle than anything Meilhac and Halévy contrived. The fun to be more sparkling than Beaumarchais, Hoffmannsthal, and Gilbert. The music to be wittier than Offenbach, Johann Strauss, and Sullivan. Nay, reader, do not think I flatter. Or if I do, it is only because criticism in this field must, if it is to satisfy the cultivators thereof, be in the nature of a dedication. And what is that nature ? Johnson, in his Hebridean small-talk, tells us. " The known style of a dedication is flattery. It professes to flatter. There is the same difference between what a man says in a dedication and a history, as between a lawyer pleading a cause and reporting it." Let this critic plead the triumph of Mr Arthur Riscoe and Miss Pat Taylor over wretched material rather than report upon the wretchedness of that material.

March 26 *Monday.* Wilfred Rouse tells me that a night or two ago his sister, who had 'flu, was drinking a jorum of hot whiskey and water out of a large balloon glass when a bomb exploded overhead. Not a window was broken, and neither she nor her husband experienced the slightest shock. But the glass in his sister's hand disintegrated into thousands of tiny splinters.

March 27 *Tuesday.* Still again Hatch :

THE TRIALS OF SACCHARISSA

CHAPTERS 13–18

(*With apologies to the Master's Diana*)

Synopsis

Saccharissa is now a dance-hostess at the Plaza Hotel in Curzon Street, where she meets and falls in love with the Hon. Hotspur Dossier, a rising politician on the Conservative side. On the verge of Cabinet rank, he is forced to resign in consequence of Saccharissa having left a particularly secret blueprint of the new battleship mixed up with her shopping-list on the counter of the Army and Navy Stores, where it is picked up by the London Correspondent of the "Brighouse Evening Sentinel," a Liberal organ of great weight. Dossier goes over to the Communist party. But before doing so he seduces and abandons Saccharissa, who stays in bed for six weeks without food or drink, comforted only by her toy pom, Crap.

Extract

It was getting cold, so Bertram, with characteristic *grandezza*, threw on the fire a few novels by Bertha Bobbins and Clorisse Cluck to promote what turned out to be a brilliant, if only temporary, blaze. The menial task accomplished, he continued, "What I mean, Cyril, is that I don't *write* that sort of play. I don't care two hoots about a story, or a plot, or who sleeps with whom. Ten years ago when I was sixteen, I fell in with Russ Kalinka, over from Prag after finishing his book on *The Tonalities of Dramatic Progression*. Russ said to me—I shall never forget his words—'Always keep your dramatic theses laterally hypomastic.' What I aim at, nowadays, is breadth of axis. You follow me, Cyril? Help yourself to the beer." "Thanks, I finished it hours ago," said Cyril. "But about this ideology of yours," Cyril went on, "it isn't new. Sven Hamsen did it years ago. What I should prefer you to aim at is something I do in my novels—the setting of the visual ellipsis against the aural elision. In my last novel, which, you remember, had no title, the characters had no names, nobody knew what anybody looked like, and there wasn't a word of dialogue. Yes, I know—the old Japanese stuff, Kokokuri and so forth—but wait. I haven't lived eight years in India for nothing. In my new book, *A Passage to Burma*, I make a concession. My hero speaks throughout in Bodo. The same when my chief woman character goes to Finland, when everybody talks Finnish. Keeps the verisimilitude upright, as it were." "Y-yes," agreed Bertram, rather half-heartedly. "But I can't do that sort of thing in my plays—you know what our actors are. The fact that most of them can't speak English hardly encourages one to entrust them with say, Afrikaans or Urdu. And then the audiences are so hopeless. Marian Bottom was telling me the other day that when they accepted that play of hers about the death of Hjaltabakki the manager of the Chute Theatre insisted on all the Icelandic scenes being turned into English. Monstrous ! " " Did I show you that article in the *Cerebral Monitor* ? " asked Cyril. " All about what we've been discussing. It posed the question : ' Is our latter-day drama catalyptic or just hyperconcatenous ? ' It made the point that Molière started out by being funistic, became cerative later, and in his last plays adopted a technique which the writer called ' the leaning-on-and-towards *netio*, the old *engaña* of Campoamor.' In a word, altro-deceptive idea-mechanisation." " I don't quite agree," said Bertram. " But let's ask Pettifog—he's a dramatic critic, he should know. Pettifog," he called to a young man who was dangling half on and half off a sofa, looking at an engraving through a pair of miniature opera-glasses, " would you call Molière a synthetist or a disthetist ? " Pettifog said, " Who the hell's Molière ? "

March 28 *Wednesday.* At supper on Friday Bertie van Thal asked me to do a book about films for his firm. On the lines of *Immoment Toys*. I tackled this on Sunday afternoon at five o'clock, " this " meaning reading through and, in Jock's phrase, creaming somewhere between nine hundred and a thousand articles, tearing them out of my scrap-books, preparing a list of contents, and writing a Preface to explain what the book is and what it isn't. Title : *Around Cinemas*, based, of course, on Max's *Around Theatres*. Delivered the whole thing to Bertie at five o'clock this afternoon.

My obsession about misprints continues. Looking casually into the H.M.V. catalogue, I find seven mistakes on one page. The piece I played to Henry Wood fifty-four years ago was Mendelssohn's Rondo Capriccioso, not Rondo " Capriccio." Raff's piece is called *La Fileuse*, not *La Filieuse*. And so on. It is all very well for Pope to write :

> Whoever thinks a faultless piece to see,
> Thinks what ne'er was, nor is, nor e'er shall be.

But that is no reason why one should not try for perfection. Even so, one is brought up against Hazlitt's dictum that a work needs defects to show up its qualities. Which brings me up against the metaphysical proposition that man, attaining perfection, ceases to be of interest. Be these things as they may, and we can be sure that they will, I am delighted to note that in *Immoment Toys* I have come across no more than two misprints. I have, however, noted over sixty inelegances which will have to be smoothed away in the next edition. What sort of inelegances ? Take for example the sente nce

"This is satire at its best, in which kind the crueller the better." "Kind" should be "sort," thus avoiding the unintended play on the words "kind" and "cruel."

March 29 *Thursday.* The *débâcle* in Germany suggests that Hitler is probably saying to Himmler what Lambert Simnel said to Perkin Warbeck in a one-act drama written by ten-year-old Master Michael Cowlen and included in A. P. Herbert's old *Riverside Nights*: "Do you not think our followers may turn on us after they have been sticking up for us for some time?"

Good Friday. That Lloyd George should be laid to rest near the stream he knew when he was a boy reminds me of some lines in an American poem, by Stephen Vincent Benét, on American names. This ends:

> I shall not rest quiet in Montparnasse.
> I shall not lie easy at Winchelsea.
> You may bury my body in Sussex grass,
> You may bury my tongue at Champmédy.
> I shall not be there. I shall rise and pass.
> Bury my heart at Wounded Knee.

Easter Sunday. Here is

ANOTHER LETTER TO MELPOMEEN

DEAR MELPOMEEN,

I regret I cannot find quite the adjective to describe your treatment of Cedric Hardwicke. "Scurvy" is hardly the word one would use in connection with a mythological lady of your eminence. Would our earthly goddess, Millamant, be acceptable to you? In which case I will describe your behaviour as "vastly filthy." Do I hear you protesting that you have not behaved at all? It is this of which I complain. You have allowed this very fine actor to turn his back on Hollywood and return to the fold and domain of the theatre without making suitable provision for him in the way of a part or parts. You have permitted him to make his *rentrée* (at the Westminster) in his old part in *Yellow Sands*. You know the sort of thing—the middle-aged ne'er-do-well, to the material eye disreputable and down-at-heel, but to the inner vision still a man of parts. As a rôle this is a good rôle—but it is not good enough for the man or the occasion. Suppose great Irving to have returned from Hollywood—may Jove's thunderbolts strike me if I think that all the millions of Pactolus Projections would have lured him there—imagine H. I. returning after some six or seven years to fob us off with Corporal Brewster!

Perhaps your sister Thalia is in part blameworthy? Very well, then, let me ask both of you ladies what you have in store for an actor whose successes include Webster's Flaminco, the Shavian Cæsar, He-Ancient, Lickcheese, King Magnus, and Captain Shotover, Besier's Edward Moulton Barrett, and Carroll's Canon Skerritt. Those who saw *Shadow and Substance*, and were not impressed by it over here, are always told that they did not see Hardwicke's performance. Well, now is the chance to let us see it. Have I any suggestions ? Yes. I suggest that this accoladed actor might like to give us a Sunday-afternoon taste of his qualities. Why not *Rosmersholm* ? I want to find out whether this rare Ibsenite bird is goose or swan. Swan, I think, albeit rather a muddled one. And since nothing could be wrong with the choice of Sonia Dresdel for Rebecca, I look to see this pair make us accept this play's ending. Can they rise to those heights at which " tragedy burns up the lamp that holds it, and flames like a star, unconditioned and absolute " ? Let Hardwicke and Dresdel prove that this play is the masterpiece G. B. S. quintessentially declared it to be.

And then, of course, there is Borkman. Dear Melpomeen and dear Thalia, unite with me in inviting this brilliant player to blow John Gabriel's horn.

Your earthbound
AGATHON

Easter Monday. Jock writes from Scotland to say that his father is dying. I am not to attempt condolences, he says.

" Some glory in their birth, some in their skill. . . ." Osbert Sitwell glories in the fact that his family tree contains a duke, a marquis, an earl, and innumerable baronets. But then, we all dote on something. I dote on the fact that my tree includes David Cox the painter, Edward Shuter the comedian and original Mr Hardcastle in *She Stoops to Conquer*, and innumerable clowns and dancing masters. *Left Hand, Right Hand!* tells us that the author was christened by a bishop, and that his father's manners were " exquisite and elaborate, about the time of Charles II, but with a touch, too, of the Meredithian baronet, Sir Willoughby Patterne or Sir Austin Feverel, clinging to them." Pure Thackeray, this. I conceive it difficult for Osbert to realise that the interest of the average chuckle-headed reader begins with his activities and not with those of Chaucerian progenitors. On the other hand, this exquisite book though not exciting or arresting, presents a picture of the England now passing away which will be of the utmost value to the social historian of the future. This first instalment of what promises to be a four-volume Life is the history of a great house and a great family rather than an " indiwidgle." (Why drag in Mrs Gamp ? Reaction from the book's near-pomposity.) There is some admirable writing; Osbert is particularly good about the painter Sargent. For example:

> Sargent matched the Edwardian Age to a nicety; he was entirely occupied with outward and superficial effects. Money, one would hazard, bore for this painter the identical Edwardian sanctity that it possessed for the City magnates, sporting peers, and old-clothes and furniture dealers whose likenesses and those of their wives he was obliged to perpetuate. Yet the fact that he was so plainly more interested in the appurtenances of the sitters and in the appointments of their rooms than their faces, from which he sought refuge in the tilted top-hats, with their sombre but water-light reflections, the cravats and fur coats of the men, or in the tiaras, flashing, stiff but uneasy, above the heads of the women, or in the brocades and velvets they were wearing, in no way detracted from his popularity with them.

Many people will like John Piper's pictures of the ancestral home at Renishaw, complete with what Sairey Gamp somewhere calls "a parapidge with chimbley pots to walk on in case of fire." But I am not convinced. I just do not believe in a gloomy pile lit exteriorly by a glare from burning stables. The illustrations have the air of a cross between Flaminck—one suspects a colour scheme of gamboge and crimson lake—and the last shot in the film of Daphne du Maurier's *Rebecca*. Stevenson says about a great novel by Dumas: "A proportion of readers stumble at the threshold. In so vast a mansion there were sure to be back stairs and kitchen offices where no one would delight to linger." I suggest that the present volume is vestibule and antechamber to a mansion which, fully entered upon, will prove a storehouse of delight. Osbert is something much rarer than an aristocrat. He is an artist, and of the most fastidious kind. His writing, as writing, is gold that has passed the "furnage."

April 3 *Tuesday.* Leo hands me this letter from his and my little Irish friend (see *Ego* 7, entry for December 22, 1944):

18 *Park View Avenue*
Harold's Cross
Dublin
29.3.45

DEAR OGRE,

I'm afraid you're an ogre with a tendency to be naughty. Why? For letting J. A. waste his leisure moments in replying to me. I know James, dear fellow that he is, can't restrain these kind but rash impulses. But you ought to have more sense. Indeed, your letters would seem far too skittish, to some people. However, I enjoy people of advanced years with a youthful sense of humour. As Elia says, " I hate people who meet Time half-way ; I am for no compromise with that inevitable spoiler." You see, I suppose, that I'm writing this letter simply for the sake of getting a reply. A letter from you now and again would keep me alive. I'm bored to death. There is nothing so boring as a conventional childhood for one who knows that there is such a thing as an unconventional childhood. People in my circle don't read anything worth while, don't say anything witty, and for a young prig like me that's unbearable. I'm in the mood at this point for giving a highly emotional outburst, but I know what effect that would have on a hardened old cynic like you. But I'm boring you now, and I'd hate to think that. Spare a few moments and reply, like a nice kind ogre.

All the best
From your clever child,
J. E. JORDAN

And I weigh in with :

*Queen Alexandra Mansions, W.C.*2
April 3*rd*, 1945

DEAR CHILD,

I have read your letter to Leo. Don't waste too much of your cleverness on the desert air of Grape Street. We spend most of our time discouraging talentless little brats. Now we think that you may have the knack of writing. Keep on at it. Read your best Irish authors. Study Swift, the poetry of W. B. Yeats, and the plays of J. M. Synge. Visit the Abbey and Gate Theatres as often as you can. Go and hear good music. Write to me once a month, and Leo will answer.

Yours sincerely,
JAMES AGATE

And then this comes from Clifford Bax :

*D*2 *Albany*
*London, W.*1
April 3*rd*, 1945

MY DEAR JAMES,

I find that I did not thank you enough for the exceedingly lively book which you so unexpectedly gave to me. For Easter I, the world's record stay-at-home, was carried off in a car to a so-called Manor in Surrey. It was really four Tudor cottages knocked into one. There was no water-supply to the bath, though a trickle flowed into the privy ; there were countless electric-light switches which ignited nothing, and the power-plugs were powerless. The rooms were so low that I hit my Tudor head countless times against those Tudor beams and, in fact, had to go into the garden if I wanted to stand up to my heroic height of six feet one inch.

So your book was a delightful companion. For one thing, only Shelley preferred to read while standing, and so, engrossed by your chapters, I kept to my chair, which was embroidered with a scene —Harold being crowned by Bishop Somebody—from the Bayeux tapestries. Yes, dear James, your fine old play discourses were balm to a much-bumped cranium. . . . Heroines are safely permitted to Draw Themselves Up to Their Full Height before Sweeping Out: but Authors should be lowly. Have you not told many a dramatist that simple truth ?

No ! I see now that, unloved as you may be, you are the least loathsome of your tribe or species. . . . Of course, you know about those HUGE ants who terrify humanity in Central America when they advance in phalanx ? When I read about them I always think of Critics at a First Night.

Well, now, your esteemed colleague Howard Spring says that the only persons who might conceivably enjoy my works are those who refuse water unless it has been filtered—did he say thrice-filtered ? So I envy you your robust enjoyment of Nellie Wallace, Robey, and the rest of them. It all goes, I expect, with a relish for Dickens ? Music-hall humour has always been, for me, as amusing as the noise of a child who keeps on slate-scratching. You yourself have granted me a pinch of wit in my composition, and I therefore suspect that these clownish players offend my sense of beauty and of human dignity. I could never see why, on the halls, women—as a rule—were allowed their beauty while men had to make themselves vulgar and grotesque ; nor could I see why the word "beer" should elicit "a safe laugh" or guffaw ; nor have I ever felt that sex union is either indecent or comic. To me it appears as a physical attempt to reproduce the greatest of all spiritual experiences, but perhaps you will smile at my Buddhism. However, to take "sex" seriously is to find most of the music-hall jokes just dreary. Suppose music-hall comedians continuously joked about "roses" or "Brahms"—you would find them simply tiresome. So I have not seen most of the people whom at the end of the book you have so adroitly outlined. . . .

But if you meet Mr Spring will you, dear James, assure him that on one occasion, put in first by a speculative captain, I scored eighteen runs from the first three balls of the match ? I suppose he conceives of me as a lily-dandling pseudo-æsthete !

Yours admiringly,
CLIFFORD BAX

P.S. Admiringly ? Yes, the notices are strewn with flourishes of wit and phrase which no other Dramatic Ant could have achieved.

Am replying :

DEAR C. B.,

But you didn't ought to write me that sort of letter. I don't mean the trowel stuff—I can take praise with anybody. It's the sex question which worries me ; it arouses a passion for amateur metaphysics which I hoped I had laid. Sex, or rather fecundity, is the one thing in the universe I feel sure of, in the sense that I feel that the First Cause intended it. Did the F. C., when it created oxygen and hydrogen, contemplate water ? Or did it give O and H the sex urge in the sense that two parts of H desired O to the point of creating water ? I can conceive that man is a fluke and that his highest aspirations are self-invented embroideries with which the F. C., like Barrie's schoolmistress, is not concerned. But fecundity, or burgeoning, or whatever you call it, is the concern of the tree outside my bedroom window. (Yes, trees grow in Holborn as well as in Brooklyn.) That amiable vegetable obeys its own natural law without any of man's sentimental refinements. I think every tree is right, and every monk and nun wrong. What should we think of a laburnum which was too virtuous to blossom ? And what am I to think of the silly woman I saw eating an ice at the Café Royal to-day ? She had on a veil which hung two inches below her chin. Every time she took a spoonful she raised her veil, and then lowered it again. I think it was the same woman that I saw the other evening at the theatre looking at *Macbeth* through a spotted cowl. I could have brained her. Far, far sooner would I cohabit with a blubber-chewing she-Eskimo or unwashed Hottentot than this veiled idiocy. How the man with her, presumably her husband, had not thrashed this nonsense out of her I fail to understand. I have improved upon Goldsmith's Mr Hardcastle. I like old manners, old books, old wine, and old women. And old friends like you.

Ever,
JAMES

April 4 *Wednesday.* Times change, but some of us don't change with them. Forty years ago Montague could write about an absurd melodrama : " The badinage ranges among such lawful topics as the corpulence of one's father's guests." Modern taste in jesting appears to regard a dead wife as a lawful topic. I am afraid I am old-fashioned in this matter. I don't think Dickens would have considered the materialisation—to use the spiritualistic word—of Dora to David Copperfield and Agnes as a theme for farce. I confess on the first night of Noel's *Blithe Spirit*, now getting on for four years ago, to being genuinely shocked at this play's second wife's remark : " Elvira was of the earth, earthy," and the husband's reply : " Well, she is now, anyway." Am I then offended by jokes about heaven and hell? It depends upon the joker. I am not offended, for example, by Hector Crémieux's libretto to Offenbach's *Orphée aux Enfers*. Nor by Halévy's little story, *Le Rêve*. The scene is Paradise, and Gaston and Raoul lay claim to the wife they have had on earth, a priest having made each this promise, one at the Church of Sainte-Clotilde and the other at La Madeleine. Raoul holds his claim to be the stronger because the priest in his case was a bishop. The Père Éternel, protesting that His earthly agents are sometimes in the habit of promising more than they can perform, tells the widow that she may choose between her husbands. To which she replies, " Si vous étiez infiniment bon, Seigneur, vous me permettriez de m'arranger avec Monsieur de Séricourt qui est là-bas dans ce petit nuage à gauche et qui me fait des signes depuis un quart d'heure." This always seems to me to be an admirable story. How comes it, then, that I can't laugh at *Blithe Spirit*? Because it is *common*! The film, which I saw this morning, is commoner still. Rex Harrison, Constance Cummings, and Kay Hammond do well enough in the Selfridge-cum-Harrod's glove-counter school of banter imposed on them by their material. But for me both the play and the film centre in Margaret Rutherford. I warn her that when, æons hence, she arrives in the Upper Regions, she will find me in my little cloud winking prodigiously.

P.S. I am wrong to attribute commonness to Noel. This is uncritical. The proper thing to say is that the age is common, and that Noel's plays mirror the age.

April 5
Thursday.
In my mail was a parcel from South Africa, in the wrappings of which I found this:

DECLARATION OF INDEPENDENCE BY FOUR-YEAR-OLD SON

He will just do nothing at all.
He will just sit there in the sun,
And when they speak to him, he will not answer them,
Because he does not care to.
He will stick them with spears and put them in the dustbin.
When they tell him to eat his dinner, he will just laugh at them.
And he will not take his nap, because he does not care to.
He will just sit there in the sun.
He will go away and play with the Panda,
And when they come to look for him
He will put spikes in their eyes and put them in the dustbin,
And put the cover on.
He will not go out in the fresh air or eat his vegetables
Or make wee-wee for them, and he will get as thin as a marble,
He will just do nothing at all.
He will just sit there in the sun.

April 6 *Friday.* From my little Birmingham friends:

438 Belchers Lane
Little Bromwich
Birmingham

10 Longmore Street
Birmingham 12

April 5, 1946

OUR DEAR JAMES AGATE,

It has been very difficult to restrain ourselves from writing as we have just discovered your novels (*i.e.*, we have only recently been able to get them from the library). We are fascinated. We started off with *Blessed are the Rich*, and it's unlike any other novel we've ever read—and that's not meant in any nasty sense. As Mark (*Gemel in London*) Rubicon says in reply to Gemel's

"Is it a good novel?"

"It's good everything else!"

So are yours, and what a lot of everything else there is! That chapter of social criticism, for example, we feel has never been excelled for lucidity, forcefulness, and truth. (Would you like us to write your "blurb" for you? We could do it with clear consciences because we really mean it.)

In the course of re-reading Caryl Brahms's *Robert Helpmann* we came across a passage of criticism from the *Manchester Guardian* on Helpmann's ballet *Hamlet*. Was it written by Jock? Certain passages have his touch—for example: "*Hamlet* has survived modern dress, Sir Henry Irving, Ambroise Thomas, and Dr Bowdler, and if a ballet-master chooses to translate it into terms of the *Yellow Book* Shakespeare can take it with head unbowed...."

Instead of riveting we are doing Inland Revenue work during our holidays. If we come across a Final Demand for you we will carefully suppress it. But we don't think there's much chance of that—by which we don't mean that we don't think there's much chance of your receiving a Final Demand, but that there's not much chance of our coming across it in Birmingham. And talking of Birmingham, have you still got ponies near Birmingham and if so would you descend to coming to Kunzle's Cafeteria to drink tea (no coffee!) and eat trifle (this is optional!)?

By the way, would you be interested in what we look like, because here are descriptions of each other. If you're not interested, skip it! BARBARA is medium height and slim, by which I do not mean skinny. She has the shape of face which Louise de Quérouaille should have had to justify the description "baby-faced." Her eyes are large and slate-grey set under thick dark brows. Her nose is snub. Her mouth is normal. Her crowning glory, and for once the title is justified, is red—not that harsh scarlet which one sees so often nowadays, but a gentle "commingling" of every red shade that ever was with a slight bias towards fair. In fact, in appearance she greatly resembles Sarah Churchill, first Duchess of Marlborough. In temperament she is very much like Horatio, and not a " pipe for fortune's fingers." HAZEL is medium height and build. Her face is an ordinary shape. Her eyes are hazel and fairly deep-set, and they twinkle! Her mouth is thin-lipped and flexible. Her nose is long and straight. Her hair is light brown and curly. She is a feminine version of John Gielgud.

Did you manage to skip all that?

Our dutiful regards.

Yours sincerely,

HAZEL YOUNG

BARBARA SIGGS

P.S. We hope you are suitably impressed by our typing. For its accomplishment we have spent many, many hours of blood, sweat, and tears. Yet we will suffer all for your sake.

April 7 *Saturday.* In my entry for Easter Monday I purposely did not give Jock's letter. As I wrote to him: The average reader does not understand that in the case of the artist perfect grief is compatible with the perfect expression of grief. To-day I receive this:

Staff Quarters
R.N. Hospital
Haslar
Hants

6th April, 1945

DEAR JAMIE,

You ask me what I " feel " about the reproduction of my last letter to you in your next *Ego*. I " feel " primarily that it is very revealing—and therefore good *Ego*. A fig for " the ordinary reader "! Where should we arrive if we for ever kept that banal-minded ideal in mind? Arnold Bennett rightly put " the ordinary reader " completely out of his mind when he set down the major part of his superb *Journals*. Hence that superbity. If he had thought of " the ordinary reader "—who is so idiotically squeamish and so sedulously sentimental about death and dying—he would have deleted his observing of the pattern of the counterpane on his mother's deathbed. He would have been utterly wrong so to delete—because the note is a flashlight on A. B.'s mind, and only the crassly stupid reader could call it " callous."

Very similarly, my fantasy about an actual skeletal Death being present by my dear father's deathbed—it was so strong an impression that it can hardly be called fantasy at all—could be regarded as " callous " only by readers unfamiliar with *Ego* (and therefore unfamiliar with *me*!). Other things happened which I did not mean to tell even you—but your letter this morning rather drives me to it. For example, I went to look at my father in his coffin, for the last time, the day before they buried him. What I first particularly noticed, and particularly remember, was the curious texture of the shroud which I had to draw apart so as to see his face. It was like very thin white lint—or still more like the super-thin layers of cotton-wool that used to be the packing of the best-quality chocolates. (We had some at Doughty Street once—it came from Heaven knows where—and I used it to pack Szigeti's recording of the Violin Concerto of Brahms when we sent it as a present to Brother Mycroft.)

I don't know why the texture stays in my mind. (But I equally don't see why I should not record the fact that it did—somewhere or other.) Similarly I may as well tell you, while we are on the subject, that my father had on his death-white face a most singularly beautiful smile, at once satirical and serene. This was worlds away from the tossed and anxious stare he had just before he died. . . . That smile stays on my mind, and comforts me in the subtlest way. He was—as you have no real means of knowing—a very remarkable person. I am sending two rather truncated accounts of him I wrote in the Ayrshire papers. But the complete truth is still to be told.

Thank you for your sympathy, Jamie.

JOCK

Here, then, is the original letter:

At Maybole

30th March, 1945
Good Friday

DEAR JAMIE,

I am at home on long week-end " compassionate " leave for the melancholy reason that my dear old father is sinking fast, and like to die any day, or any hour. I arrived yesterday afternoon, and he has not recognised me yet. He is terribly white and emaciated, and he cannot talk, only make inarticulate groaning noises. He was in a sorry enough state in December, but is much worse now. Death, in his conventional shape, sits by the bed, and politely gives me the chair when I go into the room. Death then stands—in exceptionally polite form—at the foot of the bed, with his thin arms crossed, waiting. Death is being quite exceptionally patient. But he is most undoubtedly there.

I write to you before any other of my friends—mainly, I suppose, because you once met my father : and the interview you had with him was long enough for you to sense his natural dignity and some little of his charm and odd, self-imposed culture. I am glad he has had little pain—throughout this prolonged pernicious anæmia that now affects his brain and senses. I have always, as you know, been excessively fond of him—partly through losing my mother in infancy, of course. He is almost bound to have expired by the time you receive this. Please don't bother to attempt that impossible thing—the note of condolence. Criticise me for the enclosed Sitwell review instead—an extremely difficult and ticklish review, by the way, in *any* circumstances! I should be back at Haslar on Wednesday.

Your
JOCK

April 8 *Sunday.* By mythological post:

REPLY FROM MELPOMEEN

DEAR AGATHON,

You have fallen into an error of which I should not have suspected you. Aware that the London theatre is in a highly flourishing condition, and that a playhouse cannot be got for love and hardly for money, you proceed to the deduction that the British drama flourishes also. O Agathon! You take me and my sister Thalia to task for not finding Cedric Hardwicke a job meet for his talent. How come you, of all persons, to confuse the business of entertainment with the art of drama? Revivals of Yellow Sands and Farmers' Wives will always make a lot of money.

Let me forget about box-office returns and consider drama. Where to-day are your playwrights? You can remember the time when Pinero, Jones, Shaw, Galsworthy, Drinkwater, Barker, Synge, Barrie, Carton, Hankin, Maugham, Lonsdale, Davies, Harwood, and others were cluttering up the stage with masterpieces or near-masterpieces. Anyhow, let us say thundering good plays. What have you to put against these authors now? Some have gone the way of nature; no man at all can be playwriting for ever, and we must be satisfied. Shaw has earned the right to silence; Maugham and St John Ervine have imposed silence on themselves; Priestley has turned sociologist; the tragic flame which gave you *Juno and the Paycock* and *The Plough and the Stars* is now but a flicker.

What, then, have you? Rattigan can tell a good anecdote, Bridie can string together a number of jokes, Emlyn Williams a succession of sentimentalities, and Ustinov a sequence of atmospherics, Coward still sparkles as gaily as any of these. But we skyey folk have yet to learn that five bubbles make a vat of champagne. The goddess Minerva, who knows all things, was telling me the other day about electricity, one of her points being that unless the fluid, or whatever it is, is sure of its return it will not start. Can the reverse be true of playwriting? Can it be that playwrights, in the certainty of having their efforts returned, hesitate to send them out? In the days of, say, Alexander, Wyndham, and Tree a competent playwright with the knack of fitting his play to his market was reasonably sure of having it accepted. Alexander, for example, was unlikely to turn down anything by Pinero, Wyndham anything by Henry Arthur Jones, and Tree anything by Stephen Phillips, Louis N. Parker, or any other pageant-monger. To-day the situation has changed. I conceive that it must be extraordinarily difficult for any young man to sit down and write a play to the address of Pantechnicon Productions Limited.

Then what is happening to your actors ? Mr G. is too often thrown away on parts unworthy of his eminence. To insist that he shall romp about for long periods in Valentine's dressing-gown and the get-up for Oberon, or wear the sober black of John Worthing and the husband in *The Circle*, is to ask too little from our first player. Olivier is in goodish, but not good enough, case. The Button Moulder and Astrov are perhaps not great parts, but they are something, and this actor's Richard III is, in the jargon of mortals, a whale of a performance. But that, in our airy opinion, is not enough, even if you throw in the celluloid Henry. Wolfit ? I confess that you English stagger me. Here is an actor who, in the last six years, has given magnificent performances of Richard III, Lear, Jonson's Volpone, and Ford's Giovanni, and quite good, and in places striking, performances of Hamlet, Macbeth, Othello, Benedick, Malvolio, and Shylock, with Ibsen's Master Builder thrown in as make-weight. To our cloudy perceptions it seems that of all your actors Wolfit has throughout the war period been most active in the cause of British drama. What is the result ? Nobody in London will lease our last remaining actor-manager a theatre. You tell me that the actor-manager system is dead. Very well, then, let it be dead. It may be coincidence, but you cannot deny that it was during the actor-manager's period that British playwriting and acting came to their best. I was asking my sister Thalia the other day what had happened to a favourite comedian of hers. She replied, " I think he passed on some little time ago. Unless, of course, he went into Coward's *Blithe Spirit* ! One loses sight of a player after three or four years." I do not think any actor-manager of the old days would have let his public lose sight of him !

A last word. The Muses help those who help themselves, and it *is* in mortals to command success. And now no more. I hear Euterpe calling. Something about a new concert hall, I think. Farewell !

MELPOMEEN

April 9 *Immoment Toys* published.
Monday. A letter to J. B. Priestley :

*Queen Alexandra Mansions, W.C.*2
April 9th, 1945

DEAR JACK,

Your article in yesterday's *Observer* said about some, but not all, of the younger critics a great deal that badly wanted saying.

There was, however, one passage which disquieted me—the passage about the older men. You write :

" It has been my experience that the older dramatic critics have on the whole been too hostile to experimental work. Often they grumble (as well they might) when given the same old stuff. But too often they grumble still harder when shown something that is not the same old stuff. They are too apt to think that dramatic technique arrived at final perfection about the time when they were young, and that any further refinements or twists are merely so much arty pretentiousness. They forget that an art, if it is to remain vital and engrossing, must avoid falling into routine. Writers must be for ever making fresh efforts, and so must dramatic critics. But often I have found ordinary members of the audience far more receptive and appreciative of what was new and original in a play than experienced and (otherwise) intelligent critics."

I have been looking into my records, and I give you a few out of the hundreds of encouraging things I have written concerning plays which were in some way or degree experimental.

STRINDBERG, *The Dance of Death.* " The curtain has not been up ten minutes before we perceive that we are not dealing with falsification of the familiar, but with a different kind of truth."

ANDREYEV, *The Seven who were Hanged.* " Is a great emotional and spiritual experience. . . . I ask more than that readers should take me at my word. I ask that they shall go and judge for themselves."

JEAN-JACQUES BERNARD, *The Unquiet Spirit.* " Adequately acted, this play is one of the most beautiful that the theatre has given us in the last fifty years. I regret to have to say ungrateful things about the indifferent presentation, infinitely preferring to laud the management's perception that this is an exquisite piece which ought to be put on."

FRANÇOIS MAURIAC, *The Intruder.* " Is it presuming too much to invite the playgoer who is always complaining about the mediocrity of the modern theatre to hurry up and see a piece which is head and shoulders above everything else on the London stage to-day ? "

RONALD MACKENZIE, *Musical Chairs.* " This may be nonsense, but it is unusual, plucky nonsense. If any reader sees nothing remarkable here let him attend, say, a month of London first-nights ! "

J. B. PRIESTLEY, *Time and the Conways.* " This is the place and time, and both together and one as much as the other, to say that Mr Priestley has made a play which is magnificent drama if you grasp what it is essentially about, and first-class entertainment if you don't."

J. B. PRIESTLEY, *I Have Been Here Before.* " A magnificent play. It is no argument against a sieve that it fails to hold water ; not one but fifty ideas filter through this piece."

Robert Ardrey, *Thunder Rock*. " I congratulate this enterprising little theatre on breaking ground with a play infinitely superior in craftsmanship, intellectual interest, pure theatre, *and entertainment value* to anything the commercial theatre can offer in these heart-searching days."

Now about this question of novelty. Surely a dramatist is a cabinet-maker who makes cabinets to hold his ideas ? (I confess I am not enthusiastic about a carpenter who invents new shapes of boxes and then goes about looking for stuff to justify the new shapes.) When I came to the *Sunday Times* in 1923 I found the theatre sufficiently " vital and engrossing " to satisfy me. But I gave careful consideration to every new form of presentation, welcoming some forms and rejecting others. Among the rejections was Expressionism, in which the spectator could not be trusted to gather that a magnate was a busy man unless he was shown twenty typists hammering away on twenty typewriters. I rejected that pretentiousness which made people use masks or speak their real thoughts in parentheses. Above all I rejected Pirandello. I remember asking one frenzied Pirandellist what he found to arouse his enthusiasm. He replied, " Well, I like the different angles from which the problem of reality is surveyed. I like the grouping. I like the stage patterns, the gestures and attitudes of the actors. I like Ernest Milton's bedroom slippers. Of course, there is no human interest, but I like the visual surface of the thing. I like it as ballet. I should like it just as well if it were in Chinese." " But it is in Chinese," I murmured.

Novelty is, in my view, permissible (1) when it is the only way of saying something new ; (2) when it is as good a way of saying something new, to which the charm of freshness is then added ; (3) when it is a better way of saying something old ; (4) when it is as good a way of saying something old, plus the charm of freshness. You know that I disliked your *They Came to a City*, and I know that I don't claim to be infallible. It is possible that I was wrong and that the play, which seemed to me to be endlessly boring, was in reality transcendently interesting. But I did not dislike the play *because of my lack of interest in town-planning*. The fact that I care nothing whether the water in Dr Stockmann's baths was clean or dirty has never prevented me from enjoying *An Enemy of the People*. I disliked *Johnson over Jordan* not because the presentation was new but because, while pretending to be new, it was, or seemed to me to be, a mish-mash of *Outward Bound* and *Liliom* done in the demoded Elmer Rice manner. Say that in your next play you give the characters sealing-wax ears, perch them on stepladders or suspend them from trapezes, and equip them with speaking-trumpets. That will be O.K. by me if you have something to say which can only be said in that manner. I shall merely remind you that the manner is not new.

Now about those ordinary members of the audience you find more receptive than the critics. I should not dream of denying this.

I realise that while *They Came to a City* would have had mighty little chance played to an audience of Walkleys and Beerbohms, it goes down immensely with young people devoid of dramatic perception but interested in the housing problem and wondering whether they should put their prefabricated homes together in Neasden or Gerrard's Cross.

I need hardly tell you that just as I would insist upon the modernity of such young critics as Alan Dent, J. C. Trewin, and Philip Hope-Wallace, so will I admit the conservatism of some of the older ones. I have been moved to write this letter because what I maintain about my own work I maintain about the work of men like Ivor Brown, Desmond MacCarthy, and Anthony Cookman, loyal servants of the theatre honourably bearing the brunt of a battle that never ends, critics who have never shut their minds to novelty justifying itself or containing the seeds of justification. Isn't it time, my dear Jack, that you learned to discriminate ?

I shall include this letter in *Ego* 8, and think it only fair to tell you this in case you find in it matter for rebuttal. I am not cadging for copy.

Yours sincerely,
JAMES AGATE

April 14
Saturday.

I have made it a rule, when I find an author wrong in any matters that I know about, not to trust him in matters I don't know about. Julian B. Arnold, the author of *Giants in Dressing-gowns*, fails to convince me when he calls Browning's poem " The Funeral of a Grammarian." Whereupon I desist from reading Mr Arnold on Browning and turn to what he has to say about Irving. " At the height of his fame, Irving played the character of Mathias in *The Bells* before a Bradford audience. He had reached the bedchamber scene wherein the unhappy Burgher-master, confessing his guilt in the murder of the Polish Jew, dies from the terror of his own emotions—and the great actor fell back in his chair—dead ! " Irving was *not* " at the height of his fame " ; he was *en pleine décadence.* The rest, of course, is just not true. Every schoolboy knows that the last words Irving uttered on the stage were Becket's, and that he died that night at his hotel. Our fantasist goes on to tell us that Ellen Terry died saying, " No funeral gloom, my dears, when I am gone." And so on to the end of William Allingham's poem. The facts are as follows. Ellen Terry wrote the poem on the fly-leaf of her copy of *The Imitation of Christ* and added, " I should wish my children, relatives, and friends to observe this when I die. E.T." Of her actual passing Christopher St John wrote :

> Edy sat by the bed constantly, holding that beautiful, still expressive right hand. The left one was powerless, motionless. The face had not been much changed by that cruel blow from Nature.

But the breath of life was changed. It came more and more painfully as the dawn approached. The hand, gripping Edy's, moved from finger to finger, and with a last effort the voice, not miraculously clear and loud now, but thick and indistinct, spelt out on those fingers the word "Happy," "H-a-p-p-y," over and over again.

Whereat I close Mr Arnold's book, deciding that he is not the author for me.

April 15 Priestley didn't take long to answer :
Sunday.

*B*4 *Albany*
*Piccadilly, W.*1
April 12*th*, 1945

Dear Jimmie,

Your letter of the 9th has just arrived, and I make haste to answer it.

Certainly you have sometimes praised experimental work, though some of the plays you mention do not seem to me to come into that category. And I cannot help wondering what you would have said of *The Dance of Death* if I had written it and not Strindberg. Just as, when I saw *Peer Gynt* at the New, and remembered *Johnson over Jordan* (which held and moved the audience far more and brought a far better performance out of Richardson), I could not help wondering what some of you would have said if I had written it. People fully as intelligent and sensitive as yourself have assured me over and over again that *Johnson over Jordan*, *Music at Night*, and *They Came to a City* (which has nothing to do with housing) gave them immensely stimulating and memorable evenings in the theatre ; and I do not hesitate to say that your failure—not to praise them, but to give them careful critical attention, as being the work of a mind that is at least as good as your own—was lamentable. I have an international reputation as a dramatist, and when a senior critic like yourself just amuses himself airing his prejudices then you not only injure me but, what is more important, you strike a blow at the whole poor struggling English theatre. Furthermore, when I do a unique thing and write a serious, if discursive, play for the Army, to be played by soldiers to soldiers—namely, *Desert Highway*—you do not even condescend to notice it at all ; and this was a play that soldier-authors like Linklater and Henriques, and dramatists like Robert Sherwood, praised enthusiastically. Yet you waste your time telling your readers that I am now a sociologist, merely because I make use of themes that attract and excite audiences everywhere but do not happen to interest you.

I stick to my point about the older critics, and to show you that I am quite able to discriminate I offer you a brief analysis of several known to both of us. If I disguise them by initials, that is simply because you propose to print this letter.

Critic A. Intelligent and knowledgeable about the theatre, but now bored and inclined to be wilful. Made deeply uneasy by certain themes, and tries to carry off this uneasiness with a high jocular hand.

Critic B. Also intelligent and experienced. But bored at heart, and though progressive-minded in many matters is deeply conservative in the arts, and makes little or no attempt to discriminate between the vaguely " arty " and genuine originality.

Critic C. A nice, intelligent fellow. but has no real feeling for or understanding of the theatre, and tries to disguise this lack by making small adverse points. Should not be doing the job.

Critic D. First-class on the kind of play that was thought daringly original about 1911. Wants carefully realistic plays chiefly about personal relationships, which he describes admirably, but is lost—and apt to be stupid—if the dramatist has other irons in the fire.

Let me make yet another point. You talk of yourself and your friends " honourably bearing the brunt of a battle that never ends." You have not borne the brunt of any battle. When Ronald Jeans and I, neither of us a rich man, subsidised the Westminster before the war, just to give London some intelligent productions at easy prices, your whole attitude was grudging and querulous. You have never, it seems to me, at any time carefully examined the theatrical situation in London. The theatre at this moment is briskly being ruined by the conditions of theatre ownership, the old bricks-and-mortar problem. More and more theatres are taken over by men who just want to put on any rubbish. I have recently withdrawn a new serious play—as exciting as *Dangerous Corner*—because after keeping actors hanging about and refusing other engagements for months, no theatre was available ; and it was not the kind of play I could send on tour first. My comedy for the overseas troops, *How are They at Home?* was a lightweight piece, no doubt, but nevertheless it should not have been turned out of the theatre (because of a deal) at a few days' notice to make room for a tasteless little American farce that only ran a few nights. Nor, in my view, will the serious dramatist's position be any better by creating any more new theatrical enterprises run by star actors. This is merely to return to the actor-manager system (against which Shaw fought so long as a dramatic critic) ; star actors are bad judges of plays, and cannot help looking for " vehicles " ; and so I see no hope there. Some of us are trying to make plans that may give us a chance of doing good work under proper conditions. It is too early to tell you what they are, but if and when they mature I shall be most pleasantly surprised if we receive much encouragement from dramatic critics. If you think you are honourably bearing the brunt of a battle, just try being a serious dramatist for a year or two, and then you would know what a really heart-breaking campaign is like.

Forgive this hurried stuff; I'm tired and very busy. If it sounds unfriendly, forgive that too. Remember that there was many a time when I could have hit you back—and never did.

Yours sincerely,
J. B. PRIESTLEY

Whereupon I counter:

Queen Alexandra Mansions, W.C.2
April 15th, 1945

DEAR JACK,

Many thanks for your letter. Can I put it this way—that neither of us wants to "best" the other, as we used to say at school? But you have raised a point which, with respect, I cannot allow you to make. This is the statement that I failed to give "careful and critical" attention to *Johnson over Jordan*, *Music at Night*, and *They Came to a City*, and that I merely amused myself by airing my prejudices at the expense of these plays. You are at perfect liberty to say that the line I took about them was wrong; I don't pretend that my judgments are necessarily right. What I do say is that, right or wrong, those judgments were the result of the utmost attention, and that they were based on principles of criticism which I have in part taken from my predecessors, and in part evolved for myself during the last thirty-eight years. You are entitled to say that my judgments are insensitive, unintelligent, stupid if you like. You are not entitled to say that they are not the result of "careful critical attention." Put yourself in Emlyn Williams's place and read what Ivor Brown and I say this morning about *The Wind of Heaven*. Ivor confesses himself embarrassed, and dismisses the piece with a pun—he calls it "The Passing of the Third Floor *bach*." Whereas I confess to having been deeply moved. Would Emlyn be justified in saying that I had been critically attentive and that Ivor had not? You know he wouldn't.

I am going to take extracts from the articles I wrote on the first productions of your three plays and leave the reader to decide whether those articles were critical or merely the airing of prejudices.

JOHNSON OVER JORDAN

"This play shows that Mr Priestley has been thinking a great deal about his and everybody else's approaching dissolution. Unfortunately, he has not been thinking very freshly, for though I listened hard I could gather no hint of any new thought on the subject. . . . Why harp upon physical corruption, of which no man is conscious? Even death itself ceases to exist once he who is to suffer it realises that, as the old writer said, 'either it has happened, or it is not yet.' That, as Lady Bracknell would remark, is all there is to be said about death. . . . In this, the most old-fashioned piece he has yet contrived, our author has gone back to the Expressionism of the nineteen-twenties as practised by Messrs Toller, Kaiser, Molnar, and Elmer Rice, and dead almost before it was alive. You know the kind of thing. A business magnate wants to write a letter, whereupon twenty typists appear joggling twenty imaginary typewriters while twenty office-boys lick twenty imaginary stamps. The whole of Mr Priestley's first act is a wilderness of dusty antics of this sort. It shows the soul of Johnson repairing to a spiritual clearing-house where he is put through a lot of questions. Has he gone in for regular exercise ? Has he looked after his teeth ? Did he ever take the trouble to find out what the letters T.U.C. stand for, and what is meant by Proportional Representation ? All of which is expressed in terms of ballet. Then comes a great deal of skimble-skamble stuff about Johnson's money. But by this time fog, for me, had set in, and it did not lift when an incinerator, horribly suggesting a crematorium, turned out to be the door to a night-club. Here the characters wore masks, and the point of the lugubrious orgy seemed to be the pet proposition of the asensualists, that commercialised pleasure is dull. Hereabouts one glimpsed the tremulous approach to an idea, the notion that no human being can exist to be the toy of another human being. In other words, that the meanest drab has had a mother somewhere. But even here I think that if I were put to it I could find a Victorian ditty with the same burden. . . . I do not accuse my old friend of having consciously bamboozled us ; I suggest that he has unconsciously and with complete sincerity bamboozled himself. I sat through all but the last four minutes of his play dry-eyed, unamazed, and unexcited, and as I am honest I must hold that any play, whether about death or anything else, is a failure if it does not move me emotionally, intellectually, or theatrically."

MUSIC AT NIGHT

"Mr Priestley's *Music at Night* is a play about a new violin concerto and how a number of guests are moved by it to reveal their inmost thoughts. This is uniformly depressing, because the ultimate mood of every character is a hundred per cent. black-out made up of regrets and repinings. Much has been heard of innovation with regard to this play, and it is something of a shock to find that the principal character, Lady Sybil Linchester, 'the most successful kept-woman in London,' is only Dumas's Marguerite Gautier all over again. . . . Heaven in their infancy has lain about Mr Priestley's male characters, who one by one describe how shades of the prison-house crowded upon the growing boy, whether the man he has become is a cackling imbecile of a statesman, a merchant-prince who bought his millions at the price of a secret, or a gossip-writer with a hundred-horse-power car and a hundred silk shirts. All of these tell how the vision splendid died away. . . . In the last act the company group themselves pyramidally and explain that the Greatest Common Measure of them is the Tree of Life. Whether playgoers will or will not like this piece it is not for me to say. My complaint is not that it is not a farce, but that it is not a tragedy. To dine off noble despair is one thing ; to spend the evening nibbling at a wet blanket is another. When you have heard this piece your impulse is to say of the author not 'Hey, but he's tragic!' but 'Hey, but he's doleful!'"

THEY CAME TO A CITY

"Mr Priestley divides his characters into three kinds: those who, sensing that life in the city will be like Hampstead Heath on a Bank Holiday, wish for no part in it; those who, embracing the communal part with passion, think that life on the new lines must be bully and are therefore willing to stay; and those who are so much enamoured of the brave new city that they feel they must go back to the shabby old one and tell the stick-in-the-muds all about it. One judged from the warmth of the applause that the audience *en masse* endorsed Mr Priestley's sentiments *en bloc*. Were there dissentients? One thought, very few. Did one or two ill-conditioned people coming to the theatre for pure entertainment (oh, dear!) find themselves let in for a good talking-to? If there were any such let us hope 'sitting under' Mr Priestley did them good. . . . If anybody asks me whether *They Came to a City* is good theatre I shall be forced to say no. And proceed to add quickly that it isn't bad theatre either. That, in my view, it is magnificent sermonising. Or you might put it that Mr Priestley has built himself a first-class tub and thumps on it to superb effect. What a tympanist the theatre has gained to make up for the dramatist it has temporarily lost!"

If in my reviews of your plays, of which the above are extracts, there is a certain levity, it is because levity seemed to me to be the best counter to ponderosity—if there is such a word. The unthinking cocking of a snook at a playwright of your "international reputation" must obviously injure my own. Do you, a Yorkshireman, really think that I, a Lancashireman, am such a fool as to fall into a trap of this sort?

About your fourth play, *Desert Highway*. I abstained from seeing this because I felt, rightly or wrongly, that I wasn't going to like it. And since nothing would have induced me to write damagingly about a play written to be acted by soldiers to soldiers, I just didn't go. I intended no discourtesy to one who has been, and has it in his power to be again, a great writer for the stage. Why don't you have another think about the theatre? Why must you believe yourself called upon to write dramas about the Beveridge Plan? Consider those first-rate playwrights, Jean-Jacques Bernard and André Obey. Do they weave dramas round the de Gaulle Plan? If you want to go into Parliament, my dear Jack, do so, and if you put up in my part of the world I promise to vote for you. But for Heaven's sake don't drag the House of Commons into Shaftesbury Avenue!

Yours sincerely,
James Agate

April 16 From Jock:
Monday.

Sunday, April 15*th*,
at Beaconsfield

DEAR JAMIE,
Your article this morning on Emlyn's *The Wind of Heaven* and headed " A Noble Play " is a noble article—and in your highest vein. I read it walking between New and Old Beaconsfield, and oddly enough reached its conclusion and culmination—" It is as though Lear had convoked his knights to prayer "—just as I passed the house in which that great and noble person, G. K. Chesterton, lived and died. So good morning and thank you!

JOCK

To Jock:

*Queen Alexandra Mansions, W.C.*2
April 16*th*, 1945

DEAR JOCK,
Thanks for letter. I suspect that you would have found a lot of your Dad in Herbert Lomas's Shepherd.

Have just come back from Chatham, where I talked to the staff and patients of the Naval Hospital on the theme of " Good Music is not Dull." You can imagine the wrangling Leo and I had about the choice of records. The old thing wanting me to play the boys pieces proving that good music is *duller than they thought*—things like the second movement of the Beethoven No. 8 or the last movement of the Mozart E flat.

You will agree, won't you, Jock, that for the purposes of a recital like to-day's most composers are too long in getting under way? It's the old business of the music hall; your serious actor can afford to play himself in, your low comedian hasn't a second to waste. The last movement to Tschaikowsky's No. 4 is a superb example. Give the boys that opening flourish, repeated twice, you remember, and they will put up with what follows. Take away the flourish, and the foot-shuffling starts at once. Anyhow, Leo and I spent two afternoons on the job, and presently he went off to the H.M.V. place in Oxford Street with an impeccable list of nine records, including the *Fledermaus* Overture, the *Valse Oubliée* of Liszt, and the Johann Strauss *Perpetuum Mobile.* They hadn't one of them in stock, so I had to rely on my own little collection. Surgeon Rear-Admiral Sankey was charming, and with his permission I improvised a jury of twelve members of all ratings and both sexes. Here is the result, ten marks being the maximum for any item. You will understand that there was time only for snippets of the longer pieces, and if you boggle at the inclusion of the Herman Finck I must explain that it was just to give them an " easy."

GOUNOD. Gigli singing *Salve, dimora.* (91 marks)
LISZT. Hungarian Rhapsody No. 1. (88 marks)
TSCHAIKOWSKY. Finale to Fourth Symphony. (87 marks)
CHOPIN. Two Studies, op. 25, Nos. 2 and 11. (86 marks)
CHABRIER. *España.* (85 marks)
FINCK. *Melodious Memories.* (84 marks)
HANDEL. *The Origin of Design.* (77 marks)
ELGAR. *Enigma* Variations, Nos. 8 and 9. (73 marks)
BIZET. Adagietto from *L'Arlésienne* Suite. (71 marks)

As there were three minutes to go, I gave them as an encore piece Gigli in *Bohème* singing, "Your tiny hand is frozen." About a hundred and fifty people present, there was no shuffling or whispering, and everybody stayed to the end. So I think the thing can be reckoned a success. After you have left Haslar—*but not before*—I'll come down and perform for your boys, if anybody thinks they would like it.

Ever,
JAMIE

April 17 *Tuesday.* I see from *The Times* that my old master, R. P. Horsley, has died. He was head of the Modern side at the Manchester Grammar School, and my form-master in the Modern Sixth. A terrifying little man, and exactly like Lewis Carroll's Walrus. And I think he knew it. From him I learned that in translation it is the spirit rather than the letter that matters. I remember some wretched boy standing up in form and reeling off something about the wind making love to the trees, and Horsley rapping out, "Nonsense! The wind doesn't make love. It woos or kisses!" A typical incident. When Horsley was translating he had the habit of tilting back chair, putting feet on desk, holding book, jangling keys, and combing walrus moustache with long, untrimmed nails attached to tobacco-stained fingers stuck together like fins. One day, in the middle of this, the High Master (J. E. King) walked in. Horsley's sway over us hung in the balance. Continuing to jangle and comb, he assumed his most baleful glare, and when King had traversed the long room snarled, "In future, when you honour me with a visit, be good enough to shut the door!" An extraordinary man! After leaving the M.G.S. I went to him on Sunday mornings for private coaching in Latin. One day he said, "I don't feel like teaching this morning. I'm going for a walk." He then thrust a book into my hand—it was Ian Maclaren's *Beside the Bonny Brier Bush*—and said, "Read that till I come back, and if it hasn't made you blub I'll flog you." Years later I partnered him in a golf foursome, and I remember no stroke in which he did not hit the ball bang on the top, mostly driving it into the ground. Before retiring to Devonshire he lived for many years in Disley, close to Allan Monkhouse, and at one time proposed to engage a valet, who, however, stayed only one day. Going to call his master, the man said, " What suit will you be wearing, sir ? " And Horsley growled, " Bring it in ! "

April 18 *Wednesday.* Last week I wrote about some silly piece at the Playhouse that it was " an unassuming, unpretentious, unaffected, uninteresting domestic comedy which has been played to seventy thousand troops in France, Belgium, and Holland. Judging from the reception by the first-night audience, it is likely to entertain several times seventy thousand simple folk at home." And then the pother started, the authors writing to complain that I had not sat their nonsense out. It's the old story. Playwrights and novelists can never understand that an experienced taster doesn't have to swallow a whole barrel of bilge-water to know what he's drinking. Add to this the silly fetish whereby anything happening in a theatre is taken by newspapers more seriously than anything of the same quality happening outside the theatre. My answer to all charges of deserting my post is to quote G. B. S., who, in his eighth week on the *Saturday Review*, wrote of some comedy at the Opéra Comique : " Taking advantage of the second interval to stroll out into the Strand for a little exercise, I unfortunately forgot all about my business, and actually reached home before it occurred to me that I had not seen the end of the play." In my eleven-hundred-and-second week on the *Sunday Times* I took advantage of the Playhouse interval to stroll out on to the Embankment and sit in the little garden admiring the rear of a statue to some Crimean general. Like Shaw, I could plead absent-mindedness and say that, after the manner of the couple in Stephen Phillips's *Marpessa*, Bertie van Thal and I " into the evening green wandered away." But we didn't. We went back to see whether the second half could be as abjectly silly as the first. It was. So we left.

April 19 *Thursday.* The reviews of *Immoment Toys* have been more than handsome. The *Observer* started the snowball with Ivor Brown's gratifying " a brilliant anatomy of all that isn't melancholy." One of the most interesting notices was in the *Tribune*. The reviewer, W. P. Rilla, wrote :

> It seems to me that criticism is essentially an objective function, and Mr Agate's criticism suffers fundamentally from an excess of subjectivity. Often we are told more about the critic, his likes and dislikes, his personal habits and idiosyncrasies, than about the play

or the actors he is criticising. Time and again the greater part of an article has, like the flowers that bloom in the spring, nothing to do with the case under discussion. It does always make good reading, but often it is not criticism.

May I plead that I have done my best to be objective ? For example, when I say :

Nobody who ever saw Billy Bennett is likely to forget that rubicund, unæsthetic countenance, that black, plastered quiff, that sergeant-major's moustache, that dreadful dinner-jacket, that well-used dickey and seedy collar, the too-short trousers, the hob-nailed boots, the red silk handkerchief tucked into the waistcoat, the continual perspiration which was the outward and visible sign of a mind struggling for expression.

Every critic's shelves are stocked with superb examples of objectivity. What could be better than Bournonville's account of Frédérick Lemaître in Victor Ducange's *Trente Ans, ou la Vie d'un Joueur* :

In this part he goes through all stages of the gambling mania, from the victim's twentieth to his fiftieth year ; sinks down into poverty and crime, goes about begging, a ragged, crook-backed *lazzarone*, with nothing left of all he once was—except his expressive eyes. He is given a loaf, and told to cut as much off it as he wants ; the first slice he puts in his pocket with a " Pour ma famille " that sets all hearts a-quiver ; but when, later on, after committing a murder, he brings gold home to his wife, and replies to her anxious questioning with " Je l'ai trouvé," a murmur runs through the audience, as if an abyss had suddenly opened before our eyes.

And there is Gordon Craig's wonderful account of Irving, in the first act of *The Bells*, taking off his snowy boots and buckling his shoes :

We suddenly saw these fingers stop their work ; the crown of the head suddenly seemed to glitter and become frozen—and then, at the pace of the slowest and most terrified snail, the two hands, still motionless and dead, were seen to be coming up the side of the leg. The whole torso of the man, also seeming frozen, was gradually, and by an almost imperceptible movement, seen to be drawing up and back, as it would straighten a little, and to lean a little against the back of the chair on which he was seated. Once in that position—motionless—eyes fixed ahead of him and fixed on us all —there he sat for the space of ten to twelve seconds, which, I can assure you, seemed to us all like a lifetime, and then said—and said in a voice deep and overwhelmingly beautiful—" Oh, you were talking of that—were you ? " And as the last syllable was uttered, there came afar off the regular throbbing sound of sledge-bells.

But there comes the occasion when objectivity is no more than a railway time-table in comparison with the urge the critic feels to describe his sensations in the train. It is this urge which accounts for Montague's:

> Sarah Bernhardt's faults are rank; they cry to heaven—when she is not there. Then you see her act once more, and you feel as if you were looking again at Florence from Fiesole, or at a pheasant's neck, or Leonardo's Monna Lisa, or ripe corn with poppies in it.

Sometimes, but so rarely as to be almost never, objectivity and subjectivity go together. I know one example only:

> If the Paycock and Fluther were the planets of the O'Casey plays, Joxer and the Covey were not satellites only, they were mighty in themselves, and I shall remember for ever the angular slouch, the dragging walk, and the whole apparatus of a lean yet sensual squalor which moved in the broken boots of the actor who played these parts. So surely did Sydney Morgan work himself into the essence of these crapulous corner-boys that you felt that not the boots only, but the entire creature was held together by bits of string and by such welding and cohesive power as a glass of malt can exercise upon a thing of rags and patches. Sinclair's rascal-parts were the full-blown bladders of a taproom knavery; Morgan's were the wry starvelings of the game. They dripped no fatness and larded no gutter. They were less largely droll than Sinclair's, but more actual, more terrible in their harsh and absolute rejection of the humbug which is so theatrically picturesque as to be endearing and refreshing.

Well, Mr Rilla, there you have it. There are objective critics and there are subjective critics, and we must all do the best we can in our own vein. It is not given to everybody to combine the two as Ivor Brown did in his magnificent "Tribute to Sydney Morgan."

April 20 Sent the following letter:
Friday.

To the Editor of "The Times"

SIR,

One day last week, at the invitation of Surgeon Rear-Admiral Sankey, I visited the Royal Naval Hospital at Chatham. The object was an hour's talk to the staff and patients on the theme "Good Music is not Dull." I took with me an album of gramophone records of works by Handel, Elgar, Chopin, Tschaikowsky, Bizet, Gounod, Chabrier, and Liszt, the idea being to give them a topical rather than a musical interest. Let the boys think of V Day in terms of the Battle and Finale from Handel's *Origin of*

Design. Let them, while listening to Elgar's "Nimrod" Variation, remember Roosevelt. Did they find, in the fire and vim of the opening to the last movement of Tschaikowsky's Fourth Symphony, an image of Russian impetus and drive? I admit that such an approach is strictly non-musical. But that it was effective—and effectiveness was what one was after—was proved by the fact that the boys never relaxed attention, there was no whispering or shuffling of feet, nobody dozed, and nobody left. Next morning I opened my paper to read that the London Philharmonic, the Liverpool Philharmonic, the London Symphony, the Hallé, and the Scottish orchestras are not to broadcast any more, the cause being some miserable question of remuneration. Now, sir, speaking off the book and with no pretension to technical accuracy, I understand that the B.B.C. has a monopoly of the air in this country. Since we do not grant monopolies to grocers and clothiers, the only justification for granting this privilege to the B.B.C. is the understanding, the gentleman's agreement as it were, that the Corporation shall carry out its intellectual, educational, and artistic responsibilities. Surely, sir, here is a case for arbitration. As I understand the figures, the demands of the orchestras do not seem to be unreasonable, and presumably the orchestras are prepared to put the case for reasonableness to the arbitrator. Presumably, also, the B.B.C. will maintain that anything above its present rate is not good business in the sense that vast sums paid to popular buffoons are good business. But that is not the point. The Corporation must prove that the extra sum demanded is excessive to the point at which the Corporation is justified in repudiating its moral and æsthetic responsibilities.

Some means must be found whereby this repudiation is not allowed to happen. There is plenty of materialistic discord before our young people in the immediate future, and there can be nothing better than music to resolve that discord. What is the use of instilling the love of good music into our returning sailors, soldiers, and airmen if the only organisation which can give them the best performances of that music easily and familiarly is to refuse on the score of expense? This country has recently spent thousands of millions in the arts of war; why should it boggle at a few hundreds expended in the arts of peace? The B.B.C. cannot plead that it is a commercial organisation. It is this country's voice on the air.

Hitherto nothing has frightened me more than the use of the ether for advertising purposes. But if the B.B.C. cannot carry out its moral obligations, then its charter should be revoked and the air given over to commercial firms forced by competition to deliver the goods, even when some of those goods are, regrettably, of the highest quality!

Yours faithfully,
JAMES AGATE

The Savage Club
April 20, '45

April 21 *Saturday.* How far should a writer take his readers into his confidence ? Shall I " lose face " if I confess that the *Ego* books are not the careless jottings of idle half-hours ? That I think *Ego*, talk *Ego*, dream *Ego* ? That I get up in the middle of the night to make a correction ? That before the MS. of any of my *Ego's* reaches the publisher it has been through at least a dozen revisions ? That it is only when the galley proofs arrive that the real work begins ? I suppose that when I had finished with the galleys of *Ego* 7 it would have been difficult to find fifty unaltered sentences. The reason for this is that stuff in print reads differently from the same stuff in typescript. Very well, then. The galleys have been returned to the publishers, and one sits back and awaits the page proofs in the vain belief that there is nothing more to do except see that the galley corrections have been properly carried out. Actually I made over two thousand corrections *on the page proofs* of *Ego* 7. For the reason that stuff in page reads differently from the same stuff in galley. There is another and more humiliating confession. This is that anything to which I subsequently attach value always turns out to have been an afterthought. Henry James wrote to his agent that the only way he could write was " to *overtreat* my subject by developments and amplifications that have, in large part, eventually to be greatly compressed, but to the prior operation of which the thing afterwards owes what is most durable in its quality." With me the long-cogitated stuff, once it has been deleted, is deleted for good, and no trace that I can discern remains. Whereas all my best stuff goes into the margin of my page—not even galley—proofs. I remember talking to Leo about this. He said, " Afterthought my foot ! Don't you know that Dickens wrote the whole of Mr Dick's ' King Charles's head ' stuff on the page proofs of *Copperfield* ? That those two marvellous octaves at the beginning of the slow movement of the Hammerklavier Sonata were an afterthought, sent by Beethoven to the printers ? So cheer up." Another trouble is inaccuracy, which is my *bête noire*. My passion for correctness amounts to a neurosis. Not only do I look up chapter and verse, but I compare editions, telephone to libraries, consult innumerable dictionaries and encyclopædias, ring up Embassies. And now this morning comes a letter asking how in *Ego* 6, page 132, I can say that Cora Pearl appeared at the Variétés in Offenbach's *La Belle Hélène* when I have already said in *Ego* 4, page 174, that the theatre was the Bouffes-Parisiens, and the opérette *Orphée aux Enfers* ? ! ! ! ! ! !

April 22 *Sunday.* Tell *S.T.* readers to-day that in the revival of *The Duchess of Malfi* Mr G. put up a great performance in the first half. Like a pianist pretending that Liszt's E flat Concerto is another *Emperor*. That if in the second he dwindled it was because Kean himself couldn't have done more with this mish-mash of Hamlet's " antic disposition," Edgar's " Poor Tom's a-cold," and a subtle prevision, which I take to be Mr G.'s own, of Pirandello's Henry IV. That Trouncer put up a grand show as Bosola, whether or not he knew what this mixture of Enobarbus and Thersites was up to. And that Ashcroft did teeny-weeniers, her " I am Duchess of Malfi still ! " sounding like " I am still Little Miss Muffet ! "

April 23 *Monday.* *Cocasseries, No.* 12 :
An unknown friend sends me a poem entitled *Auchmountain Glen,* which appeared recently in a Scottish newspaper, apropos, I take it, of some proposal to commercialise the Glen. My friend suggests that the sanctuary indicated in the last four lines is " even more exotic than that from which the Walla-walla bird surveyed its baffled pursuers."

Auchmountain ! ravished maid, outraged, molested !
Poor bleeding child, sunk in an early tomb ;
Thy flow'ry, fruitful produce now arrested,
Thy sepulchre—thy once proud pregnant womb !

April 24 *Tuesday.* Judging from his latest effusion, I must think that there is something in Leo's and my little Irish friend :

18 *Park View Avenue*
Harold's Cross
Dublin
20–4–1945

Ave DULCISSIME LEO !

I shall attempt to deal with your charming letter in the same logical, businesslike manner that you dealt with mine.

Firstly, " J. E. " stands for " John Edward."

Re my not getting an opportunity to talk, I meant that there is no one to talk to. At least, not in an intelligent manner. You may, Leo, go over to your desk and deliver a magnificent speech on " Art for Art's sake." But the desk remains dumb. You can get no satisfaction out of making your magnificent speech. . . .

I hope you weren't expecting a witty letter bubbling over with Noelisms, and Irish humour as typified by Our Mr Shaw. You bemoan the fact that the English have never heard of anybody. Well, they can't be worse than the Dubliners. Earthly bliss for them is realised in some awful blonde showing her hideous legs in some film, or some horrible he-man doing vulgar gyrations in a private cop's tailor-made. *Othello,* running for ten performances, broke all records. A ham thing like *Irish Eyes are Smiling* ran for nearly a month at one of Dublin's biggest cinemas. No wonder the late Mrs Shaw left her fortune for the advancement of culture in Dublin !

You must forgive my dulness to-day. There's a heat wave here and my latest short story hasn't turned out so well. Perhaps some day in the starry future I will send James one of my efforts.

There are no existing photos of me at my present ripe old age. Any at earlier ages show me as an odiously stupid child (which is exactly what I was.) Here is a rough description of me at present :

Body. Long, thin, and awkward. Lots of leg.

Hair. Once fair, now mousey, and has distinct aversion to restraining influences.

Nose. Sir Hook and Sir Bulbous fight a bloody battle.

Eyes. In colour—blue. In quality—like the last drop of very weak tea. In expression—" Insipid with veracity," as Henry James's father said about Swedenborg.

Mouth. Thick, sensual upper lip and ordinary unremarkable lower lip.

Altogether I'm like an embarrassed horse.

Reply if you get time. Love to James.

Vale, carissime Leo !

J. E. JORDAN

Lunching at the Ivy, by a stroke of luck I fell in with Hilton Edwards, the director of the Gate Theatre, Dublin. I told him about the boy, and Edwards very graciously said that if Jordan would call he would see whether he could find something for him at the theatre. He said he badly wanted an assistant stage-manager, and I suggested his starting the lad as call-boy with a view to his learning the theatre from the beginning. Nobody can make careers for other people, but a push at the start does no harm.

April 25 *Wednesday.* Letter from J. B. Priestley :

*B*4 *Albany, W.*1

April 23*rd*, 1945

DEAR JIMMIE,

Many thanks for your letter, which I would have received earlier if it had been addressed here and not care of the *Observer*.

I stick to my point, and your quotations from your notices do not unstick me. All of them seem to me too hasty and airy in their judgment. Just as you settled yourself solidly in your stall, so too you fixed yourself in your opinion of what a play should be, without really trying to understand what I was attempting or to follow my thought. I have " bamboozled myself " in a play to which I gave long earnest thought and which I re-wrote many times. Now I do not think for a moment that I succeeded here in all I tried to do; nevertheless, your notice is simply not good enough. (I have not the time or you the patience to take all three plays, so we will look at the first, *Johnson over Jordan.*)

Your notice says, in effect, this is a play about death and has no new ideas on the subject, has indeed no ideas at all, and is merely an attempt to revive the German-American Expressionism of the 'twenties. Every statement there, to my mind, is wrong. The play is not about death but about a man's life, which is presented in a new way—as if looked at outside time (as we do in dreams often), each act representing a certain level of the mind: the first giving us all the conscious worries, responsibilities, and anxieties of a middle-class urban man; the second giving us the unconscious drives; the third the poetry and deep-seated affections of such a mind. In all these acts there were, in fact, plenty of ideas; and though they may not have been wildly original (for I make no pretence of being an original thinker, and if I were I would not choose the theatre as my medium), they were ideas, and derived an emotional impact from the way they were presented. I had a lot of trouble with Act Two (the night-club) and never got it right, but to suggest, as you do, that there was only the vague ghost of an idea in it is simply not good enough. It contains, among other things, in Johnson's long soliloquy about Desire the most careful speech I ever wrote for the theatre. (Morgan singled it out, I remember.) And the third act still seems to me, as it does to many people, the most moving thing I ever wrote for the theatre. Again, it is quite wrong to say that the play is a return to Expressionism, whose object was to flatten out character, to ignore the individual and concrete instance, and to find drama in the relations of purely symbolic figures. My object was to show a real man in real relationships, but to do it outside time, to present it all, as in dreams, in a four-dimensional manner. Thus, Johnson in Act Three was reliving his past and yet standing outside the time process, again as we seem to do often in poignant vivid dreams. (Ralph suggested all this wonderfully, I thought.) It is true that some of the production, notably in Act One, did suggest the Expressionist method; but if the play should ever be revived I should have it done in a simpler fashion. Unfortunately, I had to go to Switzerland, with a convalescent daughter, while the first two acts were being rehearsed, and it was only Act Three that was done exactly as I wanted it.

Let me make it clear again what I am complaining about. I do not expect to be praised for everything I do (though I have the usual wistful hopes), but I consider myself a serious artist in the theatre, with a good technical knowledge of its resources, and I have struggled hard to bring experiment to a theatre terribly lacking in it, and I feel entitled to claim the serious careful consideration of senior critics. Finally, I have several new plays ready for production when good casts and theatres can be found for them.

Present conditions I believe to be the worst that serious dramatists have ever been called upon to face in this country. And I suggest that instead of being funny about my sociological interests, you turn your insight and wit on these conditions, which may soon leave you without a theatre at all.

Yours ever,
J. B. P.

I have replied :

Queen Alexandra Mansions, W.C.2
April 25th, 1945

Dear Jack,

Would all controversies were conducted in this spirit ! This is just to thank you for your share in our little bout, and to say that I await all or any of your new plays with the greatest eagerness. I shall bend up every mental as well as corporal agent to the terrible feat of giving them careful and critical attention. Delete the word " terrible."

Yours ever,
Jimmie

April 26 Thursday. " Now let it work. Mischief, thou art afoot. . . ." My letter to *The Times* (see entry for April 20) appeared yesterday. This morning I get a letter from St John Baptist College, Oxford, enclosing a copy of a letter addressed to the writer's City and University M.P.'s, these being the Hon. Quintin Hogg and A. P. Herbert, asking them to back me up.

The post also brings a letter from Tom Curtiss, now settled in Paris. It has taken six days to get here. He writes :

Paris is very nearly her pre-war self externally. Blue skies—chestnut blossoms—lilac—sudden showers and a surplus of G.I.'s. The food situation remains the same, and the major restaurants—Larue, La Reine Pédauque, etc.—remain closed rather than cope with the ration regulations. Drinking is a dubious business. The beer tastes like well-water aged in metal containers, the white wine is sour, the red often non-existent, the champagne usually fake, and the cognac diluted. Saw Raimu in *Le Malade Imaginaire* last night. Wonderful performance. There's a new film of Marcel Carné, who made *Quai des Brumes*. This is a story of Debureau and Lemaître, and the Paris of their day. Beautiful photography and lovely acting, but it runs for three and a half hours !

A jolly and surprise luncheon given by Hamish Hamilton, who introduces me to a bright young man intending to open a theatre. If only some one would introduce me to some one with the power to close a theatre ! The surprise turned out to be Jock, invalided, or something, out of the Navy. I gather that he has to go to Oxford or somewhere to write for a firm of University publishers a History of the English Stage. Which, bless his dear heart, he thinks he can do in three months. I once did it in three days, producing for fifty pounds a vastly filthy little book of which I have always been ashamed and which, whenever I meet it in the Charing Cross Road, I buy and destroy. To do a good job on this subject should take three years. However, I don't discourage him.

Cocasseries, No. 13 :

This is an advertisement seen in the window of a music-shop in Uxbridge :

Selection of Melodies by Chopin

From the Columbia Picture

A SONG TO REMEMBER

STARRING PAUL MUNI AND
MERLE OBERON WITH CORNEL WILDE

Arranged and Adapted for
Piano Solo by Louis Levy

CHAPPELL 3/–

April 27 *Wednesday.* The old heart-breaking subject has turned up again. A sergeant in the Buffs submits a poem, "not with a request for advice on publication, nor for suggestions of how to break into the big money, but merely for an opinion ; so as to confirm my worst fears, *i.e.*, that I am just wasting my time, or to uphold what my friends tell me, that there is merit in the effort." The letter has this postscript : "I may add, as a point of interest, that I wrote the poem whilst engaged in tank fighting in Normandy. We were standing by to go in, and it passed an hour away." The poem is valueless. I have sent the following reply :

*Queen Alexandra Mansions, W.C.*2
April 27th, 1945

DEAR SERGEANT,

It seems to me—and I have thought about it a good deal—that any work of art must have two functions. If you write a book the first function is to get something off your chest ; the second is to give pleasure to the reader. The same thing applies to a painting, a bust, or a piece of music, and equally to acting, singing, playing a musical instrument, dancing.

Your poem is valueless as regards its secondary function, which does not mean that it is valueless in its first function. I doubt if you could have been better employed during that hour before going into action. Look at it this way. Take the following lines :

> Matthew is in his grave, yet now
> Methinks, I see him stand,
> As at that moment, with a bough
> Of wilding in his hand.

And now the following :

> He trudged along through copse and brake,
> He trudged along o'er hill and dale ;
> Nor for the moon cared he a tittle,
> And for the stars he cared as little,
> And for the murmuring river Swale.

Magic is in the first but not in the second. Yet it is quite possible that Wordsworth, getting the second off his chest, felt as much relief as he did with the first. You wanted to write those lines before that battle, and you wrote them. You got them off your chest, and you felt the better for it. That means that your poem fulfilled its first function. But it is not poetry. Are you going to ask me to define poetry ? My dear Sergeant, better men than I have spent a lifetime over this and failed. Asked for a definition, that great minor poet A. E. Housman replied that he could no more define poetry than a terrier could define a rat, but that he thought both he and the terrier recognised the object by the symptoms which it provoked in them. These symptoms differ with the individual. The great critic Montague said that the sight or sound of a beautiful thing gave him gooseflesh. The form this emotion takes with me is a shiver at the base of the spine. I have no other criterion. Here are one or two specimens, and they all have to do with arms. First I choose Herbert Asquith's poem which begins :

> Here lies a clerk who half his life had spent
> Toiling at ledgers in a city grey,
> Thinking that so his days would drift away
> With no lance broken in life's tournament :

and ends :

> And falling thus he wants no recompense,
> Who found his battle in the last resort ;
> Nor needs he any hearse to bear him hence,
> Who goes to join the men of Agincourt.

Next a poem by Patrick Shaw-Stewart, beginning :

> I saw a man this morning
> Who did not wish to die ;
> I ask and cannot answer
> If otherwise wish I.

and ending :

> I will go back this morning
> From Imbros over the sea ;
> Stand in the trench, Achilles,
> Flame-capped, and shout for me.

Third and last you might like to know John Pudney's *For Johnny*, of which most effective use is made in the film *The Way to the Stars*. Here it is:

> Do not despair
> For Johnny-Head-in-Air,
> He sleeps as sound
> As Johnny underground.
>
> Fetch out no shroud
> For Johnny-Head-in-Cloud,
> And keep your tears
> For him in after years.
>
> Better by far
> For Johnny-the-Bright-Star,
> To keep your head
> And see his children fed.

I cannot tell you, nor can anyone tell you, why these things are poetry, and why

> Can this be then the purpose of it all,
> That woman shall go through the jaws of Hell
> To give another victim to the call,
> Of Naziism and the Fascist cult as well?

is not. But let me stress this equally—no man should tell you, and you must not allow any man to tell you, that the effort of writing your lines wasn't worth while. There are some things of which the act of doing is the real reward.

Yours sincerely,
JAMES AGATE

I have decided, whether it is cynical or not, to have some five hundred copies of this printed for dispatch to all those soldier, sailor, Air Force, and civilian scribblers who pester me.

April 28 *Saturday.* The Statement issued by the B.B.C. to *The Times*, in reply to my challenge, leads off with a piece of muddle-headedness. Have sent to *The Times* this second letter, after which the matter, as far as I am concerned, is closed:

To the Editor of "The Times"

SIR,

Let us be quite clear what we are arguing about. In its Statement in your issue of Friday last the B.B.C. says: "This dispute has already lasted fifteen months and has not caused any decrease of serious music in that period." Sir, why should it? The decision of the five orchestras not to broadcast takes effect only in May!

The Statement's next sentence runs: "The B.B.C. wishes to make it quite clear that the continuing of the dispute will not reduce the amount of good orchestral music available to listeners." Sir, let us take that Statement as being issued in complete good faith, and as a guarantee that every time there would have been an outside broadcast the B.B.C. undertakes to give listeners the equivalent inside one, with soloists of equal prominence.

Even so, the public will, in my submission, not be satisfied. Some orchestras are known for the excellence of their strings, some for their wood-wind, others again for their brass. Different conductors have different qualities. I greatly admire Toscanini, but I should not want all my music to be interpreted by him to the exclusion of all other interpreters, any more than I should want all my Shakespeare to be performed by Mr Gielgud, Mr Olivier, Mr Wolfit, or any other distinguished actor to the exclusion of all other actors.

I have expressed no opinion as to whether the demands of the orchestras are reasonable or not—that will be for the arbitrator to decide. If the arbitrator holds that the demands are reasonable, then the B.B.C., in so far as it is public-spirited, must pay up. If the arbitrator holds the opposite view, then the orchestras must climb down.

Here, sir, is an issue which should be kept clear and not obscured by fog or red herrings.

Yours faithfully,
JAMES AGATE

The Savage Club
April 28, '45

April 29 *Sunday.* A total stranger comes up to me in the Café Royal:

T. S. Mr Agate, why are you so ungenerous? A generous artist admires his fellow-artists.

J. A. Rubbish! Do you think Beethoven admired his musical contemporaries?

T. S. Yes, he admired Schubert.

J. A. A few songs, perhaps. If the young man had brought along a work as good as one of the Rasoumowsky Quartets the old man would have shut up like a knife. Was Wagner charmed by Brahms? Did Balzac boost George Sand? Did Whistler crack up Sargent? Did Melba rave over Tetrazzini? Was Sarah crazy about Duse? Only the second-rate artist has time for the work of others; the first-rate artist is preoccupied with his own output, to the exclusion of any and everybody else's. I'm your first-rate artist.

T. S. Do you hold yourself to be a first-rate diarist?

J. A. I most emphatically do.

T. S. To be ranked with Pepys?

J. A. To take my place beside Pepys.

T. S. Perhaps you think that, like Samuel, you ought to be Secretary to the Navy?

J. A. Go to hell!

April 30 *Monday.* I get really angry when people tell me that the dedication to *Noblesse Oblige*—" For and on behalf of SYD, ERN, CHARLEY, and their kind "—is a pose. Yesterday evening I went down to Bethnal Green to talk and play gramophone records to a club for kids. Small, clean, tidy room in the Friends' Hall, Barnet Grove, and on the wall a picture of a grove of trees—more trees than there are in the whole of Bethnal Green, that wilderness of flatness and bricks. I had been promised an audience of fifteen ; actually sixteen turned up. I have no illusions at all about this sort of thing. The street outside was full of urchins who couldn't be bribed to come in. Neither would they stop yelling. First I sent them a polite message—no result. I then sent the biggest boy to tell them that if they didn't stop their noise I should come down myself and wallop their bloody arses for them. After which there wasn't a sound. Given this material, did I start with carols by Wilbye and Weelkes ? No. The thing was to get their interest, and after leading off with a bit of Handel I went straight into Ponchielli's *Dance of the Hours* and told them to look out for the circus ponies. But what they liked best was the four sides of Herman Finck's *Melodious Memories.* Here, putting them on their honour, I asked for a count of the numbers they recognised. Somewhere in the eighties would have been the best possible ; several of them were well up in the sixties. I particularly noticed one young monkey with an astonishing power of mimicry. He mimicked me and the various instruments in the orchestra and was entirely irresponsible from first to last. The Warden told me that the lad could hardly read but is the delight of the entire school. I was so much impressed that I asked the Warden to tell his father, who, it seems, is a brewer's drayman, to get into communication with me when the boy leaves school, and that if he approves I will then put the kid in touch with Lupino Lane.

May 1 *Tuesday.* Leo comes into my room this morning and says, " This is the last you'll hear of Hatch."

THE TRIALS OF SACCHARISSA

CHAPTERS 19–24

(*With apologies to Tess and Jane Eyre*)

SYNOPSIS

Saccharissa, penniless, seeks employment as a Land Girl. Arrived at Little Strangles, Essex, she makes the acquaintance of Eric Mangold, a rich farmer who seduces her. She then encounters Seraph Cleer, a poet with vague notions of marriage. On hearing about Seraph, Eric smacks Saccharissa's face, whereupon she brains him with a hoe. Subsequent legal proceedings go in Saccharissa's favour, the jury declining to convict on the grounds that her father died in Widemoor and her mother in a mental home in Wessex. Again penniless, Saccharissa accepts another post as governess, this time to the child of a rich country gentleman, Captain Gillingham, who has a mad wife. They fall in love, and just as Saccharissa, fearing seduction, is about to relinquish her job, Mrs Gillingham, excited by drinking too much red ink, throws herself into the petrol-tank and is drowned. Gillingham and Saccharissa are united in Hymen's bonds.

Extracts

Just then Hilda Stumm drifted in, and Rollo asked her at once whether, in Bannerhof's book on the history of film technique, she agreed with Bratislav Brzcnv, quoted by him at such length. " Let me refresh your memory," continued Rollo, taking out the current number of the *Film Psychologist.* ' Any non-prescience of what Iwan Plutoff calls the barotic incalcation attains to a *simacrea* fluxing itself on the edge, as it were, of coincidentalism.' Do you, or do you not agree, Hilda ? " he asked anxiously. " With every syllable," answered Hilda.

. . . .

Hettie Spott was not, in our understanding of the word, an intellectual at all. She was just a *mouton de Panurge,* in the sense that she modelled herself on each idol before the next one dislodged it from its pedestal. So much was clearly shown on this occasion when Hjalmar Sikersen, commenting on the degeneracy of Pouputier's direction, blurted out in his gruff Nordic way, " None of these people *understands* the true montage. The effect should realise itself along lines of endemic simultaneity, through the mental superimposition of a triasis over the conventional diaporistic visulum. Eisenstein calls this audio-visual montage. But I go further. I demand an auro-cerebral montage which shall make possible the *tandis grandis,* the super-orasticism that ever lurks in the bi-symmetry of all thought-oxidisation." Here Hettie, who was spraying herself with the new perfume, " Voyou," stopped dabbing operations to murmur, " You forget, darling. Eisenstein also claims that the so-called ' double-exposed ' image is just as inherently characteristic of audio-visual montage as—as—— " " As it is for all other cinematic phenomena," completed Noel Flipp, with ready wit. To clinch the argument, René Fauchegarbe, who had not so far spoken, said, " Geometrical presentation must always be accurate—we can have no dallyings with a rutinous perspective. Just as on the ethical plane we must have a convergent horizon, so now we must pull such levers as are compatible with the world-theory of determinism." Hettie's face was aflame at this revelation ; her eyes registered unquestioning enslavement.

. . . .

What was quite unforgivable of Irene Hasseldon was that she included in the picnic a dreadful barbarian, one Sir Pilligo Gasper, a fat, vulgar man reputed to have made a fortune out of discarded goloshes. Just as Gwen and Lydia were in the thick of an argument about the respective merits of Konrad Blitz and Jean Castrate, this uncouth animal interrupted them to say, "I like films I can understand. I like the sort of picture where people lie about on beaches, thrumming guitars, waving multi-coloured palm-leaves, and singing South Sea Island serenades like:

"'Jake, I'll be trew-w-w to yew-w-w,
To yew-w-w I'll always be trew-w-w.'"

And the wretch actually sang! Not content with this, and despite the disgusted faces all around him, he continued, "I'm low-brow, and I'm proud of it. I don't care a damn about montage. I like to see pretty girls with lovely legs and as much of everything else as they like to show. I like to see them kiss and hug. I like to see the good rewarded and the bad punished. I like happy endings. In short, I am normal, commonplace, everyday. I am what has made England what she is, and what she always will be. As for you, you sissified saps and frillified floozies. . . ." "Enough, Sir Pilligo—thank you," commanded his hostess. "You were saying, Virginius?" But Virginius Booper, like the others, was choking with inarticulate rage. Searching for his pocket edition of Theocritus, which he found in his cigarette-case, he proceeded to read several Eclogues in the original Greek. . . .

Enclosed was this covering letter:

As from The Intellectual Youth Hostel
798 *High Street, Chiswick, W.*4

April 30*th*, 1945

DEAR MR AGATE,

You have, I hope, read what is my final instalment. *Are you conquered?* Will you now, please, find me a publisher? And by so doing make me the corner-stone of your immortality?

A temporary advance of twenty pounds, should you feel so inclined, can be automatically deducted from my advance royalties. But please do not cross the cheque.

No longer incognito, I now sign myself with my real name,

OLEANDER FUGGE

May 2 *Wednesday.* According to Robert Ross, Oscar Wilde "never regarded his works as an adequate expression of his extraordinary genius and his magnificent intellectual endowment." And in *De Profundis* Wilde wrote:

The gods had given me almost everything. I had genius, a distinguished name, high social position, brilliancy, intellectual daring; I made art a philosophy and philosophy an art; I altered

> the minds of men, and the colours of things, . . . whatever I touched I made beautiful in a new mode of beauty. . . . I awoke the imagination of my century so that it created myth and legend around me. I summed up all systems in a phrase and all existence in an epigram.

Suppose we have a look at these extravagant claims. Genius ? Wilde was a magnificent talker and a superb wit, and perhaps one mustn't complain that the wit all came from the same fount. A Jew, on being asked whether his dinner-table could accommodate twelve persons, answered, " Yes, God forbid ! " And in the sense that all Jewish jokes are a form of this joke, so all Wilde's jokes are basically epicene. The " distinguished name " and " high social position "—neither of which Wilde possessed—were pegs for snobbery of the worst type ; the photographs show him to have been inseparable from top hat and fur coat with an unhappy leaning towards astrakhan. Of the " intellectual daring " I see no trace. He could rattle about the philosophy of art in an amateurish way, but to say that he " altered the minds of men " is just nonsense. As for " the new mode of beauty," one might say that he touched nothing that he did not chichify. " Myth and legend " ? Gilbert's Bunthorne is the answer.

The boast about being " a lord of language." Wilde was that very different thing—the fine lady of the purple passage. Apart from his wit, he was entirely bogus. The words " art " and " artist " appear on almost every page of his writings ; yet he knew very little about the arts. In the matter of pictures Whistler was constantly putting him right. In the matter of music Wilde could make one of his characters say, " And now, let me play Chopin to you, or Dvořák ? Shall I play you a fantasy by Dvořák ? He writes passionate, curiously coloured things." No person with any knowledge of music could have written this. About his own profession :

> From the point of view of literature Mr Kipling is a genius who drops his aspirates. From the point of view of life, he is a reporter who knows vulgarity better than anyone has ever known it. Dickens knew its clothes and its comedy. Mr Kipling knows its essence and its seriousness. He is our first authority on the second-rate, and has seen marvellous things through keyholes, and his backgrounds are real works of art.

The truth is that there is more knowledge of life in six pages of Dickens or Kipling than in the whole of Wilde's scented output. All the world known to O. W. was what Pinero's Cayley Drummle called " our little parish of St James's." He was a borrower, and his show-pieces about jewels and such like—how he would have hated the last two words !—were lifted from the French. The atmosphere of *Salomé* was taken straight from Maeterlinck. He was a fifth-rate poet with one first-class ballad to his credit. His sonnet to Irving ends with the astounding image :

> Thou trumpet set for Shakespeare's lips to blow!

Wry-necked fife, yes. Trumpet, no. The plays ? He wrote the wittiest light comedy in the language ; the other pieces are stilted, wholly insincere Society melodramas redeemed, possibly, by their wit. If it were true that Wilde altered the mentality of his age then that could have been written of him which was written of Swinburne :

> He was to young men everywhere an intoxication and a passion, awakening half-formed desires, hidden longings and impulses, and secret enthusiasms, and wielding sway more imperiously over heart and sense and soul than any other man of his time did over the intellect or the reason of his disciples.

Would one have written that of Wilde ? Perhaps. But in the sense that the young men to whom he was an intoxication were of the queerest kind.

The makers of *The Picture of Dorian Gray*, which I saw this afternoon, have cut out most of the nonsense. They have forborne to present Lord Henry Wotton with his " low, musical voice, and the graceful wave of the hand that was always so characteristic of him, and that he had even in his Eton days." And they have been wise. Dickens and Kipling ? Perhaps Albert Lewin, who directed, asked himself what Trabb's boy, or Stalky, or even America's Andy Hardy would reply to a man saying to one much his junior, " You with your rose-red youth and your rose-white boyhood, you have had passions that have made you afraid, thoughts that have filled you with terror, daydreams and sleeping dreams whose mere memory might stain your cheek with shame." But all of Lord Henry couldn't be deleted ; George Sanders, condemned to present what was left, did so in a manner suggesting a bookmaker in his Ascot toggery doubled by Svengali. Dorian Gray himself ? What could any self-respecting young actor make of a character with " cool, white, flower-like hands " and the habit of " burying his face in great, cool lilac-blossoms, feverishly drinking in their perfume as if it had been wine " ? And what about that face ? " What the invention of oil-paintings was to the Venetians, the face of Antinoüs was to late Greek sculpture, and the face of Dorian will some day be to me," says the painter Basil Hallward. And his creator describes Dorian as " wonderfully handsome, with his finely curved scarlet lips, his frank blue eyes, his crisp gold hair." Some of us whistled, some of us thought of Browning's " What's become of all the gold ? " when the screen disclosed this young Hollywood actor, black of hair, sad of countenance—sad in the pastry sense—and looking generally as though he were not the master but the footman.

I shall tell *Tatler* readers that if Hurd Hatfield wants to have any success with me or any of my generation he must at once change his name, which is much too reminiscent of Mr Hardfur Huttle, "that clever writer for the American papers," whom Mr and Mrs Pooter met at dinner at Mr Franching's, and whose table-talk has been so miraculously preserved. "Happy medium, indeed. Do you know 'happy medium' are two words which mean 'miserable mediocrity'? I say, go first-class or third; marry a duchess or her kitchen-maid. The happy medium means respectability, and respectability means insipidness." And again: "We have no representative at Mr Franching's table of the unenlightened frivolous matron, who goes to a second-class dance in Bayswater and fancies she is in Society." No wonder that Mr Pooter held Mr Hardfur Huttle to be, as others held Wilde, a marvellously intellectual man "who says things which from other people would seem quite alarming." What book am I quoting from? *The Diary of a Nobody*, of course. Wilde's tragedy was a double one. He believed in the Dorian Grays, who even if they existed were not to survive the 'nineties, and could not believe in the Lupin Pooters, who existed then, and are alive to-day and for ever.

May 3
Thursday.

Am tired of all these so-called soldier letters that keep on appearing in the Press. Here's part of a real one from my old friend Flight Lieutenant Jim Parle, D.F.C., D.F.M., now stationed in South-east Asia:

> I suppose you have almost forgotten my existence, but I have been in the Far East for some time so it has been difficult to call on you as I used to. I am supposed to be having an operational rest at the moment—actually I have never worked so bloody hard in all my life. I am Adjutant, Armament Officer, and Mess Secretary, to mention only a few of my jobs. It isn't too bad, though, except it is all so bloody safe. My mind is incapable of gauging the full magnitude of what is happening. Perhaps I have become temporarily hardened to superlatives. There are, however, a hell of a lot of little yellow bastards to be finished off out here before there is any real peace. At this unit there is no blood and few tears, but a great deal of toil and six times our ration of sweat.

By extraordinary coincidence the post brought me this letter from a Flight Lieutenant at Streatham:

> Some individuals are so incredibly uncommunicative that it is impossible to follow their rather doubtful movements. You may or may not recall the pilot who assisted Jim Parle (Richard to us), to some small degree, in attaining such eminent heights in his flying

career. (We had a yarn in the Café Royal one night.) And now this knavish gunner of mine has scuttled off over the horizon, and the only news one has been able to cull from various unreliable sources is that he has got himself married, without the permission of his crew, and/or has disappeared mysteriously to the Orient. Perhaps, sir, you may have more precise knowledge of his inscrutable ramblings, in which case I should esteem it an honour if . . . etc., etc. . . . Dash it all, he was one of the best friends I ever had.

It gives me the greatest pleasure to forward the gunner's letter to his former pilot, and the Streatham letter to Asia.

May 4 Friday. When I was a boy I was entirely taken in and captivated by historical novels. I really believed that life in Pompeii was such as Lytton described, and in South American forests such as Kingsley pretended. That such were the exact words spoken by Ivanhoe to Rowena, by Hereward the Wake to the Last of the Barons. I believed, in a word, in the Hengist-Horsery of the entire business. Then came a time—and I think George Eliot had something to do with it—when I ceased to believe in the literal inspiration of the authors of these books, and read historical novels purely for their style. If I read Thackeray's *Esmond* to-day I should do so because of such a sentence as :

> Esmond thought of the courier, now galloping on the North road to inform him, who was Earl of Arran yesterday, that he was Duke of Hamilton to-day, and of a thousand great scenes, hopes, ambitions, that were alive in the gallant heart, beating a few hours since, and now in a little dust quiescent.

I should *not* believe in Esmond saying to Mr Addison :

> " I admire your art ; the murder of the campaign is done to military music, like a battle at the opera, and the virgins shriek in harmony, as our victorious grenadiers march into our villages. . . . You hew out of your polished verses a stately image of smiling victory ; I tell you 'tis an uncouth, distorted, savage idol ; hideous, bloody, and barbarous."

Then came the time when I started going to historical dramas other than Shakespeare's, and I believed in them not at all. Thackeray, when he was proposing to write *Esmond*, asked whether History was never to take off her peruke ? In the plays enacted by Fred Terry and Julia Neilson she took it off with a vengeance. Here is Montague on the subject :

> Dorothy Vernon proposes to exchange clothes with Mary Queen Scots : " I, by your leave," she says, in the metre Shakespeare used, " will wear your robes awhile." " I suppose," she subjoins, with the fine prose humour of to-day, " I must wear something."

And I myself remember a drama of the Cavalier and Roundhead wars in which an elderly Countess proposed on the day after the battle to hold her ground or flee according as her side had won or lost. "How will your ladyship get to know ?" somebody pertinently asked. And received the reply : "My gossip, who is to come hot-foot i' the morn, will bear the tidings." It was at that moment that I decided that the historical drama is not only what Stevenson and Henley called "tushery," but tushery for the million.

Next came the screen, and History took off much more than her peruke. And, of course, the film being a popular entertainment, designed expressly for the million, makers of historical films took care to present their subjects as their public would like them to have been. And quite reasonably. Neither your city clerk nor your Oxfordshire ploughboy wants to see a Henry VIII who is a subject for a doctor's case-book or an Anne Boleyn who is a slut. Nor are they going to believe that the issue of such a union is going to provide this country with the greatest ruler it has ever had. No film could be expected to tell the true story of Catherine of Russia, and we reflect that even the *Oxford Dictionary of Quotations* declines to give that famous line in which Byron sums up the lady in two epithets. No, most people expect to see of the carryings-on of the Empress no more than

> Merely innocent flirtation,
> Not quite adultery, but adulteration.

Let it be said that in *Czarina*, which I saw at the Odeon to-day, Lubitsch has presented the preposterous story with subtlety and wit. Who supplied this wit in the first instance I don't know, since the screen play is by Edwin Justus Mayer, adapted by Bruno Frank from a play by Lajos Biro and Melchior Lengyel. But the wit is there all right. Somebody coming to tell the Empress that he has heard whispers of a plot being hatched against her in the Ukraine or somewhere, the old Chancellor (Charles Coborn) says, "Why should your Majesty worry ? Always there is plotting ; one day it is the Army, next day it is the Navy. What does it matter ?" "But don't you arrange to take care of these people ?" asks H.M. (Tallulah Bankhead). "But of course," replies the Chancellor. "We paid General Papakoff fifty thousand roubles to take care of Admiral Mamakoff. We also paid the Admiral fifty thousand roubles to take care of the General." "So what ?" asks the Empress. "Everything turned out quite satisfactory," grins the Chancellor. "I have the honour to inform your Majesty that both the General and the Admiral were buried with full honours."

The story of this film is the never-failing one which Fielding immortalised in the letter Joseph Andrews wrote to his sister: "Had my mistress not been a lady of quality, dear Pamela, I should have thought she had a mind to me." I quote from memory. The authors, or somebody, have put a great deal of fun into that scene in which Catherine plies the simpleton with glass after glass of champagne, and promotes him in the course of half an hour from lieutenant to captain, major, colonel, and finally general. At his fifth or sixth glass the boy declares he has quite overcome his shyness and is prepared to venture that for which, on entering the room, he thought he should never find the courage. In a flutter of excellently dissembled modesty Catherine sinks on to the divan. The boy thrusts his hand into his bosom and produces his report on the plot in the Ukraine!

Why, among the multiplicity of his officials, does not a producer like Lubitsch have a Director of Details? Why does he not engage for the French Ambassador an actor who can speak French? Or are there none such in Hollywood? Somebody who would know that the word is "Russie" and not "Roossie"? An actor who knows that no Frenchman pronounces the name of his country as though it rhymed with the Scotch "manse"? These may be little things, but they count. Actually this film is free-er from this kind of fault than most, and it is from start to finish a very witty frolic and one in which Tallulah gives, in my view, the best performance of her career.

May 5 *Saturday.* *Cocasseries, No.* 14:

> TALENTED, DEEP FEMALE, tired of disillusionment and lycanthropic maledom, would sincerely appreciate correspondence with educated man of ideals and ideas.
>
> *New York Saturday Review of Literature.* Personal column.

May 6 *Sunday.* A few days ago I wrote a really savage letter to a stranger sending me a quotation which I used without verifying. No, not carelessness. The quotation had to go in the paper that night or not at all. The poem was an obscure one, and I just hadn't time to ransack London for a copy of it. Discovering my *gaffe*, I wrote the fellow a snorter, calling him crazy. Last night's post brings me this charming apology:

> Not crazy—not even mazy—merely hazy. I relied on my memory—the tired memory of a septuagenarian. I tried to verify the quotation; but my copy had been "borrowed" by some lewd person of the highbrow sort. Very sorry.

May 7 *Monday.* Occupied to-day putting together what Kipling's Beetle would have called a giddy par-ergon, on the subject of the Great Actor, being moved thereto by something Ivor wrote last Sunday in the *Observer* :

> Either the gods have ceased to visit us or we have ceased to accept gods. It seems odd, and even very unlikely, that Nature, after making such mighty ones as were thus sovereign upon our stage in successive dynasties, should have lost the mould. The other supposition is that, while Nature is still turning them out, we in our more critical, less emotional way are turning them down.

Here is what I propose to say on Sunday :

THE OLDEST FALLACY

Writing some years after Kean's début, Hazlitt has this : " I am not one of those who, when they see the sun breaking from behind a cloud, stop to ask others whether it is the moon. Mr Kean's appearance was the first gleam of genius breaking athwart the gloom of the stage. . . . I cannot say that my opinion has much changed since that time. Why should it ? I had the same eyes to see with that I have now, the same ears to hear with, and the same understanding to judge with. Why then should I not form the same judgment ? "

Of all theatrical fallacies the most obstinately recurring is the one which insists that the ageing critic has not the eyes, ears, and understanding he had in his youth. That to see and hear too much is to end by understanding too little. This is the fallacy which maintains that A was not, absolutely, a greater actor than B, but is so rated by the critics because they were young and impressionable in A's heyday and are exhausted and disillusioned in B's. This school holds Charles Kean to have been as great an actor as Edmund, and on the ground that when Hazlitt wrote : " For voice, eye, accent, and expression no actor has come out for many years at all equal to Edmund Kean," he, Hazlitt, was thirty-six years of age, and that when he wrote : " It appears to me that Mr Kean *jun.* will never make so great an actor as his father," he was fifty and in the clutches of senile decay. Similarly we are told that H. B. Irving was as good an actor as the Old Man, and would have been so deemed had not Archer, Walkley, and Co. been dotards shaking a few sad, last grey hairs.

A young man has written to me : " Can you adduce any instance in which an old critic has ranked a newcomer with the players of his youth ? If you cannot, then I must conclude that the falling-off is not in the actor but in the critic." I will be content with a single example, and I choose G. H. Lewes. First, I must establish Lewes's youthful enthusiasm. Very well, then. Kean died when Lewes was sixteen. Writing many years later, the by that time famous critic began his book *On Actors and the Art of*

Acting with the statement: "Edmund Kean was incomparably the greatest actor I have seen." (Note that the man placed complete reliance in the boy's judgment.) Now apply the theory of diminishing sensibility. Assuming the law (of diminishing sensibility) to hold good, we must expect Lewes, writing of Frédérick Lemaître forty-three years after the death of Kean, to dismiss the French actor as a nincompoop. But does he? Does he temporise? Does he hum and haw? No. In his first sentence he places Lemaître among "the few actors of exceptional genius." Here let me notch a point on my side of the argument. To show how nicely the critical scales can still be held when the brain is softening and the arteries are hardening, consider this fossilised critic, bound to Kean for ever, writing about another actor: "In Macready I see only a man of talent, but of talent so marked and individual that it approaches very near to genius. . . . Tieck told me that Macready seemed to him a better actor than either Kean or John Kemble." Surely, if the deterioration theory held water, Lewes would have pooh-pooh'd Macready off the stage and kept silent about Tieck and his opinions. Whereas he allows Macready as near an approach to the throne of Kean as I am prepared to allow any living modern to the throne of Irving.

To push the argument home. Did Charles Laughton's Tony Perelli suffer because of Tree's Svengali? Or Edith Evans's Millamant because of Ellen Terry's Beatrice? Do we frown upon Sybil Thorndike because of what we remember of Madge Kendal, upon Pamela Brown and Sonia Dresdel because of Clare Eames and Mrs Pat, upon Wolfit because of Benson? Did recollection of James Welch in *The New Clown* saying to the ring-master "You've hurt me!" prevent the critics twenty years later—the same critics, mark you—from hailing as a world genius that wistful little droll who in the films was to be hurt by all the world? I claim to have had my share in 'placing' Mr X and Miss Y, and always according to their merits *and my standards*. And I claim to know the extraordinary from the accomplished as well now as when I was a boy.

It is foolish to argue that Siddons would not impress us to-day. This is to overlook the power of genius to alter its dress. To-day the Siddons would use modern gestures and intonation; it is the genius which is constant. Irving standing motionless and silent, using none of the means which are subject to fashion, could with a look gorgonise or melt an audience. This is something no living actor can do, because no living actor has what it took to implement Irving's malignity and ruth. And will not have so long as critics maintain that to count the washing is as tragic and difficult a feat as to deliver Medea's speech to her children. The alleged "modern approach to great acting"? Whoever has seen a great actor knows that he is not an animal to be stalked in its lair, but a tiger leaping out upon the spectator from the bush of mediocrity and the brake of competence. That if there is any approaching to be done, it is the tiger who will do it.

VE Day.

EIGHT EPITAPHS

MUSSOLINI

A fixed figure for the time of scorn
To point his slow unmoving finger at.
SHAKESPEARE

PÉTAIN

Mes soldats morts,
Moi vaincu ! mon empire est brisé comme verre.
Est-ce le châtiment cette fois, Dieu sévère ?—
VICTOR HUGO

LAVAL

He hears
On all sides, from innumerable tongues,
A dismal universal hiss, the sound
Of public scorn.
MILTON

RIBBENTROP

Good-bye is not worth while.
HARDY

GOEBBELS

. . . like a liar, gone to burning hell.
SHAKESPEARE

GOERING

That bolting-hutch of beastliness, that swollen parcel of dropsies, . . . that stuffed cloak-bag of guts.
SHAKESPEARE

HIMMLER

May his soul die, and never-dying worms
Feast on its pain for ever.
ROSSETTI

HITLER

Und wenn dir denn auch Gott verzeiht,
Auf Erden sein vermaledeit !
GOETHE

May 9 *Wednesday.* Who is going to be the first to admit that to the writing man the last five and a half years have been an inestimable boon, since they provided him with material he would not otherwise have had ? That a measureless gulf separates the artist from the ordinary man or woman, the non-artist to whom the war happens as an actuality and not as something to be expressed in terms of an art ? Throughout the last five years I was never in any real danger ; I never saw a flying bomb, and nothing ever happened nearer than a hundred yards away. If a house across the street had been blown to smithereens I should have been frightened, of course. But presuming I hadn't died from heart failure, I should have been saying to myself, " This will make a good entry for *Ego* 4, 5, 6, 7, or 8." Like the whore to whom Hamlet likened himself, I should have unpacked my heart with words. We know from Grove that during the summer of 1809—the battle of Wagram took place on July 6—Beethoven, whose lodging was on the wall of Vienna, was much exposed to the firing, and used to take refuge in the cellar of his brother's house. And what was he doing in the cellarage ? Shaking with fright ? No. Worrying about the future of Austria ? No. He was writing the E flat Piano Concerto and the " Harp " Quartet, and probably doing all the better for the excitement. I know it works that way with me. I used to look forward to the sirens, and never heard a warning without experiencing what, if I must be honest, I must call a pleasurable thrill. Any night when there was no warning was just a bore. Is this insane ? Possibly. Was I aware that a warning meant hurt and death to other people ? Yes. Did I think I was going to be specially favoured ? No. The fact remains that during the time of the fly-bombs, and afterwards of the rockets, the tempo of life was faster than it can ever be again. I am as big a coward as anybody. *But I miss the warnings.*

May 10 *Thursday.* Letter from Jock :

33 *King Street*
Covent Garden
*W.C.*2

8*th May*, 1945

DEAR JAMIE,

I gave myself a perfect little concert for to-day's Great Occasion, and it's a pity that circumstances didn't allow me to bring the records round to play them to you in the old endeared way. I longed to. This is all of it :

BRAHMS.	" Tragic " Overture.
MOZART.	*Figaro* Overture.
MENDELSSOHN.	*Fingal's Cave* Overture.
ELGAR.	*Cockaigne* Overture.

On the reverse of the Mozart recording was the "Dance of the Apprentices" from the *Meistersinger*—but to include this would have been in much-more-than-dubious taste. Similarly the Elgar recording concludes with *Pomp and Circumstance*, No. 4 in G. But, of course, one left that out of the scheme similarly—for opposite, obvious, and poles-apart reasons.

You were charming about dear Graham Robertson's *Time Was* in the *Express* on Saturday, and more than charming—moving, indeed—on Bertie Farjeon's death in the *Sunday Times*. As some one said of you in a letter received by me last night: "He incalculably does the nicest things."

Ever,
JOCK

Have replied:

Queen Alexandra Mansions, W.C.2
May 10, 1945

DEAR JOCK,

Merely to read about your concert gives me a pang; I think of the days when we would play such a programme together.

But surely you and I have nothing against *Meistersinger*? We that have free souls, the political matter touches us not. Am I right in thinking that your objection is to the perkiness of the "Dance of the Apprentices"?

About the *Pomp and Circumstance*, No. 4. Some glory in their birth, and some in being born English. I have no objection to Teutons who have no sense of the ridiculous glorying in being born German. What I object to is that anybody should glory in being born a member of the *Herrenvolk*. Is it that you won't have the rather vulgar March after the incomparably better Overture? Please elucidate.

> For thou art all my art, and dost advance
> As high as learning my rude ignorance.

Ever,
JAMIE

P.S. On second thoughts don't bother.

P.P.S. But of course I do the nicest things and incalculably. As some one once said about me: "Si la schizophrénie n'existait pas, il faudrait l'inventer."

May 12 *Saturday.* *Cocasseries, No.* 15:

I walked past the houses on the east side of Eaton Square, Belgravia. In 1939 those houses were alive. They had personality and spirit as well as nurseries and kitchens. Now they have been occupied by the Army. They are almost as horrible to look at as the corpses at Belsen or Buchenwald.

Feature writer in daily paper

May 13 *Sunday.* I wonder whether hanging would be more congenial if the ceremony took place in the open air on some fine day in, say, Mecklenburgh Square, with windows bulging at ten guineas a seat, five to stand, and the London Philharmonic in full blast at the Funeral March from the *Eroica*, Delius's " Procession of Protracted Death " from *Hassan*, Saint-Saëns' *Danse Macabre*, and Strauss's *Till Eulenspiegel*, the programme to be so timed that the crêpe-hung car enters the Square to the grisly yet exultant strains of Berlioz's *Marche au Supplice*. My appeals for copies of Boswell's *Johnson* to be forwarded to distributing centres in Germany for the benefit of our occupational troops resulted in something like fifty sets. I am being dishonest enough to keep one for myself, a magnificently bound specimen of Croker's fifth edition in one volume. The first page at which I open this justifies Macaulay's " The editor's want of perspicacity is indeed very amusing. He is perpetually telling us that he cannot understand something in the text which is as plain as language can make it." Johnson is arguing in favour of public executions : " Sir, executions are intended to draw spectators. If they do not draw spectators, they don't answer their purpose. The old method was most satisfactory to all parties ; the public was gratified by a procession ; the criminal was supported by it. Why is all this to be swept away ? " Croker's note is : " What could Johnson mean by saying that the criminal was *supported* by the lingering torture of this cruel exhibition ? " Croker doesn't see that what would be degradation to him was glorification to the coxcombs of the Heath looking upon execution as an actor looks on an exit. The journey to Tyburn was an honoured progress, even an apotheosis. Trulls strewed flowers in the hero's path, and weeping doxies pinned a last nosegay in his ragged coat. There is a gaiety about " He went very decent to the gallows, with a clean napkin, and an orange in his hand," which modern reports lack.

May 14 *Monday.* Frank Singleton (see *Ego* 7, page 230) descended on me this afternoon. Is now editor of the *Bolton Evening News*, and I gather that what that organ thinks to-night the *Manchester Guardian* is going to think to-morrow morning. I was afraid that just as beef-eating did harm to Sir Andrew's wit, so Bolton would impair the modern Sir Toby's. Not so. Within three minutes of his arrival he had recited his new poem :

COULEUR DE ROSE

He heightened all his sins,
Saw Helen in a harlot—
Even his pink gins
Were scarlet.

There is about Frank a sense of impish fun which not even Lancashire can subdue.

May 15 *Tuesday.* In a letter from the editor of a Canadian weekly:

If most Canadians do not understand the speech of English actors it is not because that speech is incomprehensible, but because the Common Man in Canada is averse from understanding anybody but his immediate associates, and them only on the most superficial level. The *Diary* which I publish weekly is expressed with almost unbearable timidity, since vigorous or forthright criticism of the national intelligence is resented with almost hysterical ferocity. Canada suffers from artistic malnutrition: music is the only art which commands respect and general support. There is no theatre except in Toronto and Montreal, and very little there. Few Canadians have seen a play, and few have seen a movie which was not made in Hollywood. There is little film criticism, and what there is is addressed to an inexperienced audience. But there is an audience for good English films among the more discerning Canadians: they welcome a relief from the childishness of Hollywood, and the prurient-pure, daintily salacious Hays Office attitude towards sex. *Fanny by Gaslight* is causing some fuss here because the heroine is illegitimate: Canada, you must understand, is a very *nice* country. No, Canada does not actively dislike English films: it is just too dumb, as a usual thing, to understand anything which is not thoroughly familiar.

May 16 *Wednesday.* Another letter from our little Irish friend:

18 *Park View Avenue*
Harold's Cross
Dublin
Sat. 12*th May*, 1945

My dear James,
My dear Leo,

First let me thank you, James, for your very thoughtful introduction. I won't embarrass either you or myself with a surfeit of sugary nonsense. Suffice to say that I am immensely grateful. I expected the interview with Mr Edwards to last a quarter of a minute—after which I would be heaved out on my egotistical ear. Actually we talked from seven till a quarter to nine! About what? About everything concerning the theatre, from sex-appeal to sentiment. At first I informed Mr Edwards (whose affability and condescension would have won the heart of Mr Collins) that I desired to become one of that "fine body of men"—as Max Beerbohm called the critics—but I'd better not repeat what Mr Edwards said. We discussed acting, Sarah, Rachel, and other things about which

I know practically nothing. Mr Edwards invited me to come round after each show and talk with him. (Magic words, O James and O Leo !) His partner, Mr MacLiammoír, whom I used to plague with my unasked-for criticism, drifted in, pressed my hand, swore eternal friendship, and drifted out again.

And now, dear James, please forgive me if I address the rest of this bombast to Leo. Thank you, Leo, for such a charming letter. Such taste ! I'm afraid I'm like Lady Teazle at the time of her marriage—I have no taste. Well, if you really want to know : (*a*) my favourite dramatists are Shakespeare, Shaw, Synge, O'Casey, and Tchehov. I also burrow in Marlowe, Kyd, Jonson, Webster, Ford, and Tourneur. And if you're of my way of thinking you may throw in Eugene O'Neill with the last three ! (*b*) Favourite poets are Tennyson and Yeats—why, I don't know. (*c*) Favourite novelists Dickens, Jane Austen, Charlotte Brontë, and—my only concession to modern taste—Hugh Walpole. (*d*) Favourite essayists Lamb and G. K. Chesterton. (*e*) Favourite annoyances Wilde and Maugham !

Thine and James's for aye,
J. E. JORDAN

May 17 *Thursday.* Supper with Jock at the Café Royal.

JOCK. Did you get an old *Tatler* article I sent you the other day after clearing out some drawers ?

J. A. Yes. I wondered why you sent it.

JOCK. D'you remember writing it ?

J. A. Perfectly.

JOCK. Well, you didn't. *I wrote it !* You had gone to a horse-show.

May 18 *Friday.* Thornton Wilder's *The Skin of our Teeth* turns out to be yet another example of the playwright who, with almost nothing new to say, dishes out the old stuff in the new-fangled manner. Here is Wilder's recipe. Abolish Time. Pretend the Ice Age is coeval with co-eds. Have a mammoth and a dinosaur on the stage together with a telegraph boy. Bring Adam and Eve up to date. Show Cain as High School boy with football jersey and catapult. Have the alphabet, simple arithmetic, and the wheel all in the making. Show Helen, Circe, Cleopatra in the guise of Atlantic City trollops. Have Homer and Moses put in an appearance. Have scenery that moves of its own accord. Surrealism, Dali-ism, Dadaism, and Gagaism. Hotch-potch of Shaw, Pirandello, Obey, Kaiser, O'Neill. Touches of Walt Disney, the Marx Brothers, and Olsen and Johnson. Will this make a good play ? It may or it mayn't, but it'll win the Pulitzer. Will the folks walk out ? Possibly. But they'll

Photo John Vickers

Vivien Leigh in "The Skin of Our Teeth"

talk after they've walked out, which is better than staying and not talking. Actually, Wilder's nonsense did win the Pulitzer, and on the first-night in New York a lot of the audience left. In the play which I saw to-night it all boiled down to this, that the human race can survive ice, flood, pestilence, wars, depressions and all the natural shocks that flesh is heir to. Like the man in *The Silver Tassie*, I see no magnificent meanin' jumping out of that, though I suppose I shall have to find one between now and Sunday. Lovely performance by Vivien Leigh as Sabina, the hired girl. Half dabchick and half dragon-fly.

May 19 *Saturday.* Shall I *never* learn? Open my *Express* this morning and find myself telling readers, apropos of Leonard Clark's biography of Alfred Williams, the Wiltshire poet, how, while working a steam-hammer in the locomotive shop at Swindon, he rose at 4 A.M., studied till it was time to cycle to work, read during the dinner-hour, made a hasty evening meal, and pored over his books again till midnight. How he mastered Greek sufficiently to read Xenophon, Homer, Theocritus, Plutarch. How he became a useful minor poet. How—and here the devilry comes in—they, *Express* readers, can do the same thing. The truth, of course, is that they can't. Only one in ten generations of hammer-wielders has a line of poetry in him. Now say six out of the *Daily Express's* four million readers take me seriously. This means that I shall have on my conscience the ruining of six lives, or, anyhow, holding out hopes that can never be fulfilled. In other words, putting cultural ideas into the heads of half a dozen honest fellows who won't know what to do with the ideas when they've got them, and would be much better occupied in backing horses, drinking beer, and begetting children. Gregers Werle cum Samuel Smiles is written all over my column to-day, and I am ashamed of it.

May 21 *Monday.* Spent the morning playing with the notion of translating Montague's *Disenchantment* into English for the common man. What are those who would best benefit by this masterpiece going to make of such a passage as:

> "I planted a set of blind hopes in their minds," said Prometheus, making it out to be quite a good turn that he had done to mankind. And the Dr Relling of Ibsen, a kind of Prometheus in general practice, kept a whole medicine-chest of assorted illusions to dope his patients with. "Illusion, you know," said the sage, "is the tonic to give 'em." It may be, but even illusions cost something. The bill, as Hotspur said of the river Trent, "comes me cranking

in" presently, Nature's iron law laying it down that the more superb your state of inflation the deeper shall the dumps occasioned by the puncture be.

The reader who is *au fait* with the allusions in the foregoing does not need to learn the lesson of this book, which I want read not only by soldiers and Civil Servants but by the unlettered boss of every big business left in these Socialist days. What is to be done about it? The only thing that I can see is to translate the book into common or kitchen-garden English.

May 22 *Tuesday.* Two good days at Lord's Test Match as the guest of C. B. Fry. Highly distinguished company, including Arnold Bax, Clifford Bax, Edmund Blunden, Eric Gillett, Thomas Moult, and J. C. Squire. "Plum" Warner looked into the box several times, and I made fleeting acquaintance with High Commissioners and Nawabs. Fry in good form and talked well, particularly about A. C. MacLaren, who, he said, had "a superb crease-side manner."

May 23 *Wednesday.* Part of a letter referring to my recent *S.T.* article entitled "The Oldest Fallacy":

Given sustained interest, a man should be a more discerning critic at the age of sixty-five than he was at the age of twenty-five. But Nature does not permit the man of sixty-five to bring his more mature powers of judgment to bear upon a theatrical performance seen by him forty years previously. We remember a "large" room of our childhood days, and continue to regard it as large until revisiting it many years later. But we cannot revisit a theatrical performance of forty years ago.

I have replied:

DEAR SIR,

A bent towards criticism implies a sense of magnitude and proportion. At the age of six I knew exactly how big my bedroom was; I remember calculating that it would hold my cot exactly twelve times. At seven I was taken to my first classical concert, and remember thinking that Hallé's piano-playing was tame—a judgment that was afterwards ratified. (The concert took place in the Free Trade Hall, Manchester, which seemed no smaller on my last Prize-giving Day eleven years later. Nor had it shrunk when, some forty years on, I was privileged to give away the prizes.) At nine I decided that in *La Tosca* Sarah Bernhardt ranted—another judgment that Time has approved. (In melodrama she always ranted; in classic drama never.) At ten I knew exactly how many yards it was from the wicket to the wall of the croft in which during the holidays I used to get out to my father's artful slows. At fourteen I realised that the school ground was not as big as Old Trafford. Now reverse the picture. Yesterday I saw the Australian crack, Miller, put together the first Test Match century since the war; that the date is 1945 has nothing to do with my conviction that, fine batsman though Miller is, his bat does not flash quite so eye-takingly as did Macartney's.

To-day an unknown friend has sent me a fifty-year-old theatre programme. The first-night of *An Artist's Model.* Think seriously and tell me whether we could to-day assemble a cast as talented as one that contained Marie Tempest, Lottie Venne, Letty Lind, Marie Studholme, Hayden Coffin, Eric Lewis, and Maurice Farkoa. Is it because I have been looking at musical shows for fifty years that the artists of to-day must use a microphone, failing which they would be inaudible? Let me switch to something else. Is it because I first read *Pickwick* as a boy that I cannot find its equal in the lucubrations of to-day's budding geniuses?

M. Bergeret's little dog reflected that when he approached an object he grew smaller, and that when he retreated he grew bigger. Unearth me an unpublished essay by Hazlitt entitled "On How Actors Diminish with the Years," and I shall still say that I do not increase with age. Neither do I decrease. I have a photographic memory for an actor's expression, tones, gestures; and in my estimate of the great players I pass these memories, these old negatives, through, so to speak, the sieve of experience. In other words, I do not measure Irving by what I thought of him when I was a youngster (though that turns out to have been a just estimate), but by what I think of him now, using my "negatives" as the basis of judgment. The Child is father of the Man. Meaning that one with the critical bent carries in his earliest years an old head on young shoulders, and in his later days a young head on old shoulders. Whoso fails to encompass this is never throughout his life a critic, but always an emotionalist, or, if you prefer it, a rhapsodist.

Uncompromisingly,

James Agate

May 24 *Thursday.* In view of the promised visit of the Comédie Française. Some time after the last war a quiet, unsensational light, new to the English theatre, began to filter through from France. A glow lambent yet melancholy, compounded equally of dawn and dusk. I first became certain about this gentle flooding on the occasion of the 1928 Stage Society's performance of Jean-Jacques Bernard's *L'Ame en Peine* (*The Unquiet Spirit*). True that one had been faintly aware of it in *Le Printemps des Autres* (*The Springtime of Others*) two years earlier. One saw *Martine* in 1929, *Le Feu qui reprend mal* (*The Sulky Fire*) in 1934, *L'Invitation au Voyage* in 1937, and *Madeleine* last year. As one remembers certain flamboyant moments of Sarah and one or two of Duse's abnegations and subsidences, so, in the first of these pieces, I shall never forget the way that brilliant and regretted actress Clare Eames avoided contact with the stranger to whom she was for ever after to be in thrall. Four out of those six plays were in their way little masterpieces.

Another great event was the visit of the Théâtre du Vieux-Colombier, playing in its own language. Obey's *Noé* won us over at once. Fewer people saw *Le Viol de Lucrèce*. But those few who did will never forget that chamber, empty except for the bed round which the curtains were drawn. The Reciter and Recitress had mounted pulpits on each side of the stage. Then came Tarquin, stealing along black corridors and fumbling at dark doors while the Reciter explained the emotions tearing his breast. He entered the chamber and drew aside the curtains of the bed. The thing which should restrain him now was his kingship, voiced by the Reciter crying four times, "Tarquin-roi ! Roi des Romains ! Roi ! Roi ! " But in vain. In the last act the Reciter put the whole thing back in Time. " La grande Rome est en histoire. Athènes, jadis, à ses grandes heures, fut en beauté ; Babylone, en amour ; Troie, en alarmes. Un jour, Berlin sera en guerre et Paris en révolution. Rome, aujourd'hui, est en histoire ! " Yes, that was great playgoing.

And surely that was a superb moment in *Bataille de la Marne* when the soldiers who should defend Paris retreated and again retreated. Always they had withdrawn towards the footlights, and now, in the theatre, could go no further. " En avant ! " cried France, and the spectacular right-about-turn signified that the Battle of the Marne had begun. The victorious generals were saluted by name. Manoury ! French ! Foch ! Sarrail ! Castelnau ! Joffre ! One name was singled out for its beauty of sound. " Général Franchet d'Espérey ! Vous dont le nom est beau comme une devise ! " And the good British playgoer, given a schoolboy's knowledge of French, recognised in this apostrophe all the *panache* of France.

In the way of acting I still look back gratefully to the visit paid by the Comédie in March 1939. Never again can I hope to see such a piece of comic playing as that of Fernand Ledoux as the old crock in Regnard's *Le Légataire Universel*. What crackle and atmospherics proceeded from that bosom when bronchial disturbance permitted anything to proceed at all ! Did ever legs so vacillate ? And then there was another actor, Pierre Dux, who contrived to run the entire gamut of the *cocasse* without respect to clime or time, the equivalent of that English bridge which binds Jonson's scamps to Sid Field's scallywags.

The modern theatre gave us Mauriac's *Asmodée*, Cocteau's *Les Parents Terribles*, and Giraudoux's *Amphitryon* 38. And, of course,

Sacha Guitry's *Mozart* and *Mariette*. In the second play I can still see that half-bovine, half-imperial Napoleon III sitting in his box putting his heavily kid-gloved hands portentously together. I can still hear that half-whisper : " Il faut tâcher de ne pas être ridicule ! " In the earlier play I have not forgotten, though it is twenty years ago, that people were seen to cry, and by " cry " I mean shed tears, when Music's heavenly child appeared at the top of the gilt staircase and descended it to kneel at the feet of Mme d'Épinay. I think it will be only fit and proper to remind playgoers on Sunday of the debt they owe to France.

May 25 *Friday.* Southend, with George Mathew. Half-way down ran into a cloudburst and thunderstorm, the worst I remember for years. Had to wait an hour at Southend Station. No taxis, so picked up our bags and started to walk. Between two and three feet of water under the railway bridge, which meant a détour. Found the Palace Hotel unchanged, even to the crack in the drawing-room mirror—an incident of the First World War. This room and the sun-lounge, were they anywhere except Southend, would be recognised as the two best, airiest, spaciousest, viewfullest public rooms in England. The painted metal vases, bigger than Ali Baba's jars, are still here, but I miss that enormous if dingy canvas, larger than anything Benjamin Haydon painted, that used to hang in the one-hundred-and-twenty-foot passage leading to the gentlemen's lavatory. Subject ? A pride of lions.

May 26 *Saturday.* Took a car to the golf-course, now closed. Had a look at my old bungalow. Grass obviously not been cut since I lived there. But then it wasn't cut in my time —could never be bothered with gardening. Fell asleep in lounge before lunch. Snoozed after lunch. Did a little shopping—the rain sogged down all day—and slept through two idiotic pictures. At dinner half a bottle of champagne all to myself. Nodded over some new novels. Bed early.

May 27 *Sunday.* Fine, but too cold to go out with any pleasure, so sat in the sun-room and diarised. " Surely it's time people agreed to listen to Wagner's music and forget the bosh it's all about ! " George had said at breakfast. I entirely agree. Newman writes in the *S.T.* to-day : " If I know anything of him [Wagner], he would have stayed away ostentatiously from the performances [of his operas under Nazi patronage] and told Hitler and his storm-troopers frankly what he thought of them." *Frankly*, Ernest ?

I think not. I just don't see that astute little monkey in the velvet jacket asking to be sent to a concentration camp.

May 28 *Monday.* Leigh-on-Sea presented a charming picture from the train. The town was busy as a hive with scores of Ham Peggottys building and mending boats. Presently the train began to fill up, and we finished seventeen in the carriage, including an eight-months-old baby which I nursed. I am a superb nurse, and as good with children as George is with cats. And for the same reason. George and I dote on cats and babies respectively, and they dote on us. George pointed out, to the mother's great gratification—for she was a woman of education—that the kid had exactly the same hands as those of an infant in a Michael Angelo reproduction in the *Listener*, which we had with us.

May 29 *Tuesday.* From George Richards :

After carrying her young for 67 days Bluebell was yesterday delivered of five beautiful, vigorous, and lively kittens. One, indeed, which I have christened Marco, showed extraordinary initiative and maturity of mind and judgment even before the umbilical cord was severed. Solomon, the second born, has a very elegant and fine-pointed tail, whereas poor Omar, the next one, has a tail kinked like a lacrosse-stick. Rosina and Cortez, the fourth and third, both promise to have excellent points. The mother continued purring throughout her two hours' "labour," and the fact that everything went so smoothly and without any sort of a hitch was due, I am convinced, in no small measure to the fact that during her confinement only certain sorts of programmes were permitted on the wireless. Modern dance rhythms, for instance, were entirely taboo, and nearly all modern composers, Shostakovich and William Walton especially, were likewise banned as being the reverse of soothing to the nerves of the gestating and the pregnant. Bluebell, like all, or at any rate most, cats, is a keen and discriminating wireless listener, but during the past two months she has been quite content to let Lush Mush, leader of the Palm Court orchestra of the Hotel Plush, Great Slush, cater for her requirements in the way of *musique d'accouchement*.

What of the lying-in itself, you will be wanting to know ? I endeavoured in every detail to order things as far as possible in accordance with the practice and customs of more spacious and gracious times as these may be gleaned from a reading of that charming French seventeenth-century *ouvrage* : *Caquets de l'Accouchée*. For instance :

" Pour préparer à l'événement solennel la chambre de la gisante était tendue des étoffes et des tapisseries les plus belles ; une petite couchette, connue sous le nom de *lit de misère*, était placée auprès du grand lit nuptial ; un bon feu brûlait incessament ; des linges de toutes sortes, tirées des grands bahuts, séchaient à l'entour. On mettait devant la cheminée une petite table couverte de linge très fin, sur cette table trois coupes, un pot de vin ou d'hippocras, trois pains de fleur de farine et deux flambeaux qui restaient allumés toute la nuit. Dans la chambre de l'accouchée, le plus grand prince du monde s'y trouvât-il, nul ne peut servir vin ou épices, excepté une femme mariée."

May 30 *Wednesday.* " If I had my will I would live in a ship on the sea and never come nearer humanity than that." Thus Duse.

It was obvious at the " Q " Theatre to-night that Sonia Dresdel would prefer acting, under any conditions, to hobnobbing with ice-floes or getting as far away from humanity as deserts permit. Asked whether she could live without the stage, Duse replied in a shocked voice, " I have passed three years without acting." Dresdel cannot pass three minutes without acting. (Since three minutes is a long time on the stage, better say three seconds.) She acts, overacts, and then acts a little more. In the dictionary of her playing, to ask Mr Smith to stay to dinner is like Circe enticing Ulysses ; to kiss (*vb. tran.*) is to suck forth the soul, to make immortal ; a simple move to the door is a walk to the Paradise Garden ; to speed the parting guest is a dance half-way between a galliard and a coranto. This is the more regrettable because it is entirely unnecessary. Dresdel acted superbly all through to-night's second act, which could stand up to superb acting ; she should have " thrown away " the first and third acts, which couldn't. The play itself, *Wait, my Love*, was an honest attempt to grapple with the question of conjugal fidelity, viewed from the angles of Surbiton and Cairo. The soldier-husband said, " The woman's part in war is to fight against boredom and forgetfulness ; she must keep her vows. The man's part is to undergo the danger and the strain ; what happens to his vows is immaterial." To which his wife in the A.T.S. replied, " Rubbish ! " in a speech of Medea-like proportions. Not bad stuff, and very nearly good enough for town.

May 31 *Thursday.* Letter from Tom Curtiss :

Paris
May 24, 1945

DEAR JAMES,

I wrote you a " V " letter some time ago, thinking that perhaps it would reach you in quicker order than ordinary post, but instead

" V " letters to England seem to be absolutely unanswerable documents. At least, such has been my experience ; I have dispatched a score of them, and one and all are barren of replies. May this bring better luck.

VE Days I and II found Paris in a happy mood, and the Opéra, the Madeleine, Place Vendôme, and Sacré Cœur were just flood-lit in pre-war, summer-time fashion. For us, of course, the war is not over, and even the duller of the G.I.'s seem to realise this, for the Parisian high jinks, street dancing and all, were predominantly civilian on Victory night.

The Paris stage has revealed no new masterpieces. *Huis Clos*, by one Jean-Paul Sartre, had the highbrows by the ears as pretty hot intellectual stuff. A sort of *Outward Bound*, it deals with three lost souls in the Hereafter—a low-life drifter and two women, one of whom is a Lesbian. Eternity is a dreary hotel room with no windows and without mirrors. A would-be metaphysical morality play about a relentless Jehovah's vengeance, it appeals only to theatre-goers who never went to the theatre to see Molnar's beautiful handling of the same theme in *Liliom* and to those who never heard the marine sergeant's line in *Rain* : " God's a good guy." I don't think you'd like *Huis Clos*, in spite of the remarkable acting.

How is *Ego* 8 ?

Give my best regards to Leo Pavia, and tell Arthur Bates to see that you don't sit up too late, work too hard, and/or drink too much whiskey.

Always,
TOM

June 1 *Friday.* Letter addressed to me at the *Express* :

DEAR MR AGATE,

Are you a self-made man because I wish you could advise me how to be one too. The trouble is, I am a woman not a man, and I don't know how to ring the changes. You see a man has much more advantage than a woman, just because she is a woman. And it's a good job we don't all get what we ask for, or Heaven help those who don't ask for much, though they might get more, without asking.

AN INTERESTED READER

June 2 *Saturday.* I remember in Ernest Milton's Hammersmith production of *Macbeth* a young boy's remarkable performance of the Messenger who comes to tell Macbeth about Birnam Wood. The part is of the tiniest, something under ten lines. But the boy was so good and his fear of Macbeth so real that for two

Photo Angus McBean

Sergeant Tom Curtiss, U.S.A.

minutes he reduced Ernest to the status of a brilliant actor, while he himself remained real. To-day I receive this letter :

12 *Brocks Drive*
North Cheam
Surrey
Friday June 1*st* '45

DEAR JAMES AGATE,

On August 6th, 1944, in the *Sunday Times* you wrote of " a brilliant performance by a boy who will be an actor some day." Such praise for my first real work on the professional stage meant more to me than even you, with your understanding, can imagine. I had done lots of amateur work—it was my alleged resemblance to Stephen Haggard when I won the 1943–44 Finchley and Hertford Drama Festival's Prize that led to my casting in *Macbeth.*

Since then I resolved to work and work to perfect myself. I hadn't the conventional height ; R.A.D.A.—I hadn't the money ; none of the managements would see me. I turned down an engagement—would I have benefited as one of the eighteen " boys and girls " in *Jenny Jones* ?—and in desperation accepted Peter Miller Street's part in *Junior Miss.* This abomination, which in a year's tour has made me wonder how to keep sane, is at last wending its way to a pathetic end via Blackburn, Bradford, Torquay, and West Hartlepool, and I shall be out of work again.

I am in London with a week out commencing next Monday. What do I do ? How are agents and production offices to be persuaded to see me ? I have managed to save £30. Knowing that I have talent that needs perfecting through good dramatic work—should I accept the first footling part that comes along ? I know I have a long way to go, but how can I get the opportunity ?

Yours truly,
PETER MIZEN

I am writing this young man to the effect that whereas anybody in the restaurant or taxicab business would keep a register of likely waiters or drivers, in the theatre this just doesn't happen. Am advising him to go to Hull or Hereford and look upon acting as its own reward.

June 4 *Monday.* Frank Singleton dined with me to-night and then, coming back to the flat, we sat up till the small hours. I had a bit of work to finish, and gave him *Ego* 8 to look at. Apropos of the entry for May 19 he said, " One of the things I learned at Cambridge that has always remained is this. My tutor said to me, ' You come from Manchester, a city responsible for the most pernicious doctrine with which youth has ever been misled—the doctrine that work will do everything. It won't. Work will do a great deal, but not everything. Sometimes it happens that a Manchester lad coming up against a first-rater finds that the man of natural talent can do more than he can with all his hard work. This brings on a nervous breakdown. Every term I send back one such to Manchester.' "

June 5 *Tuesday.* In a letter from George Richards :

When I *did* get up this morning I found inside the front door an obliging letter from a dramatic critic, a rather stuffy letter from a modern poet, and a deliciously vulgar postcard and a jolly letter from Jock. OUTSIDE . . . alone and palely loitering, an anæmic egg laid by a rickety and mal-nourished hen which should forthwith be placed under the auspices and come within the scope of the beneficent ministrations of U.N.R.R.A.

I have been busy this morning . . . correcting with pencil, blue chalk, ink, and brush a dozen or so large bills and posters dotted about Bournemouth, Boscombe, Poole, and Christchurch announcing that at the Pavilion, Bournemouth, next week there would be performed a play by one " Oscar Wild." But England is England and Bournemouth will be Bournemouth, and had the bill-printer really been in form he would have called the play " Lady Windermere's *Fun*."

On the back of the envelope the query : " Do you think Citizen Kane a good name for a cat ? "

June 6 *Wednesday.* To-night's play at the Piccadilly, *Jacobowsky and the Colonel*, started off with a fine air of novelty. And then it began to appear that a good deal of Franz Werfel's matter, and even manner, had been dreamed of by other playwriting philosophers. For example, the deflation of grandiosity by gumption. Here the likeness to *Arms and the Man* popped up every five minutes. And what of the other four ? Well, there was André Obey. These stragglers leaving Paris with music heard in the air and Esmé Percy in a mood of soliloquy turning him into a Reciter—what were they but the very mood and mechanics of *Bataille de la Marne* ? The plot —the outwitting of the Nazis by three simpletons and a girl—could be paralleled in any one of twenty films made since the war. Perhaps there is a playwriting mind like that of certain composers. Listening to Mahler, one recognises not only subconscious echoes of Wagner, Bruckner, Schubert, Strauss, and even Beethoven, but moods and colourings which one thinks wouldn't have occurred to Mahler but for Wagner and the rest. Werfel's work is full of such echoes, moods, colourings. There was a moment when it looked as if Marianne, the Polish Colonel's French fiancée, would have to choose between the officer, who could offer her nothing but his histrionics, and the little Polish Jew Jacobowsky, whose one card was his humility and heart's need. Would Marianne take a leaf out of Candida's book and say, "That's a good bid, S. L. Jacobowsky"? And when the Gestapo man in his death agony clawed at the mechanical piano and set it going I thought at once of the same incident in *Pépé le Moko.* The truth, I suppose, is that these things are in the air. Put it this way. If in a modern novel I read of an elderly gentleman with twinkling spectacles who undertakes scientific rambles in the company of three friends and a comic servant, and later gets entangled in a breach-of-promise case, I should assume, not that the author had read *Pickwick, but that he hadn't.* And on the ground that it is easier to believe in coincidence than in a filching which must be detected instantly. Wherefore let it be conceded that Werfel has never seen Obey's play, or those two plays by Shaw, or that film, or the musical show known as *The Lisbon Story.*

Montague once said that the highest courtesy in an author is to treat his reader "as no blind horse but a man who has some wit of his own and can take a thing in." The present authors—the play has been adapted by S. N. Behrman—treated us to-night as if we were inmates of a blind asylum. And what was their point? Simply that a humble little Jew full of shrewdness and resource is of more value to society than some noisy descendant of Ancient Pistol. Well, it doesn't need two playwrights from the New World to invite the post-Shavians of the Old to remark this, let alone make a note of it twenty times. And then the comedy was tragically miscast. The Colonel is a monument of humourlessness, which means that if he is to amuse he must be played by an actor bubbling over with an inner sense of the ludicrous. An Alfred Lunt, for example. I have no doubt that Michael Redgrave tried to be funny to-night—indeed, one could see him trying. What was wrong was that he insisted on dissecting absurdity instead of warming to it. The Colonel is what a schoolboy would call a gorgeous ass; he was turned into a solemn and regrettable one, sending cold shivers down my back as though Mr Dombey had cast himself for Cyrano. The point about Jacobowsky is subservience backed by guile, and we were given Karel Stepanek, radiating distinction and charm like a Jewish Traddles enacted by Steerforth at his most dazzling. The French fiancée was, of course, pure Wimbledon. Still, the evening had compensations. Delightful scenery, charming music, and a splash of two of wit.

June 7 Here is something I hope to say in the *S.T.* on Sunday :
Thursday.

The death of Oliver Elton at the age of eighty-four takes me back to certain criticisms appearing in the *Manchester Guardian* over the initials " O. E." It was from one of these that at seventeen I learned that great actors and, particularly, great actresses either don't know the rubbish from the masterpieces or, if they do, seven times out of ten prefer the rubbish. At nineteen " O. E. " gave me the measure of Ibsen's size and importance, *The Quintessence of Ibsenism,* published four years earlier, not yet having reached my unenterprising suburb. I remember, when I was twenty-one, the Monday morning on which " O. E. " told me what to think about *Cyrano de Bergerac* and Coquelin's acting. The performance had taken place on the previous Saturday evening, with *Le Bourgeois Gentilhomme* in the afternoon. I saw both. Here are some extracts from the three notices in question :

Bernhardt

" Last year, in *La Tosca,* we could study in its simplest form the kind of play and of heroine which M. Sardou invents in order to evoke the lower gifts of Mme Bernhardt. La Tosca, through hearing the cries of her lover while the police torture him, is wrung into dishonourably revealing the refuge of a fugitive, whose blood is thus upon her hands. Her lover is the first to denounce her, and she dies. Here the joint aim of playwright and actress was simple and unlawful ; the nerves were to be violently vexed, partly by sounds in imitation of physical agony suffered by a person unseen, and partly by the sight of La Tosca's anguish, itself supposed to be created by the same cause. There was no attempt at character. Mme Bernhardt has a genius for sinking to such parts."

July 8, 1895

A Doll's House

" The repute of Ibsen, since he first created a large band of dervishes howling against him, and a smaller band who howled on his behalf at all costs against the larger, seems to have settled into something European, which can be gauged reasonably and in his own spirit, though not with his power, of severe analysis. England is one of the provinces where the dispute, so far as it has not collapsed into apathy, has remained somewhat sectarian. Those who merely mistake Ibsen's situations for trivial and his characters for grotesque, those who from an impulse of self-preservation, representing the classes he dissects, dislike the process of dissection ; those who thank Heaven that, if Norwegians are like this, they are not like Norwegians ; and those who take the stronger line of idealistic theory in art, are all still vowed in some kind of muddled alliance against others who wish to fetter Ibsen to his own characters, or to present his art as the only art of the future. Actually, Ibsen is one of the three or four living persons with a great mastery of dramatic interest and form, and one of the most incisive and critical depictors of society, not specially as it is in Norway, but as it necessarily is at this moment wherever the ideas of the French Revolution are found newly acting upon a small, discontented, and hampered but awakening community."

April 13, 1897

Coquelin in " Cyrano de Bergerac "

" *Cyrano* is kept up with half-Bacchic, half-chivalrous exuberance, and depends for its success on a heroic pitch of madness in the interpretation. It is best not read in the early morning, or in an Anglo-Saxon spirit. It is a literary play, and errs in a juster extreme than the usual literary play, which is a sterile, mulish negation of the dramatic art, and has only to be seen to collapse. *Cyrano* is hardly to be read without reference to the acting. This is only to say that it is not one of the great plays of the world, which keep their life both as literature and as drama."

June 22, 1899

Come now, you lauders of present times, let's have a show-down. Prove to me that these criticisms are superlatively good only because they appeared when I was superlatively young. Produce the modern day-to-day equivalent, and then produce it four times over, since, Elton being matched, W. T. Arnold, Allan Monkhouse, and, of course, Montague dazzlingly remain. So much for the provinces. How about London and our noble, weekly selves ? Well, we are mighty fine fellows nowadays, but I doubt whether any of us claims to write like Archer, Shaw, Max. At this point I hear an older voice booming, " Not even Shakespeare can write well without a proper subject. It is a vain endeavour for the most skilful hand to cultivate barrenness, or to paint upon vacuity." And I invite all vaunters of the present to ask themselves whether, before the theatre can look again for great criticism, it must not first bring back great drama. How about the Great Actor ? But that is easier said than done. I understand that in music, while great concertos are rare, virtuoso pianists are ten a penny. In the theatre it is different. Any plodding fellow with a smattering of sociology plus uplift can write something that passes for a great play. Only God can make a Tree.

June 8 *Friday.* Pampering is good neither for man nor for beast. A pony that finds its own food on a bare hillside will always, other things being equal, be a better pony than one knee-deep in clover. This applies to men as well as animals, and minds as well as bodies. When I was a boy—this hangs on to yesterday's entry—the sight of an unfamiliar word in the English or in any other language would send me to the dictionary. I foraged for meanings. The youth of to-day is deprived of this wholly beneficial necessity, the edict having gone forth in many popular papers that no word in any foreign language shall be used without a translation in bracket or footnote. When, as a youngster, I came across, say, *carte blanche* or *bête noire,* I would go to the dictionary and find out what the words meant. And probably discover one or two other things at the same time. Nowadays the papers are full of this sort of thing: " In a country which has always prided itself on its *amour-propre* (self-respect) a corresponding amount of *savoir faire* (tact) must be looked for. In any case a policy of *festina lente* (hasten slowly) must be pursued if a *débâcle* (catastrophe) ending in the inevitable *sauve qui peut* (save himself who can) is to be averted." Am I suspected of exaggeration ? I read in my morning paper :

> Lord Moran, Mr Churchill's doctor, said yesterday, " It is not easy for anyone to get into Stalin's mind, but as far as one can make out Stalin thinks that the Prime Minister is a broth of a boy. Stalin doesn't like a man who lives on nuts and soda water."

*** From Eric Partridge's *Dictionary of Slang*: " Broth of a boy ": Anglo-Irish expression meaning the essence of manhood as broth is the essence of meat.

June 9 *Saturday.* A letter:

Officers' Mess
North-West Army Signals
Rawalpindi
India Command

29*th May* '45

DEAR MR AGATE,

You do not know me, nor have we ever met. I have been trying to write to you ever since I landed in this extraordinary country several weeks ago—but what with the heat and Beverley Nichols, it has been impossible to concentrate on matters that did not daily surround me. However, I am now on leave, 7000 feet above sea-level, in the blessed cool of a hill station.

I had the fortune to leave England on the same ship as Donald Wolfit and his company on their way to the Middle East. Being a struggling pre-war (and, God willing, post-war) actor, I found myself with the job of Ship's Entertainment Officer. While I was in the throes of trying to organise the very assorted talent on board, Wolfit asked, almost shyly, if he and his company could be of any assistance ! Naturally, I was greatly impressed by this very generous offer. With some hectic weeks at the Winter Garden behind them, and a Middle East tour before them, Wolfit and his team had obviously been looking forward to the complete rest which is normally offered by a sea-voyage. But, confronted by a ship full of troops on their way to India, and with the knowledge that there was no theatre on board, and that all costumes and " props " were locked and sealed in the hold, there was only one thought in the great actor's mind—to do as much as possible for the troops in the time allotted.

Within what seemed a matter of hours, the ship's dining-room was packed (and I mean packed) with troops. There was a small space at one end of the room on which we had managed to focus some of the existing lights. By this time the ship had started to roll very badly; I was excited and, at the same time, puzzled—how on earth (or at sea) could a full performance of *Much Ado About Nothing* be given in this minute space, *sans* costumes, *sans* props, *sans* scenery—in fact, *sans* everything but actors in E.N.S.A. uniform? The answer was easy—to Wolfit. He made a brief speech to the effect that *Much Ado* would be played exactly as it had been played at the Winter Garden, and that all costumes, props, etc., would be imagined to be complete—also, that he believed that this was the first time since the seventeenth century that a full Shakespearean play had been given at sea. Within two minutes of the start of the play the mass-illusion was complete, the audience were held in pin-drop silence, the absence of props, etc., was not noticed or mentioned again—even old Neptune realised the importance of the occasion, and stopped rolling the ship. At the finish Wolfit and his company received an ovation such as only a mass of really grateful British Tommies can give.

Much Ado was done several times so that the whole ship could see it. This was followed by several performances of *The Merchant of Venice*—a memorable one being given on deck in the middle of the Mediterranean to a really vast audience, who were perched on every conceivable part of the ship—and for two and a half hours the only sound that could be heard (apart from the magnificently audible performers) was the slight throb of the engines, and the gentle swish of that amazingly blue sea as we sped through it. This courageous and unselfish hard work was completed by a grand performance of *Hamlet*. The success of the whole effort can be judged by the send-off that was given to this valiant company at their post of disembarkation. The ship had a distinct list to starboard as every soldier on board cheered and sang them down the gangway.

With best wishes,
Yours sincerely,
DAVID DODIMEAD (*Major*)

P.S. You may be interested to know that I have just purchased *Immoment Toys* and *Ego* 6 from the oddest little bookshop in the oddest Indian bazaar.

June 10 *Sunday.* *Cocasseries, No.* 16:

God made the land and filled it with His music,
Blessed it with blossom, gave it spring and fall,
Gave to it life and love, and tears and laughter,
But to the sea He gave no thought at all.

From a poem in a Sunday paper

I see. While the Almighty had to think about elephants, whales just happened.

June 11 *Monday.* In the Leslie Stuart broadcast to-night the announcer referred to Signor Foli, " a celebrated Italian singer." And subsequently Foli was made to speak in the kind of broken English customary with stage Italians. Now Foli was an Irish policeman of the name of Foley, and how I came to know about it is like this. My maternal grandmother was a music teacher in Manchester, married to a wine-merchant who spent his life on the sofa with gout and the plays of Shakespeare. At the time when piano lessons were twelve for a guinea, counting thirteen as twelve my grandmother did pretty well in charging the rich Greek colony, whose children she taught, a guinea a lesson, counting twelve lessons strictly as twelve. She was a woman whose determination equalled her culture. She would not take in lodgers ; but, my father being recommended to her as an earnest young man from the South, she consented that he should make his home with her and her two daughters. Then one day my father brought home one Gustave Garcia, grandson of Manuel Garcia, the great tenor for whom Rossini wrote the part of the Count Almaviva in *The Barber of Seville*, son of Garcia, the centenarian singing-master, and nephew of Malibran and Pauline Viardot, the friend of Turgenev. Into this harmonious little circle Garcia, somewhere around the year 1870, introduced Foley, a handsome Irish policeman with a fine bass voice and billed as " Signor Foli." All this, of course, was before I was born.

Some twenty-five years later I was learning the business of cotton manufacturing at my father's mill in Nelson, Lancashire, where my parents had taken a tiny house for me and installed me with " Old Jane " (see *Ego* 7, page 73). One week, when my mother was visiting me, there was a grand concert in an Institute, the artists including Albani and Foli. I called on the great bass at his hotel, told him who I was, and said my mother had charged me to invite him to supper after the concert. He declined, regretting that he could not remember any of my family ; from which position he would not budge. I was hurt on my mother's account, though the time has come when I can understand. For what could he have expected ? At the worst he would be asked to hear me sing or play. At the best he would have to answer a fire of questions : What was his favourite opera, oratorio, ballad ? His favourite composer ? What did he think of Mascagni, Leoncavallo, the later Verdi ? What was his opinion of Santley ? Was it true that Wagner was ruining the singer's voice ? And so on until he could decently take his leave. Or he might have thought that we were hard up and wanted to borrow money. I was too young then to realise the penalty of being any kind of public figure. Years later I realised that an artist, having worked like a horse to entertain his public, should be led back to some stable of his own choosing and there left to enjoy his evening feed in peace.

June 13 *Wednesday.* *Cocasseries, No.* 17 :

Lauren Bacall's approach on the screen to a male adopts the technique used on women by roués and ordinary everyday wolves. She plays a " wolverine " and attributes her success in this part to what she calls her " down-under look." It was natural with her a year ago. Now she practises it on unsuspecting newspapermen.

Warner Bros. News and Feature Service

Cocasseries, No. 18 :

" If that b—— Hitler had heard music like this he might have been a better man," an old lady of St Pancras (" twice bombed-out by the b—— I was ") told Miss Eaton, after she had heard her playing Bach's Air on the G String in the quiet Surrey village to which she had been evacuated.

From a Sunday paper

June 14 *Thursday.* To-night's public dinner to Myra Hess, in honour of her services to music during the war, was a dreadful affair. The first three speakers took up *an hour and a quarter*, and did not say one memorable thing between them. And the humour ! Elephantine persiflage about the sandwiches served at the National Gallery buffet ! As the next on the list of speakers was a former Minister of Food I left, having been told by the chairman that there would be no time for my three minutes.

June 15 *Friday.* Cedric Hardwicke accused me to-night of hypocrisy. Why did I blame him for making pictures while I myself was wallowing in them ? I said, " Boy, you've got me wrong. I don't in the least mind your making pictures. I think you make them very well. What I object to is your coming over here and reviving old successes when you ought to be creating new ones." He said, " Let's get everything clear. First, I am not one of those intellectuals who, when war was declared, ran away to America. I was in America two years before the outbreak of war, and you will remember that we met in New York in the summer of 1937. I was officially asked to stay on in Hollywood, and I stayed. They have given me a year's leave of absence, and that is why I am in England. At the end of the time I shall go back to Hollywood, because I am one of those odd blokes who think a contract should be adhered to.

When I return to England for good I shall try to do the kind of plays you want. But it will have to be with my own money. When you're tied to a management you commercialise yourself and can't help it [I am transcribing roughly] because you are in a way responsible to them for their money. This means that you have to put up with some silly ass of a producer, or play with some wildly unsuitable actress because she's box-office." This conversation took place on the way to Cedric's sumptuous flat in South Street. On arrival, found Lady H. awaiting us with wonderful cocktails and a really remarkable supper. Cedric was in immense form and full of stories. How a famous Hollywood star, who poses as a great art connoisseur, bought a vastly expensive fake Manet or Renoir—C. couldn't remember which. Only to find, when he got home, the original hanging on his walls! Apropos of a former English actor, now a Hollywood star, C. remarked, "God made him a good actor; he has turned himself into a bad one." He was full of theories about himself. "I can't act. I have never acted. And I shall never act. What I can do is to suspend my audience's power of judgment till I've finished. There are good actors and there are great actors. The great actor takes care that the audience shall have eyes and ears for no one else." I was delighted to find that he has exactly my views about producers—"They just get in the way"—and even more pleased when he confessed that from the first night to the last of the New York production of Paul Vincent Carroll's *Shadow and Substance*, in which he was such a success as Canon Skerritt, he hadn't the vaguest notion what his part was all about. We discussed my ideal cast for *Hamlet*, and C. agreed, with one exception. He said he thought the best King there had ever been was Oscar Asche. "When he looked at Gertrude the corners of his lower lip hung down like mutton chops." He said that never before or since had the atmosphere of the court of Denmark been properly conveyed. "It should be gross and licentious. Nowadays the place is so prim and Claudius so proper that you wonder what the fuss is all about." The talk then switched on to broadcasting, and both C. and Lady H. animadverted against English snobbery in the matter of sponsored programmes. They assured me I couldn't imagine the magnificence and variety of American wireless; live performances by the best orchestras, with plenty of Toscanini. "After all," said C., "what does it matter if between the movements of a Beethoven symphony you are recommended to take somebody's cure for acidity? You get used to it, and after a time pay no more attention to advertisements you hear over the air than you do to those you see in the English *Times*. What do you care if a well-written notice of last night's play is flanked by a puff of Sal Hepatica ?" We talked till the small hours ; then these nice people sent me back in a car. Snuggled in the corner of the back seat was a bottle of whiskey.

June 16 *Saturday.* J. A. is a believer in taking his good where he finds it. In other people's correspondence, perdy! Here is another letter to Leo from his and my little Dublin friend :

18 *Park View Avenue*
Harold's Cross
Dublin
June 12*th*, '45

MON CHER PAPA PAVIA,

What has this *enfant terrible* done to offend you ? Has he said something unusually stupid ? Has his spelling been more insulting than ever ? In brief, my sweet lion, why the stony silence ? I don't mind waiting two or even three weeks for a reply, but it is exactly four weeks since I wrote to you, telling of my perilous adventures in Harcourt Terrace. Or have the wretched postal authorities mucked about with my fragrant murmurings ?

Sir, you are cruel ! Each morning for the past three weeks have I patiently awaited the postman. My heart has pounded eagerly each morning ; my dreams have been coloured by gloriously witty notes in your distinctive typewriting. But alas, I have been so very sadly disappointed. My anxiety has been such that from a Paycockish state of " chassis " I have advanced into a Pepysian condition of " with child." I am afraid, gentle beast, that you are a " prevaricator and a procrastinator." So, please, don't postpone answering this effusion. Answer it now and be doubly witty.

My blood boils at the thought of those vulgar persons who write to James reminding him that he isn't as young as he used to be ; the person whom James answered in the *Sunday Times* a week ago was the subject of much vitriolic abuse from my faithful tongue. Personally, I dislike most persons under thirty-five. This includes actors and actresses. I like my actresses to be about thirty-nine or forty. There isn't a single movie actress under thirty, with the exception of Jennifer Jones, whom I would pay to see. Among my chief aversions are woman under twenty-five who smoke. This oddity of mine has caused me much embarrassment in the past. But I shall enlarge when I am writing my memoirs. These will be very Agatian and very sentimental. Sentimentality has caused me much unhappiness in my fifteen years. My sentimentality is not that of dear Sir James Barrie and his fragrant creations, drenched with the odour of spring flowers, "dewy with Nature's teardrops." It is a sticky, sludgy, sweaty sentimentality which has drained me of moral courage and the ability to defend myself. I have received countless little injuries in the past. I have for a while nourished

" slaughterous thoughts," but soon I have forgotten, to be injured yet again.

But this is all drivel, and I must not risk offending you. Were you a brilliant mathematician in your youth ? I am quite absurd in the face of the simplest geometrical problem. Probably because I am for ever thinking of other matters. You see, I am not what the lower middle classes call a " healthy-minded boy." I often wish I were. James seems to have been aggressively healthy in mind. What about you ? Please tell me more about yourself. (Even at present I'm thinking about something totally unconnected with this letter—Lady Longford's voice. Though I have never spoken to this brilliant creature, I very often " tail " her and her husband, simply to hear their voices.)

Now please reply and be intensely witty, and earn the unlimited gratitude of

Thy,
In a state of anxiety,
Very lone,
Very lorn
J. E. GUMMIDGE-JORDAN

P.S. As usual, my best wishes to the other J. E. Does the poor lamb still suffer from asthma ?

June 17 *Sunday.* Four years to-day since Leo joined me—an endurance test for both of us. But whether two people could wrangle so much and at the same time get on so well together I doubt. Concert at the Cambridge Theatre. Denis Matthews in the *Emperor* Concerto—not quite as big a performance as I should like, but very sound and musicianly—and the best rendering of the *New World* Symphony I have ever heard. Conductor, Anthony Collins. The programme also included Collins's Idyll, " This Inarticulate Hour," from the new film, *I Live in Grosvenor Square*. I should describe this as admirable Wagner-cum-Delius, *arr.* Herbert Wilcox. Matthews, his delightful wife, Alec Whittaker the oboe-player, and Tom Lishman came back to tea, after which Leo gave us a recital. He began with " part of an unpublished piano concerto by Mozart discovered by an Austrian refugee in Linz. To be exact, the refugee had only time to copy a bit of the first movement and a few bars of the slow movement, by which time the Nazis had arrived. I will play you as much as I can remember." And did so. It was the perfect pastiche. He then tackled the *Waldstein* Sonata—with frequent haltings and stumblings. " Really, Leo," I remonstrated, " you're not playing at all well." " Neither would you," he retorted, " if you were trying to play the blasted thing in D flat ! " Followed this up with another innovation—the Chopin F sharp major Nocturne transposed into A flat! And finished with a brilliant paraphrase on the *Rosenkavalier* waltzes in the Godowsky manner, not one note of which he will remember to-morrow morning. Having goggled and giggled their fill, my guests took their leave, we started work, and I dictated an article in C major which Leo's typewriter later reproduced in D flat.

June 18 *Monday.* Jock dropped in just after midnight. He shared my fury at not being allowed my three minutes at the Myra Hess jamboree. I said, " Never mind, Jock, there are more ways than one of killing a cat. I have sent what I should have said to *The Times* ! "

June 19 *Tuesday.* *The Times* prints my letter. Which is something. Perhaps I am wrong to get into a paddy about this sort of thing. The English loathe making a fuss, and their way of dealing with a great occasion is to take care that nothing shall be uttered in what an earlier century would have called " an elevated style." What's all this fuss about, anyhow ? some reader may be thinking. What did Agate want to say that was so wonderful ? Nothing at all. He wanted to *read* something Montague wrote during the last war :

> Even Armageddons are only means, and the joy of such treasures as these [*Twelfth Night*] is an end ; though the nations fight for a generation, it is to these that they will turn back in hunger at last, as they will turn to hills and the sea. Whatever else falls in this season of shaken assumptions and rearranged thoughts, the hold of great art on the mind will not give ; it will last as long as the " true and virtuous soul " that, " though the whole world turns to coal, Then chiefly lives." So it was well that Miss Horniman opened her autumn's work last night with this specimen of the undefeatable, inextinguishable treasures beside which even a 42-centimetre Krupp gun is but a fashion in hats. Peace, when it comes, would be worth so much the less to the returning soldier and every one else if the artists were only to sit down now and sigh for it.

Yes, I know that this appeared in *Ego* 4 and will appear in *A Shorter Ego*. Had I twelve tongues I would recite it twelve times ! My speech—in so far as the words were J. A.'s—would have been limited to a single sentence. All I should have said was that Myra Hess is another noble woman who has not been content to sit down and sigh for peace.

June 20 *Wednesday.* Letter from Albert Throup:

Stud Farm
Wylde Green
B'ham
June 18, '45

DEAR SIR,

You will be pleased to hear your mare has foaled a most beautiful filly (Saturday night.) I think it will be a black brown. Four white socks, star, and a little snip on its nose. A most lovely sort, walks with any amount of action, especially off its hind legs. You will be delighted with it. It is by Footlight—the brown colt that won the yearling class when we showed King Neptune just before the war.

Hoping you are keeping well,
Yours faithfully,
ALBERT THROUP

This brings back all the old fever. It looks as if I might now fulfil my last ambition. I wanted to sit at the top table of Bertram Mills's circus luncheon; I sat at the top table. I wanted to be President of the Hackney Horse Society; I am President-Elect. I wanted to win the championship at Olympia; Ego won the championship at Dublin, but the war came before he was ready for the supreme event at home. And now Olympia will come into its own again. Unless, of course, the Socialists get into power, when I understand that every animal in a Hackney class will receive the same-coloured ribbon, and any racehorse putting his nose in front of his comrades will be shot.

In the evening to see *Chicken Every Sunday*, at the Savoy. Who first started the notion of writing a play around groups of persons living in the same place, say a block of flats? The idea is simplicity itself. You take a railway train whose engine suddenly emits a loud shriek, causing the occupants of six compartments to stick out of window six heads which the oncoming tunnel neatly severs. After which the dramatist proves that these six heads were distressingly, conveniently, justly, inexorably, gratuitously, ironically removed. And, in the language of lady novelists, "out of the warp and woof of six divergent tragedies a texture of common significance is evolved." To the playwright taking the easy way the genre has obvious advantages. George Jean Nathan wrote of the New York production of this play: "With a boarding-house the playwright can bring on, without apology, any shape or form of human flesh, however anomalous and grotesque." The people gathered under Mrs Blachman's hospitable roof are: the husband, president of a bank, a line of street-cars, and a laundry, all of which are failing; three children; an idiot boy-poet and his imbecile mother; an Irishman who has strayed in

Photo W. W. Rouch

My Pretty

from the Abbey Theatre ; a drunken female vaudeville artist with a passion for yodelling ; a woman who imagines herself pursued by Indians ; a coloured maid ; a fantastic creature who is a combination of Mrs Skewton and Miss Flite ; a big-business man with a wife who thinks she is Mae West ; a clergyman ; a socially conscious young man from Boston ; a poultry-farmer, and a Red Indian. As Nathan puts it : " Only Leopold and Loeb are missing." Like some light wines, some American farces will not travel. Not all farces refuse, and certainly not sustained practical jokes like *Room Service* and *My Sister Eileen*, where there was action. In to-night's piece there was only oddity of character—Nathan's " shapes of human flesh "—the farce lacked the American players, and the cast was inescapably British, Rickmansworth and not Arizona being written all over it.

Afterwards to the Savoy Grill, to keep a date with Jock and Bertie van Thal, who had been to *Peter Grimes*. I asked them to tell me in five words what it was like. Jock said, " I'll tell you in four. It was like *Maritana* ! ! " Later he said, " If you seriously want to know about the opera, Jamie, it's a work of genius."

Drank a health to the foal, which Jock said in view of her breeding —by Footlight out of Lady Viking by Viking—I ought to call Ellida. But since *The Lady from the Sea* bores me more than any other of Ibsen's plays, Duse or no Duse, I shall compromise with Hedda. On second thoughts I shall do nothing of the sort. I don't see what these Nordic beauties have to do with an English filly. Shall call her My Pretty. Home about 1 A.M. with a delightful pre-war feeling that of the £15 with which I started the evening only ten bob remained. Worked till three.

June 21
Thursday.

Why are the moderns afraid of standing up to the ancients, since we are always being told that they are better ? People get furious when I compare to-day's writers of opérettes with yesterday's. Why do they funk reference to Offenbach, Strauss, and Sullivan, or even Planquette, Messager, and German, since they hold the theatre of the present to be better than that of the past ? I will tell them. Even they would recognise, say, *Three Little Maids from School* as Sullivan and nobody except Sullivan, if they heard it thrummed on bazookas in the Fiji Islands. But would they recognise as indubitable Leslie-Smith any extract from *Sweet Yesterday*, to-night's affair at the Adelphi, if they heard it poured out by, say, Frankie Schubert's Otiose Otaheitans in some Tyneside Palais de Danse ? I doubt it. I suggest they would vaguely attribute it to that school of composers which, between the two wars, supplied the pseudo-Viennese drama with its sound-equivalent. I note that the programme attributes the orchestration to a Mr Ben Frankel, who has certainly seen to it that the score is lush to saturation-point. What harps and timbrels! What wild ecstasy! And for the bored critic what struggles to escape! I suppose it would be naughty to ask our modern panegyrists *who did the orchestration for Offenbach and those others*? The essence of grand opera being to fill a void with teeming nonsense, I didn't expect this grand opérette—all about spying under Napoleon—to do more sensibly. Webster Booth and Anne Ziegler in good, and oh so frequent, voice. Reginald Tate and Hugh Miller exuding nobility and acumen. Doris Hare as a Sans-Gêne born within sound of Bow Bells. Wherefore in the *S.T.* on Sunday I shall suggest deletion of the line: "Does France move against England?" The answer could only be: "If it does, it will be civil war!" No, I shall invite these Mossoos and Madarms to toast each other at the boofy at Booloyne without insisting on their nationality.

June 22 *Friday.* Coming back to the flat after lunch, I found a Mickey Rooney-ish young man on the doorstep. Twenty-six, born ten miles from me, ex-Durham Light Infantry, just back from five years in a prisoner-of-war camp in East Prussia, most of the period in a punishment camp owing to two abortive attempts to escape. Has ideas about being an actor. If he could prove he could act, would I help? Being in one of my benignant moods, I asked him in, gave him a drink, and when he had finished it, said, "Now act!" "What do you want?" "What have you got?" "I can do the Chaplain's speech from *St Joan*." And began: "I let them do it. If I had known, I would have torn her from their hands. . . ." I stopped him and said, "Young man, you're an actor all right. Go on." And in half a minute, stone-cold in the corner of the room, with Leo and me for audience, he produced more pathos than . . . never mind who. A bit of Jones in *The Silver Box* was not so good, and the diction in a poem of Cowper's was a mess. But that the young man is a born actor there can be no doubt. He screwed an imaginary eyeglass in his eye and gave us a lightning sketch of George Arliss as good as Nelson Keys. Then, saying I might like to see how a person would dance who had no bones, he executed half a dozen steps with great comicality. Finally he turned a couple of cartwheels and departed. I don't think he's an Edmund Kean, but he might well be another Bobbie Howes. Bits of him struck me as pure monkey. I was considerably flattered when he said he had read one of my books. "Which?" "*Buzz, Buzz!* A fellow at Bromberg lent it me." Of course he wants a lot of disciplining and coaching, including the elimination of the Lancashire accent. And five years' manual labour hasn't helped, except to make him as strong as a horse. Anyhow, I lost no time. As soon as he had gone I rang up Elsie Fogerty, who was most helpful and at once promised to put him through his paces. And Leo says, "Saddled with another protégé, James ?"

The mid-day post brought this note from Jock :

33 King Street
Covent Garden, W.C.2
21st June, 1945

MY DEAR JAMIE,

Cave ! Don't go about our part of the town saying that I said that B. Britten is a new R. Strauss. I didn't. I wouldn't have said that even about R. S. after *Guntram* or whatever his first opera was called !

But I think this morning—even more than I thought last night just after the performance—that *Peter Grimes* is a very remarkable opera—full of strangeness, and beauty, and strangeness in beauty. It is packed with originality and subtlety, has neither tedium nor cacophony, and has many instances of pure genius. If genius, for example, did not go to the making of the unearthly music that accompanies and follows the death of the little apprentice at the end of Act II—scored principally for celesta and solo viola, if you please—then I'm an unmusical Dutchman !

What a charming supper ! And in what nice good quiet form we all were !

Your alacritous
JOCK

June 23
Saturday.

Again from our little Irish friend—this time to me :

You want to know about my family ? There's nothing remarkable. None of my great-aunts comforted Parnell in his hour of tribulation. Nobody gambled away the family fortune. I had a great-uncle, who was kicked out of the Navy for drinking, and I believe my grandfather also drank. But no man can be sober for ever, and we must be satisfied. My great-grandmother was killed in an earthquake somewhere. Which is all the piquancy in an incredibly prosaic family. Are my parents clever ? Dear people, of course. My mother wallows in the philosophy of life propounded by Ethel M. Dell, Ruby Ayres, Berta Ruck, and the rest of the talented ladies who fool all the female public all the time. My father reads the newspapers. Harold's Cross has gone to the dogs altogether. The place reeks of poor imitations of the Captain—O'Casey's, not Strindberg's—and old-age pensioners who spit tobacco all over the place. Gentility is confined to a few back avenues where everybody is as snobbish as can be, and the word " common " echoes all through the day. When I was small I wasn't allowed to play with " common " children. You will be interested to know that the cook and the second footman have given notice. At the rate things are going, the mater will have to clean the brasses herself. I asked Lady L. about lending us a butler, but she said she had murdered the last one some time ago.

June 24 *Sunday.* Ernest Newman, in a third article on the subject, at last tells me what I want to know about *Peter Grimes* :

> Complete distinctness of speech must be maintained, in a work of this kind, not only in the episodes of quasi-recitative but in the more specifically lyrical portions ; for if the words escape us in a solo lyrical passage we are necessarily reduced to listening to it in terms of melody pure and simple, and to do that is, in the present instance, to shift it into a genre to which it does not belong. It hardly matters to us whether *Dalla sua pace* or *Caro nome* is sung in English, in Italian, or in Choctaw ; even if we could follow all the words, which is not always the case, and even if they signified anything in particular, which rarely happens in arias of this kind—has one listener in a million, for instance, the smallest notion of what the words of *Ombra mai fu* mean ?—the overriding consideration is the charm of the music as pure melody, and the intellect ungrudgingly suffers the deprivation of the words because the musical ear is satisfied.

Now let's begin at the beginning. I don't want to see any poet's words mimed or danced. Or acted unless they were meant to be acted. Or sung unless they are of a triviality indicating that they were meant to be sung. I don't believe in robbing poetical Peter to provide a living for musical Paul. I don't believe in the marriage of perfect words to perfect music. To quote something I wrote twenty-eight years ago :

> Perfect words and perfect music mean words and music so perfectly charged with emotion of their own kind and so perfectly expressed in their own way that no addition of emotion is possible. You may compare them to two perfectly full glasses, neither of which can by any possible sleight-of-hand be emptied into the other. The result of setting perfect words to perfect music is that of two fine things one must inevitably be spilled or destroyed. There is bound to be a surrender, and it is the words which give way.

I don't believe that Beethoven at his most celestial can add anything to Wordsworth's *Intimations* that the poem does not contain. I don't want to hear lambs bounding to the tabor in the Pastoral Symphony manner, or cataracts blowing trumpets *à la Leonora.* I don't want Wordsworth's emotion plus Beethoven's, because it doesn't work out that way ; what I should get would be Beethoven *in place of* Wordsworth. I don't believe that Debussy, in the mood of *Nocturnes*, can add to " Now fades the glimmering landscape on the sight." Or in the mood of *La Cathédrale Engloutie* render more expressive

> Full fathom five thy father lies ;
> Of his bones are coral made ;
> Those are pearls that were his eyes :
> Nothing of him that doth fade
> But doth suffer a sea-change
> Into something rich and strange.

Nothing of Shakespeare's verse but must inevitably fade into the web woven by the composer in that job of magnificent treachery—translation. When Shakespeare wrote these words " for music " he was too modest ; the lyrics which set best are the trivial ones which fill, and are intended to fill, only a corner of the mind. Does any musical ass think he can enhance the sonnet beginning " Shall I compare thee to a summer's day ? " These things have their own music. I defy Berlioz to do more brassily and moltenly than the verse in *Antony and Cleopatra*, or more heart-breakingly than " I am dying, Egypt, dying." On the other hand, you can add a tune to " See, saw, Margery Daw," because here is only a drop at the bottom of a child's mug that is waiting to be filled, whereas those other goblets are full to the brim. Would anybody outside a lunatic asylum have wanted to add soft music to any of Sarah's dyings ? Film actresses ? But their glass isn't anywhere near full.

I know that somebody thinks to catch me with the marriage of *Pickwick* and its illustrators. They came into the world together, my dear objector. Would you have the book re-illustrated by a modern artist, and would you believe him, however clever he was ? Would you have Elizabeth Bennet drawn ? My dear sir, she has been drawn and is a horror ! Or Tess ? I can draw Tess in my own mind better than ten Augustus Johns. Would any opera-monger take Hardy's young woman for his heroine ? Let him invent a milkmaid of his own, and have her seduced in five sharps. The one excuse I can find for Britten's choice of subject is that nobody remembers Crabbe's poem except Jock, who of course has it by heart.

I don't know whether, in the higher mathematics, you can add one to infinity. The idea seems to me to be perilously near the Higher Nonsense—you cannot give a man toothache who is being drawn and quartered. Great music heightens great poetry ? I see. You can add height to all the height there is. Add Handel to Isaiah, and the price you have to pay for the Raphaelesque quality of "He shall feed His flock" is the monstrosity, "like a She-e-e-e-ep-herd." Whereas

> Angels, ever bright and fair,
> Take, oh, take me to your care!
> Speed to your own courts my flight
> Clad in robes of virgin white!

shrieks for music, since no sane person would dream of hearing it without. Wherefore I say that the function of music is not to attempt to heighten that which cannot be heightened, but to transfigure the rubbishy and the middling. *Carmen*? Bizet took a magnificently sordid tale and made of it a glitteringly romantic one. *Otello*? Verdi turned Shakespeare's drama into music-drama, and I do not think Euclid would have agreed that A+B=A. Many years ago I went out to Ealing to see Sarah Bernhardt at a matinée. Dumas's Marguerite Gautier died that afternoon about 5.30. At eight o'clock I saw Covent Garden's curtain go up on Melba's colourless Violetta and Caruso's Puss-in-Boots Alfredo. (The curious will find an allusion to this in one of my earlier books.) From that moment I had no doubt that *Traviata* is travesty. Suppose, since I am trying to look all round the question, that some musical genius takes in hand not the topless but the exquisite—say Housman's poem beginning "Loveliest of trees, the cherry now." Here again I am jealous for Housman. The more exquisitely done the less it will be Housman—the old story of Reynaldo Hahn coming in at the door and Verlaine flying out of the window. At least it is so in the world of my logic, which is as strict as Lewis Carroll's. Let us have an example away from the arts. Suppose somebody were to take my little horse Ego and dye him dark brown, which many consider a better colour than bright bay. Would he produce the same impression on the ringsider? He wouldn't. I am concerned, not with whether the impression would be better or worse, but with the fact that it would be different.

So far the argument has been against the raiding of poetry to make a musical beanfeast. Now let's see what happens when the raid has been accomplished. Let me take in turn the media of mime, ballet, and opera. I have no use for mime when it usurps the place of words. Why should an actor pull his face about when Nature has given him lips and a tongue to say what he means? I feel about your pantomimist exactly what Hamlet felt about the murderer of Gonzago wasting time semaphoring his intentions. "Pox, leave thy damnable faces, and begin." Absolute mime, if there can be such a thing? This is exhausted after ten minutes. Now about ballet. Why should I agree that a twiddle of skirts from right to left and pointing a toe in one direction mean "He loves me," while the reverse twiddle and the toe pointed in the opposite direction mean "He loves me not"? Absolute ballet? But that to me is no more than an agreeable confluence of line and movement and *chichi*, and after twenty minutes of it I have had enough. *Enfin*, opera. To be logical I must maintain that since Isolda may not tell Tristan that she dotes by pulling faces or spinning teetotums at him, so she mustn't do this by screaming her head off within an inch of his nose but with one eye on the conductor. Why, then, since ten minutes of mime cloy, and twenty minutes of ballet satiate, can I put up with four hours of opera in which I equally disbelieve? Because I am ravished by opera, *on condition that I have only a vague idea of what it is about.* In this I wholly agree with Arnold Bennett, who maintained that opera was tolerable only when sung in a language he didn't understand. And how wisely. "Voglio la mia colazione"—I must trust to my Café Royal waiter—sounds romantic. "I want my breakfast" sounds and is ridiculous. My discovery that *Ombra mai fu* was addressed to a tree robbed it of half its charm, since the things I had pretended it was about were infinitely more magical. I still curse the day when some too explicit soprano let me hear the opening words of the Liebestod:

> Softly o'er him smiles are stealing;
> how his eyelids gently open—
> see you, friends?
> See you not?
> Ever brighter beams his glory.
> Crowned with stars, on high he floats!

Floats! And as I look at some eighteen stone of supine, ridiculous beef I think of that fairy play about India in which Oscar Asche was *wafted* to Heaven! Is it objected that Frederick Jameson's translation doesn't do the original justice? It would take a wilderness of German professors to convince me that

> Wie das Herz ihm muthig schwillt,
> Voll und hehr im Busen ihm quillt?

is beautiful or even scannable verse. I don't know, and have never known, what words Salome is babbling in that closing scene. Is it some heavy-handed equivalent of Wilde's tarty "J'étais une princesse, tu m'as dédaignée. J'étais une vierge, tu m'as déflorée. J'étais chaste, tu as rempli mes veines de feu . . . ah! Ah! Pourquoi ne m'as-tu pas regardée, Iokanaan? Si tu m'avais regardée tu m'aurais aimée. Je sais bien que tu m'aurais aimée, et le mystère de l'amour est plus grand que le mystère de la mort. Il ne faut regarder que l'amour." Well, just as I can do better in my mind than this medley, as somebody remarked, of Ollendorff and Maeterlinck, so I know that my unframed ecstasy is better than whatever Gota Ljungberg is yammering in my well-worn record made with the Berlin State Orchestra shortly after the last war. *Elektra* ? My Greek drama is more than shaky. This is why, before I see Strauss's opera, I spend the previous evening with black coffee and a wet towel. But when, say, a Rose Pauly prances about the stage in that last scene putting her knee as high as Ego used to, I don't care whether Elektra is Orestes' mother, stepmother, aunt, sister, or first cousin. And, since I don't want to know what any of them is saying, I obviously wouldn't care if the whole horrible family sang in Dutch, Spanish, or Cherokee.

I suppose my three favourite songs are Giordani's *Caro Mio Ben*, Tschaikowsky's *To the Forest*, and Strauss's *Ständchen. It gives me no satisfaction to know what they are about.* I don't care two hoots whether the melodies of Schumann are hung on a nut-tree, the moon, or any number of Grenadiers. To sum up. You can't add Ravel to Keats. If you do, it is at the peril of making that foam into Lux.

POSTSCRIPT

Out of every thousand readers who have ploughed through to-day's entry 999 will say, " Why does he criticise what he hasn't seen ? " These 999 are loose-thinkers holding that an essay hung on a peg must be a criticism of that peg. I have amused myself to-day by writing on the general subject of words and music ; my first job to-morrow will be to ring up Sadler's Wells for seats. I may enjoy Britten's opera very much. I may want to hear it every other week for the rest of my life. I may become Britten's slave. Which won't alter the fact that when I am being ravished by music I ignore the words, and that when I am reading great poetry I am indifferent to sounding brass and tinkling cymbal. And here is a naughty thought. I have never read a line of Crabbe's poetry that made me want to read another. Suppose no bar of Britten's music makes me want to hear the next ? Would not *that* marriage be perfect ?

June 25 *Monday.* Sadler's Wells can do two seats on July 17.
Letter to Frank Singleton :

*Queen Alexandra Mansions, W.C.*2
June 25*th*, 1945

Dear Frank,

Please divert your mighty intellect from the great part Bolton is going to play, and is doubtless playing, in the coming Election, to help me in a little matter. Do you know the original of the little rhyme:

Le temps est beau,
Et bleu le ciel;
Doucement je vais
A mon bordel.

There are several longer versions, but the present one seems to me to say all that need be said. Nobody here knows the author. A French major whom I consulted had an idea it was Verlaine. Probably something of the sort was current in Ancient Rome.

Did you hear some learned owl on the wireless the other evening tying himself into knots trying to explain how *A Shropshire Lad* could have been written by a man who was never in love?

One thing more. Where in Boswell is that passage in which Johnson says he doesn't mind what political views a man holds so long as he votes Tory? Or isn't it in Boswell at all? For myself, I shan't vote. In my view there ought to be professional jurymen and professional voters, chosen from people competent to weigh evidence and record an opinion. The masses? Even Ruskin could tell the workman that his voice wasn't worth a rat's squeak. I should compel them to vote, of course, because of the salutary effect of voting. But I should destroy the votes, not count them.

Kind regards from
Your liberal-minded
JAMES AGATE

P.S. I feel in my bones that I've got the verse all wrong. Is there something about "La mer est belle," and taking one's hat and stick and sallying forth "au bord d'elle"?

June 26 *Tuesday.* From the Introduction to Sacheverell Sitwell's *British Architects and Craftsmen*:

Is not the life of the individual in our large towns, near the cinema and the fried-fish shop, with the air-raid shelter opposite, hideous and shameful compared with that of any savage? Is ours to be a world only of dog-races and the Cup Final? When we consider the spiritual values in our council houses, should we not envy the Papuan and the black fellow of the Torres Straits?

Which suggests the following one-act drama:

SANKAN AND SUDAKANA

Play in One Act

SCENE: *Any native hut in Borneo. No tables and no chairs. No eating utensils. No beds. When the hut-dwellers retire for the night they lie on the floor. Filth and abomination everywhere. Odour of decaying flesh.*

SANKAN. Mummy, can I have fish and chips to-night?
SUDAKANA. Certainly not.

SANKAN. Mummy, can I go to the pictures to-morrow ?

SUDAKANA. No, you can't.

SANKAN. Mummy, can I go to the dogs Friday ?

SUDAKANA. How often have I to tell you you're not going near the dogs ?

SANKAN. Mummy, can I go to the Cup Final Saturday ?

SUDAKANA. No, you can *not*. You ought to be ashamed of yourself. You're not a nasty little English boy. You belong to a superior race.

SANKAN. Mummy, *why* can't I go to the Cup Final ?

SUDAKANA. Because, my child, Daddy's going to give you your first lesson in head-hunting. Now go to sleep.

CURTAIN

June 27 *Wednesday.* Put into practice my new ultimatum to taxi-drivers refusing to wait. " I am a journalist and must please my readers. You are a taxi-driver and must please your riders. I give good tips. You must expect to wait five minutes. After five minutes I pay ten shillings per quarter of an hour or any part of it." If they reject these terms then I give them *no tip* ! A dozen or so of persons assembled in the Cromwell Road to-day to hear an altercation at the end of which the cabman, dashing his cap on the ground and saying, " You're a imbecilic—that's wot you are ! " invited me to put 'em up. No Jingle intervening, J. A. hailed another cab that by great good fortune happened to be passing. And, in the language of Tennyson's parodist, " clomb therein and sate."

June 28 *Thursday.* Letter from Brother Harry, saying that he and my niece are all set for their week's visit to London. " I have the personal assurance of the L.N.E.R. that the train will not be late on Sunday." I haven't seen Ann since she was a three-year-old paddling at Llanfairfechan ; she is now eighteen. Bertie van Thal and Jock report her an enchanting little person bristling with certificates, erudition, and fun. She has passed all sorts of examinations, and is going in for the Higher Development of Women or some rubbish of the sort. Shall tell her I'm too old to be converted. Have arranged what I hope will be good entertainment in the evenings for them. Harry's letter ends :

Owing to the fact that an injection was unwise and the fear that gas might upset my tummy, I have to-day had a tooth out without any anæsthetic ! I was assured that provided I held tight to the chair, and the handles of the forceps didn't come apart, " we shall be all right." We weren't !

June 29 *Friday.* Letter saying the writer has just read *Ego* 2 and regrets the inclusion of one or two improper stories. If I like to delete these in the next edition he will then be able to place the volume on his bookshelf. Wishes I had written after another model :

> If I should be discussed some distant day
> Say there were many things I might have said
> And did not say.
> Admired by hosts of readers, I grew old
> But honoured this conceit :
> The bawdy tales that often came my way
> I'd ne'er repeat.

Ends by asking when *Ego* 3 is coming out ! ! Leo says we must keep the existence of this and the next one from him, lest the *Contes Scabreux* and the *Nouveaux Contes Scabreux* send him into fits !

June 30 *Saturday.* Letter from Frank Singleton :

8 *Hill Cot Road*
Bolton

June 28, 1945

DEAR JAMES,

I can't place your little verse, but on the analogy of the divinity student (" I don't know the answer you ask for, but I append a list of the Kings of Judah ") I transcribe some lines that have been haunting me to-day :

> Je m'en vais seul du monde ainsi qu'un convié
> S'en va seul du banquet de quelque marié. . . .

Ronsard, who wrote splendid poetry for fifty years, would object to the view that Housman was a poet who had never been in love on the grounds that, whether he was in love or not, as a poet he had never furnished more than some agreeable samples. You remember the preface to the second slender volume in 1922. " I can no longer expect to be revisited by the continuous excitement . . . nor indeed could I well sustain it if it came." The Renaissance had more appetite for production. Lope de Vega wrote 1500 plays !

Do you know the lines in which four hundred years later the Comtesse de Noailles contemplated her own death ?

> J'accomplirai cet acte unique et solitaire,
> Moi qui n'ai pas dormi seule, aux jours de la terre.

Your verse reflects a happy adjustment to life on this imperfect planet. Mine seems all concerned with getting off it.

What Dr Johnson said was : " I don't mind what a man's politics are so long as he *behaves* like a Tory." I can't find where.

I am enjoying the Election in a circus-master sort of way. Democracy would certainly be hard pressed to defend the thesis that every one is fit to govern. But the lesson of the dictatorships is that certainly no one is fit to govern alone. In the words of the motion which I proposed as retiring President of the Cambridge Union : " This house will reluctantly continue to interest itself in politics." That is still my attitude to-day.

Yours as ever,

FRANK

July 1 *Sunday.* From G. W. Stonier's review, in *The Windmill*, of " Palinurus's " *The Unquiet Grave* :

> Nothing but praise for its short cuts, its touches of fantasy, its humour, its anthologising, its bilingual idiom ; the French quotations are as much a part as Latin is to the *Anatomy of Melancholy*.

To revert to an old sore. Why, when other people are allowed to quote gracefully and naturally, am I always accused of doing it to show off ? Do I, then, drag in my quotations ? I think, perhaps, in the *S.T.* to-day I do. Last week's play was all about a poet who lost his hands in an accident and had a pair belonging to a murderer grafted on. (On the lines of the old film called *The Hands of Orlac.*) To-day I write :

> It is natural that anybody fitted with hands which have belonged to some one else should be interested in learning how those hands have previously behaved. The sensible thing, of course, would be to make *no* inquiries. Imagine Hamlet's horror on learning his fingers have paddled in unlawful necks and pinched wanton on cheeks they should not.

This is too long, and reads as if it had been lugged in. What I wrote in my first draft was : " Imagine Lear's horror on finding that the dead man had not kept his hand out of plackets." But would the *S.T.* have liked that ? No, sirree ! But I have no doubt about " Micawber's disgust on realising that his knuckles are those he has rapped, the knuckles of Heep, the Forger and the Cheat " !

I can lay my hand on my heart and swear that normally, when I quote, it is because I can't help it any more than Bacon or Burton could, and Connolly can. Dickens quotes very little. But there are two plays of Shakespeare which are always at the back of his mind. One is *Hamlet* ; see Hamlet's Aunt and Mr Wopsle. The other is *Macbeth.* At least two references in *David Copperfield* : " The shade of a young butcher rises, like the apparition of an armed head in *Macbeth.*" Steerforth saying, " ' Why, being gone, I am a man again,' like Macbeth. And now for dinner ! If I have not (Macbeth-like) broken up the feast with most admired disorder, Daisy." In *Dombey and Son* we are told that Miss Tox's bedroom commanded a vista of mews " where the most domestic and confidential garments of coachmen and their wives usually hung, like Macbeth's banners, on the outward walls." Now was Dickens showing off, or could he just not help it ?

With me the quotation varies with the mood. The papers have been trying to scare us recently with accounts of how the Nazis were planning to destroy cities and whole countries by focusing the rays of the sun on to them. How they were going to split the atom and so destroy the world. How death and destruction in one form or other are knocking at our doors. When my nerves are not at their best my nostrum for all this is a jumble of Stevenson which runs : " A man should stop his ears against paralysing terror, and run the race that is set before him with a single mind. . . . Death may be knocking at the door ; we have something else in hand, thank God, and let him knock." When my nerves are in reasonable shape I just think of the Fat Boy and refuse to be the Deaf Old Lady.

July 2 *Monday.* The York train last night was some three-quarters of an hour late, its arrival coinciding with a cloudburst. Which did not damp my pleasure at seeing Brother Harry and Niece Ann. Harry's offspring, which I shall use as pet name, turns out to be exceedingly pretty—no make-up that I can detect—and I don't notice what she's wearing, which, of course, is right. Asked what she would like to see most in London, she instantly replies, " The Zoo and the Ivy." How she will laugh when she sees those hats like outsize dartboards !—though I am afraid she will find some of the frisky old girls a trifle pathetic. As a good little niece she enormously overrates my importance in the scheme of things, wherefore I had great pleasure in showing her a letter received from Watford this morning :

> One day last week I went to the cinema. The title of the supporting film was *East of Piccadilly*, the story of a murder in Soho. The murder takes place in a tenement, whose inhabitants include a mysterious American, a brace of what an inspector calls " daughters of joy " (!), and a mad actor. One of the " daughters of joy " is murdered, and her body disappears. The inspector questions the haywire ham and asks him if he has any bodies lying around loose. Says the actor : " Oh, yes, I have five—five dramatic critics ! They aren't dead yet, but they won't last long." He tiptoes across to a curtain and, with a burst of ghoulish laughter, flings it back to reveal five hanging dummies. " This," he whispers, " is the *Evening Standard* critic, this the *News*, and this *The Times* —he's pretty far gone, I fear. And this is Ivor Brown of the *Observer*. This "—and here he rolled the words round his tongue with marvellous unction—" this is—James Agate ! " Alone among that large audience I laughed. No one else had heard of you.

Saw them safely to the Prince of Wales's (Sid Field) to-night, and then betook myself to the New Theatre (Comédie Française). Beaumarchais's comedy still sparkles. Why? Because of its wit and power of observation? (The young fellow was not born a watchmaker for nothing.) Because of its Leftism? But Molière was before him. My guess is Rossini. Meaning that for the music's sake—and it was running in my head all evening—one is glad to hear the old words. Pierre Dux very amusing. Took H. and O., Gwen Chenhalls, and George Mathew to supper at the Café Royal.

July 3 *Tuesday.* Realising that I should be hellishly busy with the Comédie Française all week, I had asked Leo to look through some old *Tatlers* and make a list of ten of the most idiotic film plots we have seen. The Old Thing having his own way of interpreting instructions, I find on my desk this morning ten *précis*. Here is the first one:

> The rich Philadelphia couple who marry from motives of social convenience. They agree not to live as man and wife, until she explains that she is about to become the mother of twins. Her husband, piqued at first, is reassured when his wife tells him that the happy event is the result of the previous summer's visit to France and a pilgrimage to the sepulchre of St Jean-le-Canaille.

Follow nine even less printable fantasies. But none of them, be it said, as witless as the rubbish to the private view of which I took H. and Offspring to-day after lunching them at the Ivy. Imagine the following. You are a thug and have in your power and in a Bronx cellar a detective of enormous strength. But this detective is blind, wherefore he is always accompanied by Friday, an extremely powerful Alsatian wolfhound, which you let him take with him into the cellar. Presently the detective is heard saying plaintively through the door, "Friday is thirsty." He goes on, "Surely you wouldn't have a dog whine for water?" And you, being a softie at heart, get some water and take it into the cellar, and the dog at once buries its fangs in your throat. Whereupon the blind detective takes the key of a second cellar from your pocket and liberates his personal bodyguard. The Young Things in whose honour all this has happened are then united. When it was over O. turned to me and said, "Does London really like this sort of thing?" I said, "Yes, dear O."

Ruy Blas? Yes and no. It is going to behove me to step warily on Sunday next lest I fall into the error of judging the masterpieces of one nation by the taste of another. We are displeased when a French critic finds Shakespeare barbarous and Ben Jonson uncouth. Whence it follows that an English critic should not be too sure that Hugo's

Brother Harry

rhetoric is mere bombast. To the French it may—indeed, it must—be something more. Better to ask whether Hugo's drama caught the new spirit stirring in the minds of Frenchmen and, if so, crystallised it in terms of poetry. Not that I shall go as far as Swinburne, who held that Hugo, functioning as poet, eclipsed Milton and recalled " the lyric inspiration of Coleridge and Shelley, the prophetic inspiration of Dante and Isaiah, the satiric inspiration of Juvenal and Dryden." After which there was nothing left for the extravagant fellow to say of Hugo as dramatist except that he was the greatest since Shakespeare. (Forgetting Goethe, as somebody forgot Goschen ?) Again, we English are not so liberal-minded as the French. We hold in our snobbish way that the lackey who aspires to his royal mistress is a lackey still; if we pretend that he isn't it is only in a semi-serious Monsieur Beaucaire-ish sort of way. And then, phlegmatists that we are, we have little liking for the hero who is alternately braggart and sob-machine. Not Teresa del Riego herself could have dried those never-ending tears in Paul Deiber's voice to-night, though in view of the actor's youth this was a very promising performance. The composer to have kept alive this, to us, stuffed dummy of a play ? Meyerbeer in his mood of Piff-Paffery. And even then I doubt, for Meyerbeer too is dead.

Good party at the Savoy afterwards. H. and O.—who had been to the Albert Hall to hear Ginette Neveu play the Brahms—Cedric and Lady Hardwicke, Gladys Cooper, Jock, Meric Dobson, and Bertie van Thal. I asked Gladys her views about filming. She said, " They give you your part, and tell you to relax while they arrange the lights. You learn your lines while you're relaxing, and then play the sequence. As far as I know I have only seen one of my films. I go to the cinema to take my daughter, and as she doesn't like the kind of film I act in, we just don't go to them." She was in wonderful spirits and more radiantly beautiful than ever. Cedric, too, was in excellent form. " The Comédie Française is the best argument against a National Theatre." (*Not* for Sunday !) I was particularly pleased with O., who sat there mistress of herself and much less overawed than Jock, Meric, and Bertie, who did nothing but gape and gasp.

July 4
Wednesday.

A note from Jock :

33 *King Street*
*Covent Garden, W.C.*2
1 A.M., *July 4th*, 1945

DEAR JAMIE,

A mighty fine party, sir, thank you. I had an access of party-fright just beforehand in the Strand, and almost failed to turn in at the Savoy. But I am very glad I did—now.

I longed to tell you *this*, but didn't dare—I longed to come round to your side of the table to tell it to you and Miss Cooper only. 'Tis perfectly true—and it perfectly illustrates the lady's legend, which—like her beauty—is apparently continuous. Earlier in the evening I was in my local pub, " The Bird in Hand " in Long Acre, and the following brief, astonishing conversation took place between me and my old friend, the landlord, a man of sixty-odd :

A. D. " You'd never guess what beautiful woman I'm having supper with to-night."

LANDLORD (*immediately*). " Gladys Cooper, I suppose ! "

A. D. (*after a gasp*). " Right, first time. How did you know ? "

LANDLORD (*with a grin*). " You will have your little joke, Jock. What are you having ? "

And I, of course, left it at that ! Nothing more to be said or done about it.

You—and, indeed, all of us—very nicely and creditably covered up that split second of awkwardness when she came back from 'phoning to find us all with our heads together discussing her age. " Fifty-five " was the conclusion we were arriving at—" honestly and without cattiness," as Lady Hardwicke said. But I have just found on returning home—still rather dazzled with your supper combined with G. C.'s surpassing fairness—that she was born in 1888 and will be fifty-seven in December. This fact is in John Parker's *Who's Who in the Theatre*, a book which I have always found in such matters to be either admirably accurate or admirably silent. How witty and wise is she, therefore, as well as lovely ! First, in a public reference-book to have stated her unabashed age and to ensure that that age is even higher than another actress's private speculation can make it (cattily or uncattily). Second, on the Hollywood screen always to make up to the age of the characters she has played—like a sound, conscientious actress—to make herself by artificial means older even than her own age ought to look. Third, to be young in spite of years—to have the freshness of youth, with an April laugh at old Time. I don't know how 'tis done—but I was delighted with the privilege of seeing it done, so close and so wondrous.

To-morrow I shall go about vainly trying to find anyone who looks as if he or she would believe that I sat at supper to-night with Gladys Cooper. There is no one who will not look sceptical. I used to have much the same kind of experience in the Haslar days when I would let slip to some of my naval colleagues that I was going to spend the week-end with Vivien Leigh. Young sailors would throw at me whatever was handy, and tell me not to be a confounded and blankety-blank kidder, blarneyer, and liar. Such are the penalties of a lifetime of truth-telling, whole-truth-telling, and nothing-but-the-truth-telling. Wot larks !

Ever,

JOCK

Tartuffe? This wonder of the world lives because Molière satirised not manners, which are the human animal's clothes, but the animal itself. It is a moot point whether the immortal hypocrite should be played on Shakespearean (Angelo) or Dickensian lines. I suggest that the character has that universality which permits it to be exploited at either end of the scale or at any point in between. Jean Yonnel's interpretation to-night was a masterpiece, conveyed in terms of superb miming and glorious sonority of tone. Imagine our English Charles II in one of those black depressions known to every debauchee, add a touch of Oliver Cromwell, smear the whole with Oil of Chadband, and one would have a faint idea of this grand performance. Had sent H. and O. to *To-morrow the World*, which impressed them very much. Took them afterwards to supper at the Ivy, where they met Stanley and Vera Rubinstein, Donald Wolfit, and Rosalind Iden. Wolfit was very full of his visit to Cairo. About the Egyptians he said, "There are no middle classes. About 2 per cent. of the population live in extreme luxury, and 98 per cent. in incredible squalor. One person in every five is either blind or suffering from some hideous deformity. The most hopeless thing about the Egyptians is that they appear not to be aware of their misery, and are just waiting for some master-race to come along and turn them into slaves." He told me that some ten days ago he put young Peter Mizen (see entry of June 2) under contract.

July 5 *Thursday.* I hope H. and O.'s holiday is not tiring them as much as it is tiring me. The Comédie repeating a play already given, I had the night off and took H. and O. to the Ambassadors' to see *Sweeter and Lower*. Afterwards to the Savoy, where we were joined by Harry Kendall, Hermione Gingold, Norman Newman, and Alec Shanks, the stage designer.

H. gave evidence of an unsuspected talent as a *raconteur*. Here is the first of two stories he told us to-night. An old friend of his had a nervous breakdown, and his wife, who has considerable aptitude as an artist, was compelled to market her abilities at no matter what price. She was approached by a small farmer of the Dales, who suggested that she should paint his homestead, and after haggling the deal was clinched at seventeen shillings and sixpence! The finished painting was duly delivered, and both the farmer and his wife expressed themselves as delighted. Ten days later the farmer's wife brought back the canvas and said, "You've got a little girl on the front path. She isn't one of our lot; she's an evacuee and we dunna want her in. Tak her out." The artist obliged, and the picture was duly re-delivered. A fortnight elapsed, and again the farmer's wife appeared with the painting. The man driving the cart was a hind who had been sacked by the farmer. Could her husband's face be substituted ? This was done, and once more the painting returned. Within a month the farmer presented himself at the artist's house with the picture and the following command : " Tha shows me driving away from a field with the gate left oppen. I canna bide an oppen gate. SHUT IT ! "

The second story was about a valuer whose experience was entirely urban. Unexpectedly called upon to value a horse, and having no notion how to go about it, he decided to cube it. H. said to him, " Yes, my dear fellow, that's all right as regards the animal's height and length ; how did you manage about the thickness ? " " Oh," said the valuer, " I just drove it through a door and estimated the space left on each side ! "

Spent a good part of the meal explaining to Hermione, who wants to go into serious drama, that the bed she has chosen is that of revue, and that she will have to lie on it. That if she were ten times Mrs Siddons, something in her look, tone, gesture, or even walk would recall to-night's song about Colonel Hopkins and the Stirrup Pump. But I don't think she was convinced. Glad to have been able to take H. and O. at least *once* to the theatre. To-morrow is their last night, and I am looking forward to seeing how Marie Bell will negotiate that Becher's Brook for tragic actresses—Racine's Phèdre.

July 6 *Friday.* The Hippolyte of Jacques Dacqmine was a superb piece of acting ; magnificent to look at, listen to, and be moved by. The Thésée of Jean Yonnel was the acme of noble decorum. Phèdre herself ? On the revival of the film *Un Carnet de Bal*, I noted " the brilliant self-effacement of Marie Bell." But self-effacement is the last quality one looks for in whoever is to play Phèdre. Hear Lewes on Rachel :

> What a picture she was as she entered ! You felt that she was wasting away under the fire within, that she was standing on the verge of the grave with pallid face, hot eyes, emaciated frame—an awful, ghastly apparition. The slow, deep, mournful toning of her apostrophe to the sun, especially that close—
>
> Soleil ! je te viens voir pour la dernière fois—
>
> produced a thrill which vibrates still in memory.

But did Marie Bell look wasted ? She was as plump as a partridge ! Next I think of W. T. Arnold on Sarah's performance in Manchester in the summer of 1880. Why do I not quote myself ? Because of

Photo Angus McBean

Jacques Dacqmine as Hippolyte

the *Manchester Guardian*'s " One thinks one is tired of Mr Agate on Bernhardt."

> The great Phèdre has hitherto been that of Rachel. It is useless to dilate upon Rachel's tragic power. Her performance alike in the second and in the fourth acts is declared by all competent critics to have been all but perfection. The doubtful question is rather whether she was capable of rendering the tenderness and the infinite piteousness of the hapless woman as she rendered her transports of passion. We can conceive Rachel as having been better than Mme Bernhardt in the denunciation of Œnone ; but we should like to know how Rachel said such passages as this :
>
> Œnone, il peut quitter cet orgueil qui te blesse ;
> Nourri dans les forêts, il en a la rudesse.
> Hippolyte, endurci par de sauvages lois,
> Entend parler d'amour pour la première fois :
> Peut-être sa surprise a causé son silence ;
> Et nos plaintes peut-être ont trop de violence.
>
> The inexpressible tenderness with which those lines were sighed rather than spoken was all Mme Bernhardt's own. This line again :
>
> Et l'espoir malgré moi s'est glissé dans mon cœur.
>
> And this, when she has discovered the love of Hippolyte and Aricie, and contrasts their affection with her own guilty passion :
>
> Tous les jours se levoient clairs et sereins pour eux.
>
> These were the passages which Mme Bernhardt marked with the most personal and enduring charm, and in these we cannot believe that she has not surpassed her forerunners.

Marie Bell to-night showed competence, but in this play competence won't do. Great line after great line went by, and we were not moved. Surely

> On ne voit point deux fois le rivage des morts,

must conjure up the image of death or it is nothing ? Surely

> Dieux ! que ne suis-je assise à l'ombre des forêts !
> Quand pourrai-je, au travers d'une noble poussière,
> Suivre de l'œil un char fuyant dans la carrière . . .

should breathe the very spirit of heart-break ? Marie Bell gave us nothing of this. Her countenance, refusing to be ravaged, brought to the sullens of Wastwater the petulance of Buttermere. The truth is that her *moyens* are not tragic, and there is no more to be said.

Small party afterwards at the Ivy for H. and O., who had been to the Coliseum. Ivor Novello told us a story about an ageing actress examining the menu at the full length of her arm, and some friend saying, " Millicent, dear, oughtn't you to get some glasses ? " The actress retorted, " Don't be silly, Virginia ! There's nothing wrong with my sight. It's just that my arm isn't long enough ! "

P.S. In Leo's typescript Phèdre is made to say :

" Soleil ! je te viens voir pour la *première* fois."

July 7 *Saturday.* Took H. and O. to Louis Sterling's luncheon-party at the Savoy. This is their last function before going to spend a quiet week-end with my sister May.

July 8 *Sunday.* In last week's hurly-burly I seem to remember :

1. An orgy of what George Mathew calls " collective stupidity." Meaning the General Election.

2. Letter from a Lady. " In Tangier what you say about the drama is practically gospel."

3. Discussion on beards at the Café Royal. I said that as far as I am concerned I know only four natural and legitimate beards—Shaw, Augustus John, Clifford Bax, and Beecham. That all the rest are unnatural and ridiculous, particularly those grown by pale young men at sea. Leo said, " You ought to have seen the beards of some of the Wagnerian singers of my youth. They all had them ; it was the convention. Tannhäuser's beard came down to his navel ; he had to brush it on one side when he took up his harp to sing to Venus. Tristan had a beard, and longer, if possible, than King Mark's. Indeed, in some of those German opera-houses you couldn't tell one from the other except by their voices. And fat ! They were all fat and they all had beards. Often it was difficult to pick out Isolda, who, by the end of the Liebestod, had probably grown a beard herself. Some of those German women were very hirsute."

4. Seeing that the Editor recently tore out of the paper my review of Peter Quennell's book about Gibbon, Boswell, Sterne, and Wilkes on the grounds that *Express* readers had never heard of these great men, didn't want to hear about them, and wouldn't be the better for hearing about them, I had very little hope of succeeding with a straight review of Newman's third volume about Wagner. But there are more ways of killing a cat, etc., and the result was the better part of a column. I began by saying the life would make " an admirable subject for a novel, always on one of two conditions. One. That the author knows everything about music. Two. That the author knows

nothing about music, and knows that he knows nothing." I then divided Wagner's life into four books, and I ended :

> Wagner returns from exile and builds a theatre in Bayreuth, where his *Ring* is produced. Cosima, a masterful, narrow-minded aristocrat, now rules the roost. She is a vitriolic anti-Semite and Jew-baiter. Sarah Bernhardt, being a Jewess, strikes her as " an old she-ape." Wagner dies in Venice in 1883, probably the fourth greatest composer the world has known and the first in his own line of music-drama. Well, what about it, you English Werfels and Feuchtwangers ? What better subject than this sharp-nosed little fox who wrote some of the most glorious music the spinning globe has ever heard ? And think of the money you will make when Hollywood buys your story, forgets that Minna ever existed, and transforms the horse-faced Cosima into a nitwit blonde, and Richard into a handsome uplifter of the Spencer Tracy class with a gift for writing theme-songs !

Very artful, if you ask me !

5. Death of Elsie Fogerty at the age of seventy-nine. In accordance with her promise she saw my young actor-friend—who, by the way, is called Frank Cowburn—though too ill to let him do any of his stuff ! She was sympathetic and encouraging, and said there was something about him that reminded her of her favourite pupil, Laurence Olivier.

6. Note from Cowburn, saying that he started last week in *Strike It Again*, the Sid Field revue at the Prince of Wales's.

7. Note from my little Irish friend, with his photograph, in which I trace something of the spirituality of Stephen Haggard combined with the truculence of the Irish navvy. He writes, " I am so glad you and Leo don't quarrel. There is something so poetic about two old gentlemen passing their days together in peace and harmony. . . ."

8. Alexis Kligerman, about to give a recital, and coming to play to us thirty-two Beethoven Variations that I don't want to hear. Also that filthy Sonata, Op. 31, No. 2, that was hammered into me by old Beyschlag in Manchester, eight Chopin Études, the F minor Ballade, the A flat Polonaise, and the inevitable Liszt. It should be said that while this is going on Leo is frantically typing in one room, I am frenziedly correcting in another, with K. in a room between. I have no doubt he has made great strides. But while this maelstrom of work is on the only strides I am interested in are those *away from Alexandra Mansions*.

9. Letter from my young friends in Birmingham, saying, " Miss Ashcroft seems to have taken your ' Little Miss Muffet ' rebuke to

heart. We were in London recently, and her 'I am Duchess of Malfi still!' seemed to have graduated to the Lady Bracknell school."

10. Lunch with Meric Dobson, who was highly excited about his new novel. I gathered that while the plot is as yet non-existent and the characters are vague, he has decided on the locale. This is divided between Great Whipping and Little Whipping, both in Dorset.

11. Letter from Jack Priestley, containing the following:

> There came a cable this afternoon from Alexander Tairov, the famous director of the Kamerny Theatre in Moscow, to say that my new play *An Inspector Calls*, which, as they say, "so fascinated Moscow with its high merits," is having its première there to-night. I only sent them the script of this play, by plane, just over two months ago. Meanwhile, we have been waiting *six months* to find a theatre for it, without success, in London. So will you please remember, when you are reviewing these second-rate farces from America and the revivals that H. M. T. insist on doing (*Lady Windermere's Fan*, for instance, which wasn't a good play when it was written and is plain rubbish now), that all the time you are being deprived of seeing a good new play by me?

12. Talk over the 'phone with J. B. P., as the result of which I wrote him this:

> I have been thinking seriously about whether I ought to let myself be roped in on this question of theatres. I am a dyed-in-the-wool Tory with streaks of ultra-red. I hold that when Labour rules the world all elegance will vanish and good manners will be a thing of the past. Except, of course, *natural* good manners, which, O. W. would have told us, are the worst sort. But have you, my dear Jack, occasion to use taxis these days? If you have you will have noticed the manners of the taxi-driver now that he is on top. I dread the time when on six days of the week I shall be herded in a communal eating-shed where the food is thrown at me with the indifference that booking-office clerks use to their customers, and on the seventh must take my turn at dishing out the food. My ideal working man is a sturdy, independent creature with a dash of servility.
>
> Now for the ultra-red streak. I believe that everything *of which the supply is limited* should be nationalised—land, water, noblemen's parks, coal-mines, hospitals, lifeboat institutions. There are, however, certain things to which nationalisation would be fatal—newspapers, for example. Another is the theatre. We have one national newspaper—*The Times*, and if anybody wants *one* National Theatre I don't mind. But I would not allow commercial speculation in theatre property. I would not allow anybody who

was not in the theatre in some artistic capacity or other to own so much as a single brick of any playhouse. This probably means a return to the old actor-manager system. And why not? The theatre was at its healthiest under that system. I do not see why players like John Gielgud, Laurence Olivier, Sybil Thorndike and Lewis Casson, and others should be at the beck and call of syndicates.

And then there is another matter. Let X be a syndicate owning half the theatres in London, and let Y and Z be a young actor and actress trying to make good, and regarded by some of us as players of undoubted talent. Now if the powers that rule X do not share this view of Y and Z, the result must be that X will never cast them. But suppose the twenty theatres to be governed, not by X, but by all the letters from A to T, one letter in control of one theatre. Then I submit that Y and Z would have a reasonable chance, and that if they fail and have to betake themselves to the provinces it is just too bad! Obviously there is a similar case to be put for playwrights Y and Z. Why not a sumptuary law whereby no man shall own more than, say, two theatres, or have any interest in more than two companies of players?

But to come to the point. All this is theatre politics, and I don't see how, as a dramatic critic, I can afford to interfere in theatre politics. I know that I can disapprove of X's owning twenty theatres and like his latest production, or approve of X's owning twenty theatres and dislike his new show. I know, and you know, that I can keep each of these things in its proper compartment. But since neither X nor the general public is in a position to be aware of this, there is a danger that if I take sides in questions of this sort my criticisms will be held to be coloured by my political opinions. Now I put my critical integrity, and the reputation for it, above everything else, always, all the time. Wherefore, dear Jack, please leave me out of it. If you can prove me wrong, and prove it to my satisfaction, I will come over to you publicly. Until then, "Break, my heart, for I must hold my tongue!"

Yours ever,
James Agate

July 9 *Monday.* I am a waltz fan. I grew up revelling in Johann Strauss the elder, delighting in Lanner, going into ecstasies over Johann the younger. I love them still. What I don't love is the dreary pastiche masquerading as the real thing. The vimless, pepless, tuneless rinsings in which these pseudo-Viennese films are soused. The latest, *Waltz Time*, at the Empire, is an example. Vienna, indeed! The film should have been called *Tales from the Wimbledon Woods*. I am glad H. and O. have returned home. Bored with yet another version of the old story about the young Empress who flirts with a young officer, goes to a masquerade, and gets herself arrested, with the usual accompaniment of ravishing Mädeln (obviously from Streatham) and dashing Kavaliere who wouldn't understand a word spoken in Swiss Cottage, I fell asleep. I had had a surfeit of three-four time, and finding myself snoring in six-eight time, I left in double-quick time! But not before I had realised that Carol Raye tra-la-la'd very prettily, and Peter Graves swaggered about like a British subaltern between chukkas at polo. I suspect that Tauber was somehow mixed up in it all. But the person I most envied was some one I took to be Brefni O'Rourke, though as he was recumbent on his Imperial death-bed and I saw only the actor's chin and the tip of his nose I can't be certain. Anyhow, he was soon out of it. Lucky dog!

July 10 *Tuesday.* To-day I became President of the Hackney Horse Society. Enjoyed last evening more than any other since the war. Occasion: a reception given by the French Ambassador and Madame Réné Massigli to the actors of the Comédie Française—I owe my invitation to the fact that my French goes a little beyond that of the young gentleman with the lumpy forehead at Mr Podsnap's party who said "*Esker*" and then stopped. I sat in a corner for two hours with Jean Yonnel and Pierre de Rigoult. Yonnel, off the stage, looks every inch an actor; you couldn't possibly mistake him for anything else. Wit and the grand manner, to which must be added his superb voice. Said that to put paint on one's face, learn another man's words, simulate another man's passions, and go on the stage to court the applause of an ignorant rabble must always be a despicable business unless the actor knows and holds himself to be in touch with beauty. Said his first appearance had been as Hippolyte to Sarah's Phèdre. "I have played Hippolyte to many Phèdres, and with all the others I felt that when the Queen had declared her passion there was no reason why I should stay to hear the rest of the speech except that I was paid to do so. With Sarah it was different. She hypnotised me—I couldn't move. It was only when she took her eyes off me that I recovered the use of my limbs." Said later that when he was finished as an actor he had one ambition—to be a concierge. "In that profession there is no housing problem." Presently Pierre Dux joined us and asked whether I knew any witty English comedy which would translate. Tentatively I suggested *The Importance of Being Earnest*, of which he had never heard. Delightful evening, the champagne taking second place to the elegance of the setting and the fascination of hearing great artists discuss themselves and their art. "X is exactly right as Hippolyte; his voice is not dark enough for Ruy Blas." "Y has the voice for R. B. but not the shoulders." And so on.

July 11 *Wednesday.* The Eskerites were in great force at the British Council's treat last night. Again a notable absence of critics. Perhaps they are saving themselves for Lord Bessborough's party on Saturday? Got jammed in a corner with the charming but voluble gentleman who runs the principal theatre in Cairo, in which I had to simulate interest.

July 12 *Thursday.* The only way with miracles is to make them happen. When I first conceived the idea of luring Tartuffe and Hippolyte to Angus McBean's studio I renounced the idea as altogether too ambitious. To ask of overworked actors that they should transport themselves and their props, make up and pose for the benefit of *Ego*, seemed to me to ask too much. And then I took my courage in both hands and went all out for it. I addressed a supplication to the Contrôleur-Général, in which I suggested that since the *Ego* books go all over the world, my account of the visit of the Comédie, embellished by such photographs as McBean proposed to take, would help to spread knowledge of civilisation's most precious possession—French culture. As a letter of this sort must be elegant, and as my written, as well as my spoken, French leaves something to be desired, I sent the letter to a translation bureau and received in return a screed which the French Académie could not have bettered, and far more ornate than my draft. Gaily I signed this, and sent my houseboy with it to the theatre. It was only when the messenger was beyond recall that I remembered that the envelope bore the stamp: "Berlitz School of Languages"! On my arrival at the French Embassy that evening Yonnel came up to me and said, "J'ai grand plaisir à rencontrer l'auteur d'une prose si majestueusement belle!" The séance at Angus's took place this morning, and succeeded beyond expectation. After which we adjourned to the Ivy, where we were joined by Pierre de Rigoult, the Contrôleur-Général. Luncheon was a trifle hurried—they were due at a matinée—but *very* gay, though I am not quite sure that I liked Angus saying, "I understand Mr Agate's French, but not anybody else's." If there is such a thing as a terrestrial paradise then I inhabited one to-day. There had been a moment in the studio when I raised Hippolyte's arm an inch. Dacqmine said, "You find it better like that?" I said, "No, young man, worse!" "Then why?" "So that I can write in my diary: 'To-day, July 12, 1945, I directed the Comédie Française!'"

July 13 *Friday.* To-day has been hell. I told Angus McBean that I should call last night some time after eleven to see the negatives of the French players. I called, and at my first knock all the lights in the place were turned out ! I knocked half a dozen times, but nobody answered. This morning I began getting into touch soon after nine o'clock. Hopeless. I tried the 'phone ; no reply, though I could hear the ticking of the clock on the wall, which meant that somebody had taken the receiver off. I sent messengers. No admission. Finally, I sent Leo over. Not at home. All day we got the most conflicting reports. Angus was sick. He was lunching with a duchess. He had gone to photograph a herd of Hereford cattle. I was in despair until, very late at night, he turned up at Alexandra Mansions to explain the whole thing. It seems that, twelve out of twenty exposures being ruined owing to a faulty box of plates, he hadn't dared to meet me until he had developed the remainder. He then produced eight superb heads—seven of Dacqmine and only one of Yonnel. But what a one it is !

July 14 *Saturday.* Excellent supper at the Savoy, given by the Franco-British Society to the French players. We ate *Les Quenelles de Saumon Nantua* (only mine was lobster), *La Volaille en Cocotte Grand'mère*, and *Le Mont Blanc aux Fruits Frais*. Asking whether I would take *vin rouge*, the waiter whispered, " It's the same thing as red wine, sir." I demanded whiskey and soda. The seating arrangements were, in my view, entirely right and proper. Lord Bessborough had on his right the wife of the French Ambassador, and on his left Phèdre, and then me. Phèdre, who was dressed entirely in black, turned out to be of the Hamlet's Aunt persuasion, and I got through by enlarging upon the one line in which she had been better than Sarah—the one favourable point in to-morrow's notice. She inclined her head and said, " Votre Lady Macbeth n'est pas un rôle difficile." To which I replied that some of our English actresses found it difficult enough.

No sign of the critics, who, throughout the entire stay, have put up an extraordinarily poor show, the Critics' Circle, from which I resigned some time ago, doing nothing whatever about our visitors, and most of the popular papers ignoring them. Knowing that they were feeling strongly about this, I intimated that I should like to say a few words. What I proposed to do was to remind our French guests of, and acquaint our English hosts with, the story of John Philip Kemble's visit to Paris in 1800, and the dinner given to him by the Théâtre Français. The conversation turned upon the respective merits of English and French drama. The French actors being

Photo Angus McBean

Jean Yonnel as Tartuffe

for Corneille, Kemble naturally countered with Shakespeare. Whereupon one Michot said, " Molière, sir—whom have you to show against Molière ? " " Oh," said Kemble, " but Molière is not a Frenchman." " What ! " said the actor. " He is an Englishman, perhaps ? " And Kemble replied, " No, sir, he is not English." And then, according to Auger, Kemble went on, " Les petites divisions de royaumes et de siècles s'effacent devant Molière. Tel ou tel pays, telle ou telle époque, n'ont pas le droit de se l'approprier. Il appartient à l'univers ; il appartient à l'éternité." Yes, I had it all nicely memorised. It would seem, however, that what I call the Agate-As-Public-Speaker Resistance Movement is making progress. Anyhow, I wasn't called upon ; and perhaps the evening was running late. Arthur Christiansen, Henry Wood, Myra Hess, the Comédie Française—I see here the nucleus of a little book on " Speeches I Have Not Been Allowed to Deliver." Recovered my equanimity on emerging from the Savoy into the biggest thunderstorm for years. Even I don't pretend to compete with the elements !

July 15 *Sunday.* Leo arrives this morning, asking whether I heard the thunderstorm last night. " Heard ! " I snapped. " It kept me awake all night." " Did it ? " says he. " It sent me to sleep. I haven't slept so well since the Blitz."

The *Observer* has let the French players depart without a word. Nothing about the quality of the Tartuffe, or the Phèdre. And I turn up the little book entitled *The Manchester Stage* 1880–1900 : " The line was taken that a city such as Manchester could claim the application of the strictest standards, just as if it were London or Paris." The line I take is that a capital such as London should apply to an august company of players from the most famous theatre in the world the standard of criticism ruling in Mancester when I was a boy.

They do these things better in France. Here are some extracts from an article by Robert Kemp on the visit of the Old Vic to Paris :

> La visite que la très honorable " Old Vic Theatre Company " de Londres vient de rendre à la Comédie Française a enflammé la curiosité des gens de lettres. On a applaudi à la technique précise, à la diction colorée et forte de la troupe. Laurence Olivier, Ralph Richardson, Sybil Thorndike, Joyce Redman, Margaret Leighton, nous sont devenus chers. Nous leur cherchons des " correspondants " parmi nos comédiens vivants. C'est difficile. Ils stylisent et ils fouillent le détail plus que les Français, qui visent à la spontanéité.
>
> . . . .
>
> *Richard III* a été plus fécond en enseignements qu'*Arms and the Man*, de Shaw, ou que *Peer Gynt*. J'ai vu à cette inoubliable soirée,

Gide, Mauriac, Duhamel, Émile Henriot transportés d'enthousiasme, et une grande comédienne-auteur, Mme Simone, près des larmes !

. . . .

Shakespeare, peu à peu, devient notre chair, notre sang. Nous l'absorbons, nous l'assimilons. Aucune comparaison avec Goethe ! Goethe, on l'admire de confiance. Sauf *Faust*, avouons que la majorité des Français ignorent son œuvre. Ils ont, naturellement, boudé *Iphigénie en Tauride*, pendant l'occupation. . . . Ils commencent juste à goûter Strindberg et Tchékov, Ibsen s'éloigne. . . . Le succès du charmant Pirandello paraît n'avoir été qu'un feu de paille. Tandis que Shakespeare, de jour en jour, gagne en autorité, et soumet plus d'âmes à ses sorcelleries. On ne l'aime pas par soumission aux dogmes, à l'enseignement des professeurs, à une tradition. On l'aime d'un amour direct, spirituel, et charnel.

Clifford Bax, unburdening his heart about the critics, recently wrote : "The fact is, though nobody has perceived it, that a professional play-critic is a monstrosity—a sow with five legs or a man with four thumbs. Nature did not intend him, and that is why we have to conceal our repulsion when he confronts us. A keen playgoer may see, perhaps, ten, fifteen, or even twenty plays a year, and it is for him that dramatists write and that managers dangle their bait. Your newspaper-critic may see a hundred productions in a year. The result is—let me put it with unmistakable simplicity—that he does not see any play as a normal citizen would see it. He is therefore as fantastic a freak as the Yorkshireman who ate half a dozen ordinary breakfasts. However, I must give you an example of my contention. Some years ago I glanced at a play-notice by X.Y.Z., whose conceit would be pathetic if it were tolerable, and in his notice he wrote, 'Then the usual quartet of lawn-tennis players came on, with the usual racquets,' and, we deduce, immediately bored X.Y.Z. Not until I had read these words did I realise, being only an average playgoer, that several playwrights must have recently used the convenient device of a tennis-party for getting their characters on and off the stage. Does not this example demonstrate in a twinkling that X.Y.Z. may black-mark a play for some effect which will seem to me and you unobjectionable and even adroit ? He sees too many plays, eats too many breakfasts, is a monster." For "play-critic" read "film-critic," and I imagine that C. B.'s complaint still holds. Far be from me to admit that my old friend, throughout a long and distinguished career, has ever been right except about three things—the compelling fascination of Henry VIII, the wit of Nell Gwyn, and his own passion for clumping indifferent bowling out of the ground for six.

Nevertheless there is something in what C. B. says. My proposed holiday found me pegged down to London. Did I try to get away? Yes. Could I get anywhere to go to? No. If I had found anywhere, could I have got there? No. Would any railway guarantee that its employees, taking matters into their own hands, would not shove me into a siding at Nuneaton or Taunton and leave me there for a fortnight? No. This golden land of ours is blessed with more petrol than ever Jerusalem had milk and honey. But could I get a few teaspoonfuls? No. So I sat at home, twiddled my thumbs, and when I got tired of twiddling, betook myself to the pictures. And there I found myself in a state of enjoyment foreign to me in my critical capacity. I enjoyed myself as much as filmgoers who had paid. And on one occasion, it being Sunday, I did pay!!!!

In an amateurish sort of way, therefore, I shall venture to opine that *They Knew Mr Knight* is a British film good enough to be American. It tells a credible and extremely interesting story, and it contains that superb actor, Alfred Drayton. I have admired Drayton ever since his Carl Peterson in *Bulldog Drummond.* His Arthur Fenwick in *Our Betters* was a superb performance. Here, one thought, was a great actor in the making. And then, alas for the English theatre, Drayton fell in with "Bunny" Hare, for whom he has stooged ever since. I use the word "stooged" advisedly. Drayton is a grand actor who can act, whereas the British public has always preferred a funny man who can't help being funny. I don't imply that Hare cannot act; what I say is that the whole of him does not act as much as Drayton's little toe, and that, to hold the scales impartially, the whole of Drayton will probably never be as droll as one of Hare's aghast eyebrows. Nevertheless the fact remains that when Drayton went into farce the serious theatre lost a fine actor. "O the pity of it, Alfred! O Bunny, the pity of it!" And then I went to see *Mr Skeffington*, and rejoiced that all the film critics, with the exception of Campbell Dixon, whom I have not read, failed to find the one unique and pat quotation. The film, as most people know, is all about a vain flibbertigibbet who, despite the beauty parlours, finds herself at sixty a wrinkled, string-throated hag. I find it almost unbelievable that no film critic should have bethought him of Austin Dobson's

> With the coming of the crow's-feet
> Goes the backward turn of beaux' feet.

Nor was there the slightest mention of Mrs Skewton with her rose-coloured curtains for doctors, girlish laughter, and skeleton of the Cleopatra manner. And when Skeffington, now blind, returns to the wreck that was once his wife and finds her as beautiful as ever, not a line about *The Well of the Saints* ! Well, well, my colleagues, who know their business, must have come to the conclusion that to-day's readers are just not interested in Dobson, Dickens, Synge.

In the meantime I continue to dote on Hollywood, which sends me this piece of information :

> Janet Blair thinks she has invented a new type of sleeping ' suit.' It is the jacket of an ordinary pyjama set, but is a foot longer than the usual pattern, and she doesn't wear trousers with it. She calls it a ' sleeper coat,' and will introduce it in a scene from *Tars and Spars*, if the Hays office lets her.

In the Café to-night. Corduroy Trousers came up to my table and asked my opinion of *Peter Grimes*. " I'm making a piano transcription of it." I said, " For the left hand, of course ? " Trousers said, " That's an idea ! " And, unbidden, sat down and started drumming on the tablecloth with unwashed Bloomsbury fingers. I am not antagonistic to youth. I expect young people to come knocking at my door. But why are the knuckles they knock with invariably filthy ?

July 16 *Monday.* A messy day. In the morning went to the Test Match at Lord's. In the afternoon, in the capacity of godfather, to a christening at Westminster Cathedral. The priest having some difficulty in finding the right place in his prayer-book, I very nearly asked him the question Jack Worthing put to Dr Chasuble : " I suppose you know how to christen all right ? " In the evening to *Salome—Where She Danced* at the Leicester Square, an appalling film about Generals Grant and Lee and a Viennese bubble-dancer who was lured to a mining town in California where she sang *Der Tannenbaum*, accepted the offer of a Rembrandt, and went off in a Chinese junk, the captain of which spoke with a Scots accent, having been a medical student in Edinburgh. Supper at the Café Royal, and read myself to sleep with *Dombey and Son*. Am writing this in bed at 5 A.M., fearing the repetition of a nightmare in which Paul Dombey, who appears to be me, goes straight from his christening to Lord's, where he bowls out K. R. Miller when he is one short of Hutton's record, and is promptly lassoed by a Chinese thug, hauled off the field, and hanged from the clock-tower.

July 17 *Tuesday.* The other day I met a highbrow (non-musical) and played him my record of Strauss's *Also Sprach Zarathustra*. When it was over he said, " Is it a faithful interpretation of Nietzsche's philosophy ? " I said, " My dear fellow, I'm not interested. I shouldn't care if it were called *Also Sprach Spinoza* or

Also Sprach Jeremy Bentham." Since I listen to music for the sound of it and nothing but the sound, and since even Newman admits that there is nothing in *Peter Grimes* worth listening to *for its own sake* and divorced from Crabbe's situation and words, I am obviously the last person who ought to have gone to-night to see Britten's opera. Three hours of diabolically clever scoring, all of which I would willingly have exchanged for a single tune as good as *Cherry Ripe* or *Sally in our Alley*. The "Peter Grimes! Peter Grimes!" chorus was effective, and the monody with foghorn accompaniment suggested that Britten has only to get his brains out of the way to write something I can listen to with pleasure. The rest? "A blank, my lord!" I spent most of the time wondering how much longer theatres and opera houses are going to lag behind the cinema, where you get an unimpeded view of the screen. Sitting in the fourth row of stalls, I got the impression that the floor of Sadler's Wells rakes downwards and backwards. There was a large man in front of me, blotting out half the stage, so that I saw only the right and left corners; if I wanted to know what was going on in the middle I had to lean my body at an angle of forty-five degrees, and peer round him. Since I am too old for these acrobatics, I never at any time knew what was happening. Occasionally I caught some of the words. For instance, I heard one Boles sing:

> "I have to go from pub to pub,
> Picking up parcels, standing about.
> The journey back is late at night."

And presently, looking at what I could glimpse of the Peggotty-like setting, I found myself making notes for an opera whose title should be *Barkis is Willin'*.

July 18 *Wednesday*. Leo, who hadn't the courage to come to *Peter Grimes* with me last night but weakly listened to it on the wireless, also seems to have been struck by the Peggotty atmosphere. He arrives this morning with something he pretends he took from the postman. I recognise the familiar typing, read, and after some titivation present the following:

999*b Acacia Road, W*.3
July 17, 45

DEAR MR AGATE,

I am pleased about this revival movement in English opera. No doubt you have heard of the latest work in this genre, the Opera Mimetica, *David and Dora*, after C. Dickens. The composer is a young Australian, Herman Guntz. The librettist is Conchubor

Doyle, an undergraduate from Dublin University. Personally I was very much impressed, although, from what I remember of *David Copperfield*, some of the incidents seemed a little strained. Perhaps you would like to hear something about it.

Act I. Miss Trotwood's salon in Piccadilly in the year 1815. It is dawn, the birds are singing in Hyde Park (bass tuba and tenor drum), and Mr Micawber is brewing punch. The sun appears, and various people dance in from several doors, including Mrs Micawber with the twins, Traddles and his dearest Sophy bearing aloft a cake-basket, the Misses Lavinia and Clarissa Spenlow, Mr Jorkins, who later turns out to be a *basso profundo*, the Peggottys carrying a boat, and finally Mr and Miss Murdstone, who dance a fandango. So far nothing but ballet. But now David, dancing in at another door with Dora, explains in forty-eight *entrechats* that he is in love with Dora but that Agnes, who has made more sober entry (harps), has the prior claim, her father having lent him some money. Agnes, a deep contralto, seeing Dora among the dancers, commences to pray. Dora, a volatile mezzo, is always accompanied by a greyhound, and dances most of the time ; the greyhound is also an expert dancer. There is a flourish of trombones, and the Traddleses, the Peggottys, and the Murdstones dance out to meet Miss Trotwood, leaving the stage empty except for Micawber, who brews some more punch, Dora, who sings some coloratura, Agnes, who is praying, and David reading aloud the shorthand notes he has just made of the Prime Minister's speech. This forms a very effective quartet, whereupon the stage fills again and Miss Trotwood describes in dumb-show her visit to Doctors' Commons, which the dancers illustrate balletically. The act ends in a choral fugato on the words " Janet, heat the bath ! " rising to a splendid climax of dramatic tension.

Act II. The Traddleses' garden at Deptford. Miss Trotwood explains in mime why she thinks Dora an unsuitable wife for David —she dances too much. She agrees, however, that Agnes is too much addicted to prayer. (Here the double bassoon has an eloquent solo.) Which shall it be ? (Two muted piccolos echo her thought.) Several people now dance in, including Mr Micawber, who resumes brewing punch. Now David enters with Dora and Agnes, and announces that he has just married Dora. Guitars are heard, and a boat is seen approaching, out of which step Lord Byron, Shelley, and Leigh Hunt, who echo Micawber's words : " My dear, another glass ? " and make a dancing trio of it. Dora is in tears, she has lost her dressmaker's bill ; presently we find the dog has eaten it. Agnes now suggests a game of rounders, and all join in to Bacchantic music, Micawber continuing to brew punch. A thunderstorm threatens, and Peggotty and his family get into a boat and row back to London. The act ends with a prayer by Agnes to the accompaniment of harmonium and tenor tuba, after which she is rowed away by the three poets. The dog, left alone on the stage, dances a seguidilla, holding a red parasol.

3

carrying a ~~boat~~ which Mrs Gummidge suggests will make a nice coffin. The dog ~~is melancholy, feels there is~~ something wrong, ~~and dances a bolero. David 's dancing is also heartbroken.~~ Dora, rallying ~~a little,~~ sings about ~~the~~ her inability to open oysters without a knife, ~~and the dancers express their grief in a solemn Polonaise. Dora now dies~~ after drinking a glass of punch ~~offered to~~ her by the faithful Micawber. ~~Solem dance (Pavane)~~ ~~David and Agnes are united and sing a love-duet.~~ Dora is carried out in ~~the boat in which Micawber with tears places the bowl of punch. All the dancers point~~ upwards ~~with their hands, Agnes sings a last prayer, and~~ the sound of distant drums ~~is heard.~~ It is the eve of the battle of Waterloo. Left alone on the stage the dog executes a few ~~dismal~~ pirouettes and falls down dead. In the moonlight ~~we see~~ Micawber steal~~ing~~ in ~~cautiously in order~~ to finish what is left ~~in the glasses~~ of the punch. ~~The Trumpeters blow the Last Post.~~ A Cat walks in, sniffs at the dog's dead body, walks contemptuous~~way~~ and settles down to sleep on the bed on which Dora has died. Curtain.

~~You will see from the above rough precis that the union of allied arts is here brought to something like perfection.~~

Yours sincerely

Adolar de Bunk.

Photo Sydney W. Newbery

Collaboration

Act III. Bedroom in David's lodging in the Temple. Dora is dying; Micawber is brewing punch. The Peggotty family dances mournfully in, carrying a small skiff which Mrs Gummidge suggests will make a nice coffin. The dog, feeling that something is wrong, goes into a routine which includes a bolero. Dora, momentarily rallying, sings about her inability to open oysters without a knife. But at last she dies, after refusing a glass of punch poured out for her by the faithful Micawber, who, to conceal his emotion, drinks it himself. David executes a masterly *pas de deuil*, Miss Trotwood a *marche funèbre* in mime, and Dora's body is borne off (strings *ppp. col legno*) with Agnes pointing upward. The curtain is now dropped for a moment, and rises again to the sound of distant drums. It is the eve of the battle of Waterloo. In the moonlight Micawber steals in to finish what is left of the punch, but, finding that Mrs Gummidge has been before him, steals out again. Left alone on the stage, the dog executes a few pirouettes and falls down dead. A cat walks in, sniffs at the dog's dead body, walks contemptuously away, and settles down to sleep on the bed on which Dora has died. Curtain.

Even from this rough précis, you will realise, dear Mr Agate, that a sincere attempt has been made to weld three arts together in the service of the mistress art of Opera Mimetica.

Yours sincerely,

ADOLAR DE BUNK

July 19 *Thursday.* Opened the second Sixth Form Conference of the Schools of King Edward's Foundation at the ghastly hour of ten-something. Audience of about three hundred. Spoke for sixty minutes, after which they—both the boys and the girls—heckled me for ninety more. Some fifty questions, of which here are the first ten.

1. *Q. What is a good play?*

A. A play which doesn't make you yawn or fidget is a good play relative to you. A play at which only a numskull would yawn or fidget is a good play absolutely.

2. *Q. Must a good play have a moral?*

A. No. *Twelfth Night* has no moral. But no play can be *great* unless it sends you out of the theatre feeling you have undergone a spiritual experience.

3. *Q. What are the rules of dramatic criticism?*

A. Only two that matter. One. Decide what the playwright was trying to do, and pronounce how well or ill he has done it. Two. Determine whether the well-done thing was worth doing at all.

4. *Q. Is radio drama feasible?*

A. If you mean: Will plays written for the stage be effective on the radio, I say yes in the sense that a blind man presumably gets pleasure out of going to the theatre. If you mean : Is drama specially written for the radio feasible, I reply that I have heard of a new art called radio drama. Whenever I unwittingly run into an example of this I switch off. I don't pretend that this is fair or critical.

5. Q. *Is it a sign of weak intellect to like ballet?*
   A. Not if the ballet limits itself to the agile and the graceful. But to believe that six young women hauling a young man round the stage by his hair signify Retribution overtaking Lust, and that this was in Schubert's mind when he wrote the *Wanderer* Fantasie —this is pure Harpo Marx.

6. Q. *Would you stage Vanbrugh or Farquhar in modern dress?*
   A. No.

7. Q. *Did Shakespeare or Bacon write the plays?*
   A. Both. In collaboration.

8. Q. *In view of the fact that so many French and Austrian operettas are masterpieces of wit and musicianship, why is English musical comedy what it is?*
   A. Because the English like it so. As a nation we admire any playwright, composer, actor, clown, who has no talent and is modest about it.

9. Q. *Do actors need brains?*
   A. If they can act, no. If they can't, yes.

10. Q. *Must a good play have professional actors? Or will amateurs do?*
    A. A professional is a man who can do his job when he doesn't feel like it. An amateur is a man who can't do his job when he does feel like it.

The conference may or may not turn out to be a feast of reason; at lunch the only flow was soul! This annoyed me so much that when K. P. Tynan, my boy-chairman, told me that the programme included a concert, a cricket match, and a performance of *Hamlet* with himself in the title-rôle, I said, " And how, pray, will visitors know which entertainment is which ? "

July 20
Friday. Letter to Hamlet (*see above*), who had asked my opinion of a prose poem on the subject of " L'Art pour L'Art."

*Queen Alexandra Mansions, W.C.*2
July 20*th*, 1945

My dear Hamlet,

Of course you can write. You write damned well. You write better than I have ever attempted to write. The mistake you make is the old one of trying to do too much. Why sow with the whole sack ? Why say : " The *avant-garde* harks grimly back to the *splendours and miseries* of de Sade " ? Must you drag in Balzac ? Why, when you are in full spate of discussion about Huysmans, lug in Voltaire ? Why tell us that Mallarmé " was passing proud, and rode in sorrow through Persepolis " ? I see no connection between the French poet and the Elizabethan one.

I don't believe George Moore ever thought of Rimbaud as " a consumptive youth weaving garlands of sad flowers with pale, weak hands." Rimbaud described himself at that period as " surly of aspect, ungainly of figure, with huge red hands like a washer-woman." And I conjure you, now and for ever, to put a stop to your punning. Say, if you must, of Guillaume Apollinaire that " devout and donnish, here was Phœbus Apollinaire turned fasting friar." But to say that " Verlaine was always chasing Rimbauds " is just *common.* Like cheap scent.

My dear boy, in a prose poem of less than a newspaper column's length you undertake to tell us about Gautier, Montesquieu, Heredia (without the accents, please), de Sade, Huysmans, Moore, Verlaine, Rimbaud, Proust, Apollinaire, Mallarmé, and Flaubert. Don't you think that these are enough without dragging in Balzac, Voltaire, Meredith, and Marlowe ? If it helped I should be the last person to object. But it hinders. Read what Montague in *A Writer's Notes on his Trade* has to say about quotation, and be guided by him. It is only old cripples like me who have to use the crutches of another man's wit to get along from paragraph to paragraph. You don't need this.

One more small thing. Remember ' Saki ' : " Stephen Thorle said, 'The gratitude of these poor creatures, when I presented them with a set of table crockery apiece, the tears in their eyes and in their voices when they thanked me, would be impossible to describe.' ' Thank you all the same for describing it,' said Comus." Why talk of Proust as " indescribably leisured " and then go on to describe that leisure ? " The jaws of his memory were ponderous indeed and marble." Even so, what possible connection is there between Proust's memory and the tomb of Hamlet *père* ? This is just plain showing-off. Take my advice. Absent thee from quotation (four syllables, please) a while.

Yours sincerely,
JAMES AGATE

July 21 *Saturday.* Wire from Birmingham : " I shall in all my best obey you, madam. Hamlet."

When Bertie and I were making out the list of people we thought should be asked to contribute to Home and van Thal's series of " Letters " Clifford Bax was the first person we thought of. The MS. was delivered in due course, and I took violent exception to one passage in it—about the critics he has known—which Bertie invited him to delete. But he wouldn't. Wherefore, in to-day's *Daily Express*, I clump him for six :

> Mr Clifford Bax's view of the theatre's function is much higher than that of Shakespeare, who, turning history and legend into thumping good plays, didn't care two hoots whether his Elizabethan audience was edified or not. But there is one respect in which Mr B. is inferior to Mr S. ; he has not the older dramatist's knack of popular success. Mr B.'s plays have hardly ever been *that*—indeed, his best play, *Socrates*, cannot get a hearing—and Mr S.'s plays were almost always a wow.
>
> Now this riles Mr B. exceedingly, and looking about for somebody to blame he pounces on the critics. He tells us that a critic earns his living " by selling his opinion of what ten, twenty, or thirty other persons, each of them more gifted than he, have striven to build up into an attractive evening." This is flat nonsense. Edmund Kean was more talented than Hazlitt—but only in the way of acting. Ten, twenty, or thirty of Kean's co-players, putting their heads together, could not have written one of Hazlitt's notices. Then take this passage :
>
> " Among play critics I have known only two who were not publicly ludicrous on account of an immeasurable self-esteem. The self-esteem of the rest is so embarrassing to any normal person that I, for example, hardly know where to look when I have to converse with one of them, because it is precisely as though I had to speak, with an air of inferiority, to a ridiculous and bedizened tart."
>
> Besides being nonsense, this is unnecessarily rude. Among the critics Mr Bax has known are Shaw, Archer, Walkley, Max Beerbohm, and Charles Morgan, and I leave it to him to decide which two out of the five are exempt from affront. I regret having to say this. Mr Bax is, besides being a witty and exceedingly elegant playwright, a very good cricketer. But it was never his habit, I think, when he saw his stumps shattered, to turn round and abuse the umpire. Why cannot he play cricket in the field of drama ? I am sorry to have to write this about a little book that is otherwise entirely admirable, and contains some excellent advice to young playwrights. I recommend this book—on condition that the purchaser obliterates pages 12 and 13. A convenient way to do this would be to gum them together.

July 22 *Sunday*. Heard last week from Harrap's that five thousand unbound copies of *Ego* 7 are in a railway siding somewhere between Edinburgh and London and have been there for some days, the railway being cluttered up with more important commodities. Remembering the time during the last war when I dispatched hay to Salonika and knew all about trucks standing in sidings, I said, " Are they well and truly *bâche'd* ? " " Are they *what* ! " said Harrap's, and I explained that *bâche* is the French for tarpaulin. They reassured me, and said they hoped to get the sheets to the binders in a day or two. Binding will take a month, after which I shall have to wait six weeks while enough girls and string can be found to send the thing to the bookshops. Publication in October may therefore be possible. Since I handed three-quarters of the book to Harrap's last October and the balance on January 1, it seems clear that nowadays twelve months are required between delivery of a book and its issue even by the most expeditious of publishers. But of course the Labour Government which we are obviously going to get may change all that, and I can see future *Ego's* treading on each other's heels and people saying, " *Can't* the old fool keep quiet ? " The answer is : No, the old fool can't. And in any case, who grumbles now because Mozart turned out the E flat, G minor, and Jupiter symphonies in six weeks ?

July 23　　Postcard from Clifford Bax :
Monday.

At your age you must try not to write rubbish. Shaw and Morgan are not celebrated for diffidence, modesty, and lack of self-esteem. Item, I do *not* know Beerbohm and never saw Walkley. Prepare a place for a new writ in the writ-drawer. Item, *The Rose* has had something like 250 performances ; *Polly*, my first success, had about 360. Wherefore, a WRIT for belittling my professional position.

Come to Fry's box for the next Test Match—if he secures one. We missed you at the last Test.

C. B.

Have replied :

All right, all right. Then which of these five practising critics are " bedizened tarts "—Ivor Brown, Anthony Cookman, Alan Dent, J. C. Trewin, Philip Hope-Wallace ? I imagine that the two you except will view your pronouncement with an auspicious, and the others with a dropping, eye.

Yes, I'll come to the Test Match with pleasure.

J. A.

Cocasseries, No. 19 :

There was a name outfit for the straight dansapation, and a Cuban combo which sold the Latin stuff.

ROY COHEN, *Sound of Revelry*

July 24　　From Moray McLaren :
Tuesday.

Gilgal Hospital
Perth, Scotland
21/7/45

MY DEAR JAMES,

I think it would amuse you to learn that, remote and lonely here (recovering from a nervous breakdown), the only person who will cash my cheques locally is—The Undertaker. Whether this is done out of kindness of heart or to ensure possible future custom I don't know. But it's true.

I am recovering hand over fist, writing hard, and enjoying being an individual, not a cog in a machine. Do write a line and tell me that you have not forgotten one who has drunk so much champagne, both verbal and vinous, at your expense.

MORAY McLAREN

To which I have replied :

Queen Alexandra Mansions, W.C.2
July 24th, 1945

MY DEAR MORAY,

You, of course, remember your Lord Ogleby in Colman's *The Clandestine Marriage*. How on his dressing-table were drops for the gout, waters against the palsy, and cordials against matutinal depressions. But how about me, who have for three weeks sauntered forth with smelling-salts against faintness, ampoules against my head flying off, and powders against whatever fit impends ? To-day I consulted my doctor, who happens to be in hospital after what he calls a tidying-up operation. He said with some acerbity, " You didn't come to see me yesterday as you promised. I suppose you were feeling better." I then spilled the beans, and he has put me on a diet—no work, no whiskey, a little champagne, and, if I won't go away, visits to the Zoo and the Ballet. I am different from you, my dear Moray, in this respect—I am tired of being an individual, and would welcome being a cog in a machine.

Of course I have never forgotten you. It was you who argued with me that claret was the proper thing to drink with fish, and, as evidence, produced two exquisite bottles of Pontet Canet. This was in Edinburgh some fifteen years ago. We went up the West Coast afterwards, if you remember. It was during this trip that I had my one and only psychic experience. It was eight o'clock in the evening, we were out walking, and I suddenly saw our chauffeur bob up in the middle of a field. We moved towards him, and he at once disappeared. We searched the field and found nobody ! Returning to the hotel, we questioned him, and he swore he had been indoors all the time and had never left the bar. I also remember you showing me a mountain-range some six miles long which every evening at sunset turned itself into a recumbent Highlander. If I don't dream, we also visited the Pass of Glencoe. I remember that in spite of your kilt you looked and talked throughout the trip exactly like Dr Johnson.

Since too much letter-writing falls into the category of Norman Newman's " work," I must stop. Let us meet soon, and I will produce two bottles of whatever there is to be got.

Yours ever,
JAMES AGATE

All my papers having given me a fortnight's holiday, it is up to me to stop working forthwith. There are, however, letters which have got to be written, and here is one :

To the Editor
"*The Times*"

Sir,

The author of your admirable leader, "Stubborn Illusion," says there is "still a lively conflict of evidence" as to how the heroic Richardson took his failure to break the Australian last innings defence in the Manchester Test Match of 1896. I have the best of reasons for stating that the conflict is one of opinion only, the evidence being strictly on one side.

It all begins with a passage in Neville Cardus's *Days in the Sun* (1924) :

"He stood at the bowling crease, dazed. *Could* the match have been lost ? his spirit protested. Could it be that the gods had looked on and permitted so much painful striving to go by unrewarded ? His body still shook from the violent motion. He stood there like some fine animal baffled at the uselessness of great strength and effort in this world. A companion led him to the pavilion, and there he fell wearily to a seat."

Sir, my old friend, now in Australia, confessed to me when I challenged him that he never saw the match and gave me his permission to say that he never saw it. Again, it was to me, talking cricket between the acts of a dull play, that H. J. Henley boomed, "I won't have it ! After the winning hit Tom legged it to the pavilion like a stag and got down two pints before anybody else." Henley was fourteen, and may well have seen the match.

Sir, I was nineteen. I saw every ball bowled, and for the last innings sat directly behind Lilley keeping to Richardson. I saw him miss Kelly. I saw the winning hit. Now, sir, the Old Trafford crowd in my day never invaded the playing area except at the end of an exciting match, a habit known to visitors as well as to the home team. In the mind's eye I can see two Australians and eleven Englishmen legging it to the pavilion with the tall figure of Tom Richardson leading by many yards. If a historian should tell me that Napoleon remained rooted to the field of Waterloo hours after the battle was lost I should know that he was speaking essential truth ; that he skedaddled as fast as post-horses could leg it is correctness of a lesser order. Cardus, who watched the great match at the age of seven from behind the bars of his nursery window some miles away, had the secret of the higher truth. But on the lower ground he tarradiddled.

I am, sir, yours, etc.,
James Agate

Holborn, W.C.2
July 24th, 1945

And who could resist this from a boy in the Air Force ?

2245367 *A.C. Zakon, C.B.*
28 *S.P., c/o* 115 *Wing*
R.A.F., M.E.F.
15.7.45

DEAR MR AGATE,

With the conceited ambition so familiar to youth I have tried to foster an appreciation of sincere literature within myself over a period of the last few years. To that end I have read a little of Charles Morgan, Compton Mackenzie, D. H. Lawrence, Rabelais, Bromfield, Thackeray, and several of the other incomparable giants, as well as a welter of the rubbish that is becoming increasingly popular to-day.

Fortunately, however, my present station boasts a tiny library to which I habitually turn for mental nourishment.

Recently I discovered a book by W. J. Locke; namely, his *Morals of Marcus Ordeyne*, which you, in your infinite erudition, doubtless read long ago. I had heard of Locke as the author of *The Beloved Vagabond*, but the person who told me of him dismissed him cynically as a hopeless sentimentalist. When I had finished reading *The Morals* I was convinced that it was only a little short of genius, and certainly the most enchanting story I have ever read.

Now, Mr Agate, I am one of those mad dogs of Englishmen forced by circumstances to go out in the midday sun ; also a lengthy sojourn away from home may have rendered me a little too easy to please.

In fine, I should like your opinion, as I respect your Olympian wisdom in these things, and I hope sincerely that you will spare me a little of your precious time to reply. To that end I am enclosing a stamped addressed envelope.

Yours sincerely,
C. B. ZAKON

Some cynical reader may say that not to reply was easy. Well, nerve-storm or no nerve-storm, I cannot disappoint a lad who tells me in a P.S. that his camp is situated four hundred miles south of Khartoum ! And we at home grumbling at a minor heat-wave ! So here goes :

*Queen Alexandra Mansions, W.C.*2
July 24*th*, 1945

MY DEAR BOY,

I am sorry not to see eye to eye with you in the matter of W. J. Locke. Oddly enough, the first piece of dramatic criticism I ever wrote for the *Manchester Guardian* was about the play which he made out of his novel, *The Morals of Marcus*. According to my recollection, Marcus was an ass who gave chivalrous hospitality to a young woman in circumstances which pointed to her being his mistress, and when the neighbours disapproved became werry fierce and sarcastic. A drivelling, fatuous piece! Years later I met the author, and committed the deadly sin of contempt. I thought he had a mind like a stingless jelly-fish. He was a worse *writer* than I am, and that he was a better man is neither here nor there. Unless we hold with à Kempis:

> Au grand jour du Seigneur sera-ce un grand refuge
> D'avoir connu de tout et la cause et l'effet?
> Et ce qu'on aura su fléchira-t-il un juge
> Qui ne regardera que ce qu'on aura fait?

If you can't translate this write me and I will translate it for you. There's something about a 2/3000 mile correspondence that your Holborn-Paddington post-bag lacks, don't you think?

Yours sincerely,

JAMES AGATE

Then I must acknowledge a note from my sailor-friend, Ivan Plowright (see entry for January 9), who writes from China to say he received the books, and hopes to see me in a couple of years or so.

Then there is the gentleman who writes from Leamington Spa to complain of my habit of "shoving gobs of French all over the place. Why? Have you the presumption to suggest that the sense of this French is so exquisite that it would not be possible to translate it into the language Shakespeare used? Might I suggest that you write your books in the language that most folk in this country understand?"

I replied:

SIR,

Are you a potman that you should use the language of the spittle-strewn public-house bar? Of course there are things in one language that will not go into another. Find me the French for:

> Downy windows, close
> And golden Phœbus never be beheld
> Of eyes again so royal! Your crown's awry;
> I'll mend it, and then play.

And then find me the English for:

> Tournant sa tête pâle entre les cheveux bruns
> Vers celui qu'enivraient d'invincibles parfums,
> Elle tendit sa bouche et ses prunelles claires;
> Et sur elle courbé, l'ardent Imperator
> Vit dans ses larges yeux étoilés de points d'or
> Toute une mer immense où fuyaient des galères.

What goes for Shakespeare and Heredia goes for me too.

People who want to read my books must learn French. If they won't the loss is theirs, not mine.

JAMES AGATE

July 25 *Wednesday.* Just as an economy campaign always starts with more expense—for example, a calf-bound ledger in which to record one's economies—so any rest-cure must be preceded by straightening-up operations of vast complexity. Worked myself to a standstill yesterday. Then tuned in to the Proms (*Siegfried's Rheinfahrt*) in time to catch that little twiddle in the clarinet, taken up later by flute and violins, that haunted Wagner from *Rienzi* to the Liebestod. The old, old story. Siegfried is a preposterous, sword-brandishing (the equivalent of sabre-rattling) Teuton in whom I have no interest. Yet I never tire of the *Rheinfahrt.* Peter Grimes is an Englishman in whom I am supposed to have every interest. But do I want to hear " Peter's Orefahrt " ? Ten million times no. Supper consisted of two bits of spam and a bottle of Bollinger 1928. (Six pounds odd, but economy works that way.) Came back to the flat and put on my thirty-year-old record of *Siegfried's Journey,* followed by the Funeral March. As the next record in my cabinet was the Overture to *Meistersinger,* I played that too. Old Ludwig had the right notion. The ideal way to listen to music is late at night with no audience except oneself and a houseboy to put the records on, with five shillings to compensate him for his broken slumbers. About 2 A.M. I reached my Richard Strauss section. Why has nobody perceived that the jollification at the beginning of Britten's third act is just watered-down Baron Ochs ? Towards 3 A.M. I heard myself say, " Always remember, Arthur, that in the theatre the clotted cream of pure sound is better than the vinegary lees of sour intellectuality." Arthur said, " Righto, I won't forget. Now what about me putting away the whiskey and you going to bed ? "

The afternoon post brings this from Jock :

Tuesday, July 24

DEAR JAMIE,

These past two days I have been at my old self-appointed task of reading the entire criticism of the *Manchester Guardian* since its beginning in 1821. The war impertinently interrupted this when I had reached the middle of 1896. The files are kept, as you know, at the B.M. Newspaper Place, Colindale. It is pleasant—nearly country ; the sun shines, birds sing, and haymakers make hay outside the windows.

I knew all was going to go well yesterday morning because the first thing my eyes fell on (oddly enough after our long midnight telephone conversation about *Frou-frou* the night before) was this :

July 1*st*, 1897. " Madame Sarah Bernhardt last night repeated at the Adelphi her well-known performance of *Frou-frou.* In all the quieter scenes of the play she was delightful, but she has gradually come to overact very decidedly the more violent passages, such as the scene with Louise in the third act, and with de Sartorys in the fourth."

In the following day's paper I found :

July 2nd, 1897. " At the Lyric Theatre last evening Madame Réjane appeared, for the first time in London, as Frou-frou, thus directly challenging comparison with Sarah Bernhardt, who is playing the same part at the Adelphi. It cannot be said that either actress is distinctly superior to the other. Madame Réjane's performance is in many ways more artistic than that of her great rival ; but Madame Bernhardt certainly gives to some of the chief scenes a greater depth and variety of colour."

So that was that. And I had a rare day's hunting.

To-day began not nearly so propitiously with my eyes falling on this (in December 1897) :

" Rarely have the lobbies of the Palais Bourbon presented so animated an appearance as to-day, when the latest developments of the Dreyfus case were discussed with passionate excitement. The opinion was expressed on all hands that the letters attributed to Major Esterhazy were monstrous, if genuine ; but there was considerable disposition to doubt their authenticity. M. le Blois denies the assertion made by the *Eclair* that he drew up a statement of the case for M. Scheurer-Kestner in collaboration with Lieutenant-Colonel Picquart."

This, of course, took me away back to another hot July of ten to twelve years ago when you locked up poor Brother Edward and me in Briar Cottage, Beaconsfield, for three days and nights so that we might sift the contents of Schwarzkoppen's wastepaper-basket, reduce the Veiled Lady's score of letters to two at most, and Scheurer-Kestnerise generally on behalf of your damned Dreyfus play—while you gallivanted in London ! (I never liked you less !)

However, after so disconcerting a start (and in spite of occasional headline interruptions like " The Dreyfus Scandal " and " The Dreyfus Uproar " and " Trial of M. Zola " and " M. Zola Mobbed " and " A New Dreyfus Sensation ") I had another morning full of events much after my own heart—visits to Manchester of Olga Nethersole, and Irving and Ellen Terry (in *Madame Sans-Gêne*), and Forbes-Robertson in *Hamlet* (first time). And finally—just when the bell was ringing for the half-dozen dusty researchers to pack up and go home—there occurred the one far-off divine catastrophe to which the whole *M.G.* creation was in those days moving. In short, in May 1898 Mr Gladstone died—and his life and death were described in how-many-d'you-think columns of that mighty paper ? THIRTY-FOUR COLUMNS AND A QUARTER ! ! !

Your exhausted

JOCK

P.S. Proust's charming M. Swann, sered, old, and gnawed by cancer, gently remarked to a sympathetic friend, " I should not like to die, you know, before seeing the end of the Dreyfus Case ! " I shall still be reading something about the old business in the last paper I pick up in this life !

P.P.S. And my God ! d'you see the headline of the *Express* this morning : " J'accuse : by Daladier."

I raise my eyes and see on the wall the framed issue of *L'Aurore* for Jeudi 13 Janvier 1898, which an unknown friend gave me for the first night of my " damned play."

LETTRE
A M. FÉLIX FAURE
PRÉSIDENT DE LA RÉPUBLIQUE

MONSIEUR LE PRÉSIDENT,

Me permettez-vous, dans ma gratitude pour le bienveillant accucil quc vous m'avez fait un jour, d'avoir le souci de votre juste gloire et de vous dire que votre étoile, si heureuse jusqu'ici, est menacée de la plus honteuse, de la plus ineffaçable des tâches ?

Vous êtes sorti sain et sauf des basses calomnies, vous avez conquis les cœurs. Vous apparaissez rayonnant dans l'apothéose de cette fête patriotique que l'alliance russe a été pour la France, et vous vous préparez à présider au solennel triomphe de notre Exposition universelle, qui couronnera notre grand siècle de travail, de vérité et de liberté. Mais quelle tâche de boue sur votre nom—j'allais dire sur votre règne—que cette abominable affaire Dreyfus ! Un conseil de guerre vient, par ordre, d'oser aquitter un Esterhazy, soufflet suprême à toute vérité, à toute justice. Et c'est fini, la France a sur la joue cette souillure, l'histoire écrira que c'est sous votre présidence qu'un tel crime social a pu être commis. . . .

And then the old names start—Mercier, Sandherr, Henry, du Paty de Clam, Boisdeffre, Esterhazy, Picquart, Scheurer-Kestner, Mathieu Dreyfus. . . .

Also this from " Curly " :

1803621 *Sgt. Bowdery, J. C.*
341/116 *H.A.A. Battery, R.A.*
B.L.A.

17*th July*, '45

DEAR JIMMIE,

I am writing from Hamburg ; a city half-razed by incredible pin-point bombing. Would that the peoples of Coventry and Bristol, Plymouth and London, and all those places so ruthlessly savaged by the Luftwaffe, could tour the ruins that are Germany to-day. Let them look closely: they will see that houses, sliced by bombs, are still inhabited. Many Germans are living in rooms which have but two walls, sleeping high up on a precarious perch dislodged easily by a powerful wind. And in those few buildings which have escaped the fury of the R.A.F. there is overcrowding on a scale difficult to picture: eight and ten and twelve existing in rooms that four would crowd. There is little food: black, puddingy bread, greasy milk, poisonous cigarettes, endless queues that even the English housewife has not experienced. What an utter, final defeat, you think. But is it?

The Germans seem resigned to the occupation of the Fatherland. I have known no open acts of hostility directed against us, some civilians smile as you pass, bid you good-day or raise their hats. German soldiers salute, although as they get used to us and our foolish, easy-going ways these salutations decrease daily. But glimpse the look in German eyes when they are off-guard, and you will read an intense hatred. I have seen this manifestation of their true feelings too many times for my piece of mind. They don't consider us their conquerors. We are a nuisance which must be endured until the day dawns when we leave their country, outmanœuvred by a race whose clever cunning even now has not been appreciated. We are losing the peace—I'm sure of it. In trying to prove to these sadists (you've only to watch the children at play to understand the Hun) what little gentlemen we are, we're becoming laughing-stocks. The German will understand the discipline of blows and whippings and shouted commands—and no other.

Two minor disturbances have taken place during the past week, directed against the Italians, of whom two, I believe, were killed. The populace was punished by the imposition of a seven-thirty curfew for three evenings. Last night movements were heard in the garden of the house in which we are billeted. One wag in my room observed, "Don't be alarmed—no one would dare come in and kill us—they'd get a week's early curfew!" Life as a garrison soldier in Germany is not good. I'm longing for my release, which will, I hope, come at the year's end.

You are well, I trust, and not overdoing things.

Regards to Leo.

Sincerely,

CURLY

Black Thursday. My first reaction to the Election result was to make the following entry in my Diary:

Death robbed Roosevelt of his triumph, and now the mob has stolen Churchill's glory and trampled it underfoot. "The decision of the British public has been recorded in the votes counted to-day. I have therefore laid down the charge which was placed upon me in darker times." Words which should make Englishmen blush for a thousand years.

My next reaction was to 'phone Edgar Lustgarten and tell him that I was applying for naturalisation as a Patagonian. He said, " I shouldn't if I were you—they might make you President ! " And then I pulled myself together. There is no question of scurviness towards the greatest Englishman since Queen Elizabeth. The seed of to-day's affair was contained in something Lady Oxford said at lunch at Gwen Chenhalls's a few days after Churchill became Prime Minister : " Winston is the one man who can lead this country to victory. When he has got it he will cry like a baby. He is a fighter who loves fighting ; nothing else really interests him, though he may pretend it does. He is the last man to handle the reins of peace." Many electors must have asked themselves this question : Am I to vote for Winston and abandon my principles, or should I stick to my principles at the risk of seeming ungrateful ? For once in a way Churchill seems to have lacked a sense of the stage. His proposal, turned down by the Socialists at the Blackpool Conference, that the Coalition should continue until the end of the war with Japan, when there should be an election, was a mistake. What he should have said was : " Leave me in power till we've finished off the Japs, when I will retire and not embarrass the country with any nonsense about gratitude." He should not have risked defeat. Incidentally, it is no use the Tories thinking they are going to get back in six months' time because the Socialists are going to make a mess of things. The new Government won't make a mess of things, and there is enough way on the ship to keep it going for a year or two whoever is in control on the bridge.

Having written the above, I rang up the head waiter at one of my favourite restaurants and said, " Listen to me carefully, Paul. I am quite willing that in future you address me as ' comrade ' or ' fellow-worker,' and chuck the food at me in the manner of Socialists to their kind. But that doesn't start until to-morrow morning. To-night I am bringing two friends with the intention that we may together eat our last meal as gentlemen. There will be a magnum of champagne and the best food your restaurant can provide. You, Paul, will behave with your wonted obsequiousness. The *sommelier*, the table waiter, and the *commis* waiter will smirk and cringe in the usual way. From to-morrow you will get no more tips. To-night you will all be tipped royally." The head waiter said, " Bien, m'sieu." That was at a quarter-past six. At a quarter-past nine I arrived and was escorted by bowing menials to my table, where I found the magnum standing in its bucket, and three plates each containing two small slices of spam ! Who would have thought a head waiter to have so much wit in him ?

July 27 *Friday.* Letter from Hamlet:

229 *Portland Road*
Edgbaston
Birmingham 17
25.7.45

Dear Mr Agate,

You have dealt with me very temperately. But may I (it shall be for a few moments only) have leave to quibble? My prose poem exudes booksiness because the characters I limn in exude booksiness. Its atmosphere is their atmosphere; and its faults are their faults. My mistake, I take it, is not that of trying to say too much, but of seeming to know too much. I have, as you must know, never read de Sade (the nearest approach to him I have made is that best of bedside books, *Psychopathia Sexualis*); I have only seen the glow of Balzac refracted and dimmed by upstart crows of critics; and of Meredith I know only *The Egoist.* My prose poem is impressionism at its worst—literary impressionism. Its sufficient beauty is to conjure up by stealth from books an image of the wordy marvels that were burgeoning in France after 1850. And if I consider that a line of Marlowe may be perverted to apply to Mallarmé I unhesitatingly pervert it. The only connection between the two is: there is no connection. Just as my only rule is: there are no rules. Art laughs at locksmiths. My quid-pro-quoem is irritatingly derivative and allusive because the Symbolists were; it is criticism in their own rarefied cloud-country.

I know what Rimbaud looked like; I don't think George Moore did. The lines I quote, which he, impossibly, used to describe R. L. S., might easily represent his own over-idealised concept of the young jesting pirate. And as to the "ponderous and marble jaws" of Proust: when I note that Shakespeare has coupled two words which by their pompous sonority suggest weight it is a sign of my own innate breeding and modesty that I prefer using his phrase to coining one of my own.

Like Sterne, "I begin with writing the first sentence—and trusting to Almighty God for the second." But my quotation-book never leaves my side. My principal fault (and it is quite unforgivable) is expounded by Nietzsche:

> "What is the characteristic of all literary decadence? It is that life no longer resides in the whole. The word gets the upper hand and jumps out of the sentence, the sentence stretches too far and obscures the meaning of the page, the page acquires life at the expense of the whole—the whole is no longer a whole. The whole has ceased to live altogether; it is composite, summed-up, artificial, an unnatural product."

My work is a chain of soft phrases. I can only thank my Muses that it is the writer's privilege to have his chain tested by its strongest link.

Yours sincerely,
Kenneth P. Tynan

My reply :

Queen Alexandra Mansions, W.C.2
July 27th, 1945

My dear Hamlet,

Now and again fact draws level with fiction, and you appear to me to approximate very closely to my—or perhaps I should say our, since one Leo Pavia was the real begetter—Oleander Fugge, alias Durance Hatch. (Who this personage is you will learn from the pages of *Ego* 8.) In the meantime, my dear boy, there is this difference between us. I never go to my quotation-book except for the purpose of verification. I think you are wrong in likening yourself to Sterne. You begin by writing the first sentence, and then trust to the *Oxford Dictionary of Quotations* for the rest. In your flirtation with verbal surrealism I, as an old fogey, cannot follow you. And will not.

> Costly thy language as thy thought can buy,
> But not express'd in fancy ; rich, not gaudy :
> The style, says Buffon, oft proclaims the man.
> Farewell : my blessing season this in thee.

Polonius

July 28 *Saturday*. An unknown young man writes from the Mediterranean:

My obeisances to the ubiquitous L. P. Could he not write a few more Strindberg studies ? I think I should like him. As *Ego* 6 is the first I have read, he appeared before me like Minerva from Jove's brow—or rather, like Gargantua rampageous from his mother's (father's ?) left ear.

Feel like writing to the young man to say that I wish L. P. would devise some means of retreat along these or any other lines. He moans that he is deaf and cannot hear what I dictate. He laments that his handwriting is illegible, and when I ask him why he doesn't make it legible, replies, " What's the good ? I'm too blind to read it anyhow ! " In addition he has the paper-saving mania, which means that his notes are taken down on the backs of old notes for old articles, fifteen words to a page. When the dictation is finished he gathers up some forty sheets and strews them, paperchase-wise, along the thirty-yards stretch between his desk and mine. Presently he retrieves and proceeds to type them in the order in which they have been picked up, without regard to sequence. Here is something he laid before me to-day :

Mr Wolfit's revival of *King Lear* finds me on tenterhooks. Tenterhooks about what ? Remember, I receive some twenty to thirty manuscripts a week which my secretary returns automatically. Your play is not in my flat, and I can only conclude that it has been returned. Tucked away in Hazlitt's lesser-known

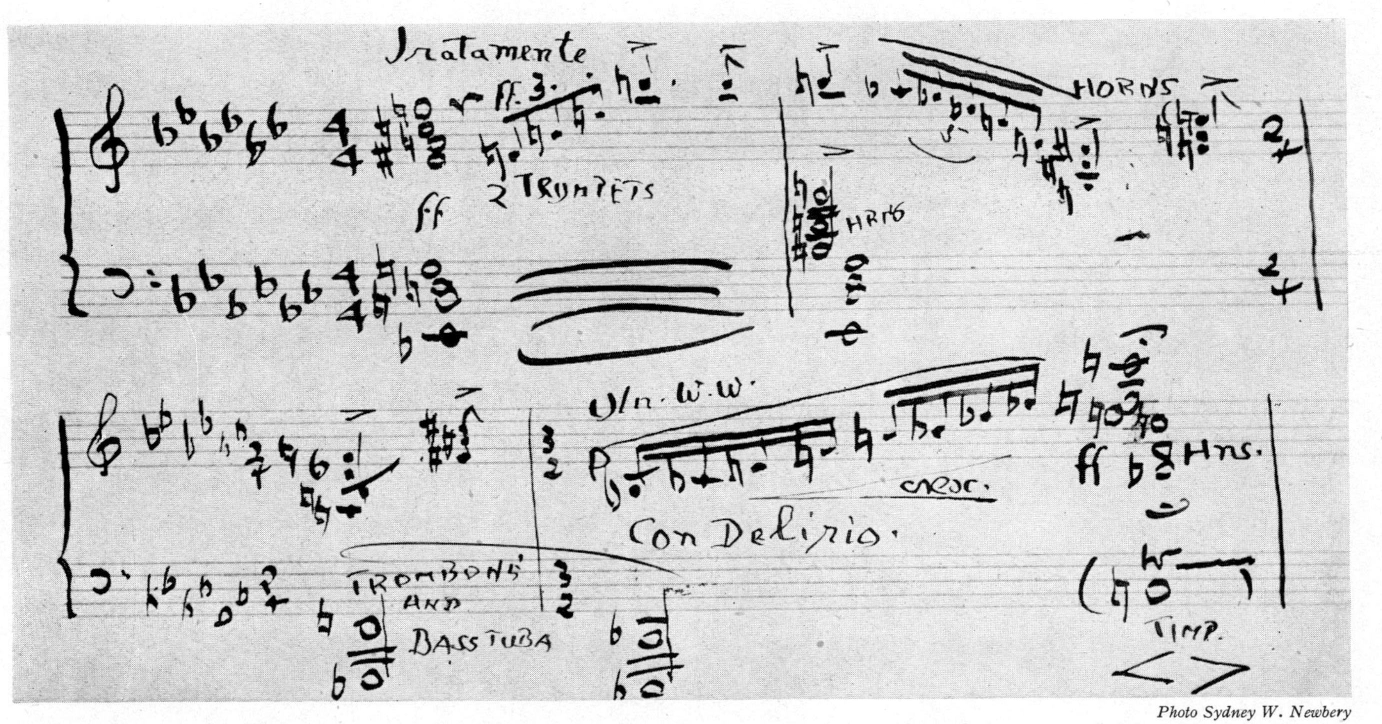

Photo Sydney W. Newbery

From "The Evacuees"

essays there is a curiously grudging account of Goldsmith's masterpiece. But this actor, although most musically inclined, is not a Liszt. To me, all microphones look and sound alike. Nine years now go by.

Fuming, I ask, " What the devil is this rubbish ? " and L. P. says imperturbably, " I thought it was rubbish when I was taking it down." He is both cause and cure of my *énervement* ; nobody else has his twofold genius for annoyance and stimulation. All the same, I think it was for the best that we couldn't get into the hotel at Southend. " If you think I'm going to sit on my behind for four days," said Leo, " looking at that mud and that mob, you're mistaken. I shall take the typewriter ! "

My trouble is that I can't stop working, the most I can do in that line being to change the work. Yesterday I had arrived at the last sentence in the last of the articles I am to write for three weeks—I am comparing Irene Vanbrugh and Nancy Price with the film actresses who have to be shoved into seventeen different positions before the camera-man can take a shot that isn't ridiculous :

> When you hear those voices, watch those gestures, note the faultless timing and the virtuosity attained by the simplest means—when either of these superb war-horses takes the stage we say : She paweth in the valley and rejoiceth in her strength. She swalloweth the ground with fierceness and rage. She smelleth the battle afar off, the thunder of the leading man and the applause.

I wrote this out by hand, partly because I was pleased with it, and partly because I knew Leo would make the ground swallow the war-horse. Half an hour later I was sitting at the Embassy Theatre, looking at and very much liking Joan Temple's *No Room at the Inn*, a play about a sadistic slattern who ill-treats five children billeted on her, one of them a little boy of ten, and is murdered by them. Fine performance by Freda Jackson. When I got home I turned up my cutting-book and found something from *The Times* in the 'eighties :

> However lamentable the fact may be, there is undoubtedly a class of playgoers whose notions of dramatic art are satisfied with the reproduction upon the stage of the sordid scenes of low life they see every day around them. A coster's barrow with a load of vegetables, or a free fight carried on by roughs whose merit it is to look as if they had walked straight upon the stage from the purlieus of the Borough of St Giles, has for these people an attraction which the highest efforts of literary or poetical genius would fail to exercise.

The word " Borough " struck a note, and I decided that to-night's play, under the title of *The Evacuees*, is our next English opera. Consider the last scene. The slattern, having come to the end of her vocal resources, throws herself on the bed on which she is presently to be smothered, and mutters, " Sod the little swine ! I'll teach him to ruin my new hat ! " Leo, saying, " And what you hear in the orchestra is something like this," seizes a piece of music paper and jots down half a dozen bars with which I would undertake to spoof any living conductor, not to mention the musical critics.

Lunch to-day with André Bernheim, who told me some lovely stories. About Lucien Guitry going with his mistress to his hatter's. Each hat was pronounced too big, too small, too grave, too gay. At the tenth she said, " Ah non ! Pas celui-là. Tu as l'air d'un vieux maquereau ! " With a shrug Guitry handed the offending felt to the shopman and said, " Celui-là me vieillit ! " About Galipaux, in a comedy by Sacha Guitry, drawing up his will and leaving 30,000 francs to his native town of Cherbourg, 20,000 to his wife, 40,000 to his mistress, 10,000 to an illegitimate daughter, and suddenly interrupting himself to say, " Bon Dieu de bon Dieu, où est-ce que je vais trouver tout cet argent-là ! "

Wind up my first day of rest-cure with another letter to Hamlet :

*Queen Alexandra Mansions, W.C.*2

July 28*th*, 1945

Expectancy and Rose of the Fair State,

I am very anxious not to mislead a clever pen like yours. What exactly is the point of " jesting pirate " ?

I have made some study of the matter, and the result of my thinking is that anything quoted must *go the same way as the author's stream*, whereas your quotations—and allusion is a form of quotation—peg the reader back. Here are passages from four great dramatic critics, showing how they used embellishment. I will begin with Shaw. He is writing about *Her Advocate*, a play by Walter Frith :

" Just as another Frith frankly said, ' I cannot do you an artistic picture like Botticelli's " Primavera " or the like, but I'll do you a railway station or a Derby Day to the life ' ; so the author of *Her Advocate* seems to have said, ' I cannot write you a dramatic poem, like *Twelfth Night* or *Pelléas et Mélisande*, nor do I pretend to any of the qualities of Molière or Labiche, Goldsmith or Sheridan, Ibsen or Sudermann ; but I'll do you a criminal trial that will be as delightful as the real thing.' There is a sort of greatness in this frank recognition of one's limitations. In the National Gallery it is quite possible, after breathing the finest ether of the true artistic atmosphere among the early Italian pictures for an hour, to spend a few minutes looking at ' The Derby Day ' without resenting its absolutely prosaic character any more than you do that of the fire-hose. It is the same with *Her Advocate*."

Now take Walkley on the subject of Dumas *fils* :

" How to qualify him ? A dramatist who can give Scribe and Sardou points and a beating at their own game ; a prophet who has brought down new Tables of the Law from a Sinai hard by Mont Valérien ; an apostle whose prefaces, pamphlets, articles, are so many Epistles to the Lutetians ; moralist, philosopher, mystic, dabbler in occultism, deist, socialist, conservative—to be thus prodigal of differences is to be a mere centre of perplexity, a rallying-point of the bewilderments. To Montesquieu's Persian or Goldsmith's Chinaman his whole theatre would seem one prolonged nightmare. . . ."

Here is Max on Duse :

" I have often wondered why Sydney Smith said he 'would as soon speak disrespectfully of the Equator.' After all, the Equator is a mere geographical expression. It casts no weird spell of awe over mankind. On the contrary, seafarers, when they come to it, put on false noses and play practical jokes. For ' Equator ' read ' Duse,' and then the remark has point. There never was an influence so awe-inspiring as Duse. At her coming, all the voices of the critics are hushed. Or rather, they are uplifted in unisonant dithyrambus."

And lastly Montague on Tree :

" Isidore Izard, the ' hero,' is a predatory financier on the grand modern scale, no mere maggot skulking in the cheese, but a really first-rate beast of prey, with the City for his jungle, and ranging it royally. The type, excellently conceived, is acted by Mr Tree with buoyancy, observation, and inventive ingenuity. His Izard has the fine, flamboyant, blackguard geniality of one of Lamb's ' higher race of men,' only that he does not borrow, but takes ; he gives you the right impression of rollicking invincibility at his own game ; he is the true taxer, ' who calleth up all the world to be taxed ' ; he is as ' the sea, which taketh handsomely at each man's hand.' Mr Tree acted the man's self-enjoyment to perfection in the second act—much the best scene in the play—where two lesser rogues tackle him, and he ' does ' them with a tranquil gusto almost romantic, singing bits of songs by the way, like Cyrano improvising a ballad while he pinks a less efficient swaggerer."

Well, here are four critics who were masters of all I mean by " quotation " instead of borrowers allowing quotation to be their master. Shaw, Walkley, Beerbohm, Montague—each ornament swells its author's stream and becomes part of it. No, I do not want you to write like any of those four great critics. I don't want you to write like Desmond MacCarthy. Or like Ivor Brown, Alan Dent, me. I want you to make for yourself a style—which can be done only out of your own bowels and nobody else's—that will make readers say, " That's Tynan," just as people say, " That's

Hazlitt" or "That's Lewes." Let me assure you that poking about in books of reference is no way of attaining the one thing that matters in all the arts—individuality. At the moment I see little more in you than blown youth blasted with other people's ecstasy. So chuck it, and start life on your own!

POLONIUS

July 29 *Sunday.* True to form, the B.B.C. faded out Ginette Neveu last night ten bars before the end of the Beethoven Violin Concerto. But then they would have no compunction in fading out some reciter of verse at the line:

> At last he rose, and twitch'd his mantle blue . . .;

though they would prefer:

> To me the meanest flower that blows can give . . .

Some day Broadcasting House will come into its own and fade out Hamlet at:

> But I do prophesy the election lights
> On Fortinbras: he has my dying voice;
> So tell him, with the occurrents, more and less,
> Which have solicited. The rest is . . .

The Concerto was cut short by the news telling us that Mr Potsdam has gone to Attlee! Or something of the sort. The news that our Daniel has gone to put his head in the Russian lion's mouth may well be more important than any concerto. But why doesn't whoever is in charge of the Proms go into the artists' room ten minutes before the concert and say, "You know you're being broadcast?" (Conductor and soloist signify that they know.) "You know the nine o'clock news is a MUST?" (Both assent.) "You know you've got forty-five minutes for the concerto. How long did it take at the rehearsal this afternoon?" (The conductor: "We finished dead on time.") Here whoever is running the concert should do a bit of quick thinking. He should remember something a famous conductor said to me about a famous opera-singer: "The Volga Boatmen, hauling away with a rope, couldn't have hurried that cow up." So my manager would say to conductor and artist, "Dead on forty-five minutes won't do. I must have two minutes to spare. The applause greeting Madame may delay the start. Or Madame's violin may break a string. Or Madame may have a sneezing-fit in the middle of the slow movement." And if I were the Prom manager I should turn to the soloist and say, "Look here, Madame What's-your-name, if you don't get through that concerto in forty-three minutes you never show your face at *my* concerts again!"

Lunched with Jock, who said there was a Dreyfus letter for me in the post. Told me that when he took H. and O. to Rules he tried his game of 'Preferences' on Harry, who answered every question without a second's hesitation. Here are his answers:

Favourite Words

Pink
Shandygaff
Eschscholtzia

Likes	*Dislikes*
Tschaikowsky	Wagner
Sousa	Brahms
Chopin	Sibelius
Shakespeare	Tennyson
Kipling	Burns
Whittier	Wordsworth
Jan Van Eyck	Turner
Hogarth	Holbein
Corot	Gainsborough
H. G. Wells	Meredith
Dickens	Thackeray
Rider Haggard	My Brother James

Favourite Line in Poetry

"Gentle Jesus, meek and mild."

July 30 *Monday.* The papers made a fine showing on the death of Lady Oxford. The best notice, *of course*, was in the *Manchester Guardian*, which always does anything worth doing better than any other paper. This makes up for doing things that aren't worth doing worse than any other paper. To-day it prints some two thousand words which ought to go into any anthology of modern English prose. Nothing could be better than:

> Margot was a wonderful hostess and a wonderful talker. She even on occasions knew when not to talk, though she always had ten thousand things to say. Many even of those who normally disliked to be silent could sit happily listening by the hour to her piquant reminiscent monologues. Her talk was never tedious for an instant, except when it concerned the subject-matter (as distinguished from the personalities) of politics. Then, indeed, it could be infinitely tedious. She rarely exhibited even a modest grasp of a political or economic problem, and so she could be as tiresome and as impervious to argument as any other echo.

Since I shut my ears to people who knew Bernhardt only in her old age, so I feel that nothing I write about this great figure and brilliant creature can have any real value. I never knew Margot, and

I never knew Mrs Asquith. My acquaintance began with the Countess of Oxford and Asquith, when, soon after her husband's elevation to the peerage, Viola Tree took me to lunch at her house somewhere in Bloomsbury. I had met her unofficially some weeks before, when I sat next to her at the Everyman Theatre on the first night of a play by her daughter, Princess Bibesco. I remember that for days afterwards my side was blue, owing to the proddings of the maternal elbow as each supposedly witty thing came along. At the Bloomsbury luncheon I remember only Asquith, sitting at the head of the table, quietly smiling while the Countess was explaining to some Russian dancer how to chalk her shoes so as to prevent slipping. And how the rest of us said nothing, and I left wondering that a man like Asquith could tie himself up for life with a tornado. Some years later she came up to me at Lord's and said, " You won't know who I am. Can you direct me to Lord Baldwin's box ? " I said, " As I don't know who Lord Baldwin is, how can I ? " She said, " If it isn't our dear, clever Mr Agate ! " I said, " If it isn't our dear, foolish Lady Oxford ! " At the same time administering a gentle slap. Whereupon her daughter said, " Mr Agate is quite right, dear ; you deserved it." Mostly we got on famously. I can be a good listener, and am all for solo performances. If there is a good talker at the table then I stay completely mum. At many of Gwen Chenhalls's luncheons *à trois* she and I would say nothing and listen to Lady O. laying down the law about politics, literature, art, science, Mr G.'s acting, and her parlour-maid's corns. She was a woman of extraordinary refinement of mind. You couldn't tell her a story which was in the least *risqué*. I made one attempt, and the reception was such as Mrs Pipchin would have accorded Master Bitherston.

And here is Jock's letter :

Colindale
Friday

DEAR JAMIE,

Your damned Dreyfus Affair interferes with my work in spite of myself ! (It must, of course, fascinate anybody with a mind—even me !) In July 1898 M. Zola declares the whole tangle to be " frightfully absurd." But on September 2nd I find a startling turn under the heading : " The Dreyfus Scandal : Colonel Henry's Suicide." And in the same issue the *Manchester Guardian* speaks up nobly in a long first leader :

" With all that one knows of the life and character of Captain Dreyfus before his trial and of the distinguished men who have championed his cause so bravely against a fanatical and foul-mouthed opposition supported by the majority of Frenchmen, one is practically forced at this stage to believe in the prisoner's innocence. . . . It is equally clear, we hope, that the first step towards reorganising the War Office and re-establishing public confidence in its actions will be at once to recall Captain Dreyfus from his desert island and give him a fair open trial wherein he may demonstrate his innocence. Nothing less than an immediate revision of the scandalous trial of 1894 can repair the injury that has been done, not only to Captain Dreyfus, but to the fair fame of his country."

On September 22nd there is another short leader to say that Colonel Picquart has had a charge of forgery trumped up against him, and that these uneasy goings-on in France "awaken the suspicion that even now a powerful party at the War Office is sparing no pains to obscure the truth about the Dreyfus Case."

At the end of October there are violent anti-Dreyfus demonstrations in the streets of Paris. In the middle of November Dreyfus himself is (falsely) reported dead. In December there is a report of Picquart's trial, and renewed agitation. And at the very end of the year—where my time was up !—Captain Dreyfus was reported to have embarked for France again for the second trial.

I cover, you see, about six months a day—and this particular day has been the least exciting of the three I have spent at the job this week. And yet not so very unexciting either ! Leaving public affairs *and* the theatre and music out of it, you wouldn't—would you ?—as *Express* book critic call six months "unexciting" which gave you Kipling's *The Day's Work*, the first complete edition of Meredith, the first general printing of *A Shropshire Lad*, Henry James's *In the Cage* and *The Turn of the Screw*, Mrs Garnett's translations of Turgenev, Monkhouse's *A Deliverance*, and Hardy's *Wessex Poems*.

In the Drury Lane pantomime at the end of the year, *The Forty Thieves*, with Dan Leno, etc., there was a specially successful burlesque interlude called "The Zoological Gardens" in which many figures in the public eye were "vociferously recognised." These included Lord Salisbury and Mr Chamberlain and W. G. Grace and Tod Sloan (who was he, please ?) AND Zola and Esterhazy and Dreyfus !

Ever,
Jock

P.S. It would be pleasant, though hardly possible, to finish the mighty task by October 15th this year, which will be the *tenth* anniversary of my becoming the *M.G.*'s London dramatic critic.

July 31 *Tuesday.* Yet again, without fuss, the *Manchester Guardian* calmly manifests its superiority over every other paper in the world. It gives this morning a detail, 8 inches by 7, of a picture by a forgotten artist, H. Jamyn Brooks, in the possession of the National Portrait Gallery, showing Margot Tennant attending the private view of the Old Masters exhibition at the Royal Academy in

1888 and walking round the room with Mr Gladstone. Other figures are Lord Jersey, Holman Hunt, John Ruskin, Lord Spencer, Sir Charles Tennant, Marcus Stone, and G. F. Watts. No other newspaper, except perhaps *The Times*, would have thought of reproducing this, and *The Times* didn't think. Every other paper, even if it *had* thought, would have turned it down.

Note from Hamlet:

229 *Portland Road*
Edgbaston
Birmingham 17

DEAR MR AGATE,

I believe in artifice for art's sake.
I do not believe in sincerity or profundity.
I believe in superficiality. I believe in shallowness.
In fact, *quand même*, I believe in

KENNETH P. TYNAN

This is immediately followed by a telegram in reply to one from me saying I hoped to spend most of next week at Sutton Coldfield and would he come to the show at which I am judging?

POX DEVOUR ME FOR HAVING ALREADY ARRANGED TO BE IN LONDON AUGUST 3RD TO 12TH WHAT NOW LETTER FOLLOWS—HAMLET.

The Post Office, staggered by the basic English of the first three words, repeats them to make sure.

Note from Tom Curtiss, now in Berlin:

I visited the Führer's Reichskanzlei residence this afternoon, and found the great man out, along with the roof, the windows, and most of the walls. I managed to unearth a whole collection of medals, from the Iron Cross (first class) to the German Mother Award presented to women bearing more than five children at once, or something of the sort.

At lunch run into Pat Kirwan, film critic of the *Evening Standard*. Pat says that in spite of knowing nothing about music or cricket he greatly admires Neville Cardus. " But tell me," says Pat, " phwat does he mean by saying some pianist put his leg in front of a straight wan?"

Modern manners. Leaving the Café Royal, J. A. hails a taxi:

TAXI-DRIVER (*hefty, bellicose and quite obviously out for trouble*). Put yer stick dahn! Oo d'yer fink yer wavin' at?

J. A. Sorry. Drive me, please, to Partridge and Cooper's, the stationers in Fleet Street. (*Is driven there; driver has altercations with two bus conductors.*)

J. A. (*descending*). I shan't be two minutes, and then perhaps you'll be good enough to take me to Grape Street.

TAXI-DRIVER. I ain't doin' no bloody waitin'.

J. A. (*patiently*). When I say two minutes I mean two minutes.

TAXI-DRIVER. I don't care wot you says and wot you means. Pay us off, will yer ?

J. A. If you wait you'll get paid and well paid. If you don't wait you won't get paid at all. Here's where I live. (*Hands him an old envelope and goes into shop.*)

TAXI-DRIVER. ! ! ! ! !

J. A. (*reappearing after the stipulated two minutes*). Grape Street. (*Driver says nothing, and on the way saves the life of a jay-walker by a miracle of skill and awareness.*)

TAXI-DRIVER (*arriving at Grape Street*). There oughter be a lor agin them effin' pedestrians. Thenks, Guv'nor. No 'arm meant.

J. A. Smart bit of work ! (*Taxi-driver grins and drives away.*)

Aug. 1 *Wednesday.* Every lifetime has its peak days, and yesterday was one of mine. At 2 A.M.—I was working at *Ego*—the telephone rang. It was Pierre de Rigoult, Contrôleur-Général of the Comédie Française, saying he was just back from Scotland, and that he and Pierre Dux, the Administrateur-Général, wanted me to dine with them that night as they had something to give me. The dinner took place at the Ambassadors, and I was presented with a scroll signed by all the members of the visiting company of the Comédie in order of seniority.

The conversation over dinner—the food was exquisite—was very animated, if sometimes a little difficult. My hosts plied me with embarrassing questions. " Is Gielgud a great actor ? " (They had seen him the night before in *The Circle*.) I got out of this by saying that the piece is not one by which they should judge Mr G., who is not a comedian. De Rigoult said, " You can't see his eyes." Next question : " Has he the scaffolding for a great actor ? " I told them that Mr G. has more poetry than any other actor of our day. " Have you any great actresses in the sense that Clairon, Rachel, and Bernhardt were great ? " I wriggled out of this by asking whether there are any of that kind in France to-day. " Who is your worst good actor ? " Ten names trembled on my lips, and I suppressed them all. (De Rigoult gave a lightning and instantly recognisable imitation of the worst of modern good French actors.) " What, M. Agate, has been your greatest moment in the theatre ? " I said, " Bernhardt as Pelléas rushing on and saying in reply to Mélisande's ' Qui est là ?,' in a voice half-way between famished tigress and strangled dove, ' Moi, moi, et moi ! ' " " And your next greatest ? " I replied, " Any moment in all the hours I spent watching Henry

Irving." De Rigoult said, "You meant that Irving's worst was better than anybody else's best?" I said, "Je vous le jure!" They made the point that to them our English actors have no "jeu." That they do nothing with their lines *qua* actor, and are content to speak them as the author wrote them. I agree, with the exception of Seymour Hicks. Not one English playgoer in a hundred will understand what is meant here. In boxing a blow starts at the back of the heel, travels along the entire torso, and culminates at the point of contact. A French actor delivers each and every line with his whole body, from his toes to his eyebrows. Our theatre is manned by signposts; theirs has the animation of a puppet show. On the political side I gathered that while there is a 1000 to 1 chance that Laval was aiming at circumventing the Hun by *roublardise* (I don't think they believed this), Pétain is the resolute, unforgivable traitor. As for de Gaulle, he is a *maître-gaffeur*, whose career is over.

Having arranged for a car, I enticed my hosts to the Maison McBean, where the Presentation of the Scroll was photographed. Then bundled them with Angus to Grape Street, where we toasted each other's countries in my last bottle of champagne, brought over from France by "Curly," who had charged me to drink it only on a noble occasion. And then I showed them round the Musée Sarah. Dux had not seen S. until the year after her operation, when, in Racine's *Athalie*, she was brought on in a palanquin. (He surprised me by saying that the drama of Corneille is more alive than that of Racine. About the latter: "C'est la tragédie de salon." I told him Edmund Gosse's remark about Racine's verse: "Poetry in silver chains.") De Rigoult didn't see S. until just before her death, and both were very anxious to hear my record of her in *Phèdre*, saying that, so far as they knew, nobody in France, and certainly not the Comédie, possessed it. Now I have two records of this: one very old and worn, the other, hardly used, given me by Ivor Novello. It was, of course, the latter that I presented to Dux, who formally accepted it on behalf of the Comédie. Further libations being indicated, my last bottle of whiskey but one was now requisitioned. Here I had the happy idea of ringing up Jock, telling him to jump out of bed, huddle into some clothes, and run "like the swift hare" to Grape Street. This he did, saying, on his somewhat breathless arrival, "If it's to meet anybody less than George Nathan or Pare Lorentz I'll be gey fashed wi' ye." He was, of course, enchanted, and talked to my visitors in excellent French, with not a little of his native brilliance. The party broke up about 1 A.M., Dux and de Rigoult having to be at Croydon Aerodrome at seven o'clock this morning. By the way, they took with them a certificate from me

Photo Angus McBean

With the Comédie Française

assuring the Censor that Racine never wrote anything subversive or in any way connected with current affairs! Dux has enormous charm—but it is almost as though there were no face of Dux but merely a rallying-ground for all the scamps in Molière. De Rigoult speaks little, but to the point.

The others having departed, and the last bottle of my whiskey now handsomely in action, Jock says, "Jamie, you've ten minutes in which to write down the names of the hundred best players, male and female, of all nationalities since Roscius. And I'll do the same." We finish on time, and comparison shows eighty names common to both lists. There are gaps, of course—I forget Stanislavsky, Joanny, Mrs Oldfield, Sada Yacco, and Adrienne Lecouvreur. Jock's omissions include Macklin, "Little" Robson, De Max, Kitty Clive, Mrs Jordan, Jeanne Granier, and Duse (! !). The concernancy? An idea Jock is going to put up to the Imperial Tobacco Company against the time when they resume their cigarette-cards. To bed about 4 A.M., entirely sober, which I attribute to the greater intoxication keeping the champagne and whiskey within bounds.

Aug. 2 *Thursday.* I have this year delivered two lectures—the first to working lads, the second to a collection of earnest female school-teachers. I propose to reproduce a part of each.

OF KINGS' TREASURIES

I want to talk to you about success. And I am to tell you that it is in the power of every one of you present to achieve success in some capacity. I give the lie to Addison. It *is* in mortals to command success. With this proviso—that if your talent is for bricklaying it is no use trying to write poetry, while if you are a poetic genius you will probably be a poor hand at laying bricks. Don't misunderstand me. I don't say that Burns couldn't plough a straight furrow, or that Bunyan didn't know pot from pan. But can it be doubted that their minds were elsewhere? And this is the point I want you to get. *The wish to be an artist is a blessing if it is coupled with the power to be one. The wish without the power is a curse.* Moreover, the power must be a lasting one. Somerset Maugham has a passage in which he lays it down that every young person possessed of any kind of sensitivity has the power to write one story, paint one picture, compose one tune. Maugham goes on to draw a tragic portrait of the young man who spends the rest of his life trying to force his brain to give something it cannot yield.

It is the practice if not the rule of the medical profession not to tell a patient that he has an incurable disease from which he cannot recover. The notion is to give the poor fellow the heart to go on living. Does this, and should this, apply outside medicine?

Should a critic of books, plays, art, music, tell a young aspirant that he is suffering from the incurable disease known as lack of talent, and will never get better ?

The other day I received a letter from a man at Weston-super-Mare saying :

" Will you have a look at my novel ? It has been returned by sixteen publishers, but I take comfort in the fact that Jane Austen's *Pride and Prejudice* was turned down by as many. However bad you may think it, do not tell me that there is no hope of improvement. I am twenty-four, and shall go on writing until I am eighty. I do not want a wife and children or even happiness. I shall be content to write and starve. There are no sacrifices I am not prepared to make for my work, and I have the constitution of a Balzac. So please let me know what you think about my *Greyhounds in St Paul's*."

I have read this young man's book, whose real title I keep back. Or at least read as much of it as I could endure. The plot was a farrago of absurdity, the characterisation nil, the dialogue null, and the style porridge. The young man was, you see, suffering from the prevailing malady of the age—ambition without qualification. You are anxious to know what I told this young man. I told him the truth. But I also copied out for him something written by my friend James Bridie about a third-rate artist :

" He paints dreadful daubs in a third-rate studio on a third floor. He is full of theory and spleen. He knows that his work is bad and that the world is right in despising it, but this is no comfort to him. He is an artist ; and if he is cross-eyed, colour-blind, and afflicted with the shaking palsy, he must still express the urge which is in him, even if it means insult, blows, and starvation."

I amplified this by saying that the artist to whom painting is its own reward must be satisfied with that reward and not look to have his pictures hung on the line. And therefore I say to all of you, if your daubing and scribbling gives you pleasure, or is a form of self-expression which you need as you need food and sleep, then by all means go on with your daubing and your scribbling. As Chesterton said, I think about golf, if a thing is worth doing at all it is worth doing badly.

I have before me a book entitled *The Truth about Writing*. This is by Mr Cecil Palmer and is published by Heinemann. It contains this passage :

" The point about any book since the world began has not been that the author desperately wanted to write it, but whether somebody could be induced to read it. That some young man or young woman with an itch for scribbling must get a novel out of his or her system is no reason why the poor mutt with an itch for reading should absorb that novel into his system."

Let me elaborate. The only criterion about a book is whether it is good or bad. If it is a bad book, it is of no account that the author lived for six years on bread and water in order to write it. If it is a good book, it doesn't matter that the author wrote it between bouts of drunkenness and on the backs of unpaid bills, keeping himself the while on bread snatched from the mouths of the widowed and the fatherless.

Now I come to the young man who is possessed of genuine talent. And I have to tell him that talent alone won't do. That he is under a moral and artistic obligation either to market his talent or to get somebody else to market it for him. I have no sympathy with the Schubert who could write an immortal work, throw it into a drawer, go out and get fuddled, and leave it to chance to rescue his masterpiece. And I have not the beginnings of sympathy with the theory that the world is full of undiscovered genius. If it is genius it will be discovered. And I have less than no sympathy with the view that people who have made their way in the world owe their success to luck. In what follows I am going to be egotistical, not, I assure you, in order to give rein to my vanity, but because I can speak from facts of which I have first-hand knowledge. It offends me to the very soul when I hear some one saying "Agate has had all the luck." I assure you that any success I have achieved has been striven and plotted for.

I began my writing career first as dramatic critic to the *Daily Dispatch* and then to the *Manchester Guardian*. In those days there were no repertory theatres in Manchester, and the plays were all London successes. The curtain fell at eleven o'clock, the notice had to be in by one, and I was a slow and unready writer. For seven years, and in case I should dry up, I never went to the theatre without having in my pocket an account of the plot derived from the London newspapers on the occasion of the London production. (I never used one of these "insurance" articles.) I then walked about the streets of Manchester from one o'clock in the morning till three in order to correct the proof, and I was at my business of selling calico the same morning at nine o'clock. Was I lucky in that my parents had given me a constitution which could stand this strain? Yes. But I gave my constitution the backing it needed. I did not smoke till I was twenty-one, and had no sex experience until I was twenty-five.

After the war of 1914–18 I kept a shop in Lambeth. Learning that the post of dramatic critic of the *Saturday Review* was likely to become vacant, I asked a well-known dramatic critic whom I met at a dinner to C. P. Scott, editor of the *Manchester Guardian*, if he would introduce me to Filson Young. He said no, so I introduced myself and for twelve months contributed a weekly article over which I took three days, re-writing it as many as six and seven times. I do not think that when Leonard Rees, the editor of the *Sunday Times*, appointed me to succeed Sydney Carroll he asked for the Telephone Directory, closed his eyes, and made a dab with a pencil.

How did I become film critic to the *Tatler* ? In this manner. Learning that the post of film critic to that paper was about to become vacant, I decided to apply. But what chance had I who had no film criticism to show ? So I hatched a little plot. I was dramatic critic to *Eve* at the time, and I suggested to the editor that it would be a novelty if for one week I and the charming lady who did the film criticisms should change over. This was agreed to, and I was cute enough to choose a week in which Emil Jannings appeared in one of his great films. I put into my article everything I knew and more. Armed with this, I marched into the office of the *Tatler* and got the job.

The *Express* ? Some time in the early summer of 1931 my friend Reggie Pound, who was then the feature editor of the *Daily Express*, told me that the position of book-reviewer on that paper was likely to become vacant at any moment—would I keep in touch ? For a fortnight Reggie took no meal alone except breakfast ! About a quarter to twelve one evening at the Club of which we were both members Reggie said, " Can you come over and see Beverley Baxter ? " I said I could and would. I was shown into Baxter's office soon after midnight and came out at half-past twelve the official book-reviewer to the *D.E.* Was that luck ? But I will not weary you. When the publisher of my first *Ego* refused to take my second I found another firm. When the second publisher refused to publish the third *Ego* I found a third publisher. And if I had not found George Harrap I should have had the thing printed and bound at my own expense, and pushed it round the town on a hand-cart. In my time I have been published by eighteen publishers, each of whom I have approached and none of whom has approached me. Is that luck ? I served the B.B.C. as dramatic critic for seven and a half years, beginning with a fee of three guineas a talk and ending with a fee of nineteen guineas. I leave you to guess whether they increased the fee out of pure generosity or because I insisted on it.

To sum up. I may have some capacity as a writer. The fact is that for the last quarter-of-a-century I have worked eleven hours a day over sheer writing and not counting the time I have spent on attending theatres and seeing films and reading books for review. I entirely hold with Thomas Edison, who said, " Genius is one per cent. inspiration and ninety-nine per cent. perspiration." An American novelist has just been asking : Where would Lindbergh have been if he hadn't made Paris but had just dunked himself in the Atlantic and got himself saved and fetched back to Boston on a boat full of codfish ? The answer is that he would have had another go and made Paris. And if he hadn't he wouldn't have been Lindbergh. Wherefore I tell you this. The world is so arranged that you can all make a success of something, while a man who fails has only himself to blame. Remember, too, that while there is only one way of succeeding there are hundreds of recipes for failing—idleness, inattention, carelessness, the notion that "this'll do," lack of initiative, want of drive, absence of tact and patience. But the list is inexhaustible. There is an old saying: Nothing succeeds like success. A great wit once altered this to: Nothing succeeds like excess. Let me tell you boys that nothing is more likely to win success than the will to succeed. Unless it be excess of the will to succeed.

OF QUEENS' GARDENS

The difficulty, my dear young ladies, is that I am the last person who ought to be addressing you to-night. Do I mean that you would have done better to invite my opposite number, Mr Ivor Brown? No. Or that brilliant young critic who will probably be my successor on the *Sunday Times*—although I haven't gone yet—whom I used to call Jock, but now, with the reverence of the master for the pupil, call Mr Dent? Certainly not. Or my revered predecessor, Mr Sydney Carroll, now amply and benevolently presiding over this meeting? No. Let me then reverse my preamble and put it that whereas I am the right person to address you, you are the wrong audience for me to address.

Do you remember that passage in *The Importance of Being Earnest* in which Lady Bracknell asks, "Is this Miss Prism a female of repellent aspect, remotely connected with education?" Dr Chasuble replies, "She is the most cultivated of ladies, and the very picture of respectability." Whereupon Lady Bracknell has her famous "It is obviously the same person." You ladies remind me of this passage, with this difference: that you have the most attractive aspect and at the same time the closest possible connection with education.

Now I have a very limited belief in education. I hold that the indiscriminate use of it does more harm than good. I believe that when Wilde wrote, "Ignorance is like a delicate exotic fruit—touch it, and the bloom is gone," he intended something more than a mere witticism. In my view nine-tenths of, I won't say the human race, but London children, are the worse for education. And for the reason that the education they are given is the wrong sort. So far as I can see, modern education leads the child out of the darkness of healthy ignorance into the denser night of soul-destroying commonness. I do not believe that instruction in my time has had any effect except to increase the number of ways in which the young people of to-day can be common. You teach a young girl to read; and she reads nothing except the film magazines. You give her music lessons; her only interest in music is the bilge spewed by crooners. You teach her to write; at twenty she can hardly spell her name. You teach her deportment; she jitterbugs. You tell her that cleanliness is next to godliness; she covers her face with messes and her nails with filth. Explore her mind to its inmost crannies and you will find nothing there except curiosity about the latest hair-dye.

You have not begun to teach the average London child how to speak its own language. So far as I can observe, no child has been taught not to say, " You was at the pictures last night, wasn't you ? " And I am under the impression that " between you and I " is in more general use than it was when I was a boy. You have not even taught these young women to speak up so that they can be heard. I am a constant user of the telephone, and I am not deaf. Yet twenty times a day I have to say to the young woman at the other end, " Speak up, miss ; who wants me ? " You have not taught the young girl to believe that the ladder of culture is more important than ladderless stockings. She is content to be common. You have not persuaded her not to want to be common. You have not convinced her that education is a good thing.

And now I am going to leave this question of education, merely remarking that if I had my will, young girls would be taught nothing but cooking, sewing, and how to keep a house clean, and young boys no more than the trades by which they ultimately hope to support the young girls. This as to nineteen-twentieths of the youthful population. It would be left to the discretion of teachers to pick out the odd five per cent. who can be educated. For note this. Before you can educate a mind you must have a mind to educate. It is a part of democratic cant to pretend that Nature has been fair and equitable in her distribution of mind. She has not ; she has been infinitely capricious. Nineteen-twentieths of the population in this country has no more mind—I am not talking of soul—than a lamp-post.

Now let me be logical. I am talking of the cultural potentialities of the mob, which has no more connection with the ultimate value of culture than the shape of the mob's nose or the size of its feet and hands. I agree that the common people, to use a convenient term, have put up, are putting up, and will put up as long as there is a man or woman of them alive, the most heroic battle in our history, on sea, on land, and in the air. That does not mean that they are susceptible to culture. I also agree that a young Bloomsbury æsthete who can quote Eliot and Joyce by the yard may be an unspeakable skunk. I say that education should aim at teaching nineteen-twentieths of the young the best way of making beds, ploughing fields, and being good citizens generally. And limit anything more complicated to the odd twentieth.

And now I realise that what I have been asked to talk about is not education but the drama. Well, what do you want to know about the drama ? Must I tell you the plots of Shakespeare's plays, how many times they have been performed, and who acted in them ? Or give a list of the minor Elizabethan and Jacobean playwrights ? Or tell you that Wycherley came before Congreve, and not the other way round as most people think ? Or how there was a long dull period in the nineteenth century in which nine-tenths of our plays were borrowed from the French, or, as Henry

Morley said, were translated, or adapted, or freely altered from the *Pomme Pourrie* of MM. Péché and Bonbon? How, on December the 9th, 1892, the intellectual theatre was inaugurated by the first performance of Mr Shaw's *Widowers' Houses*? How, six months later, this was followed by *The Second Mrs Tanqueray*? How, in 1906, Galsworthy with his *Silver Box* ushered in a new era of play-writing? And how, simultaneously, the Irish movement, headed by Lady Gregory and J. M. Synge, brought enchantment to our shores? But all of this—indeed, any of it—would be dull talking for me, and dull hearing for you. Besides, I very much want to talk to you about something else. In a word, I want to discuss with you my own educational limitations.

Let me confess that my spiritual home is the Café Royal; at least I sup there every night. And every night I hear the young people around me talking an art-jargon I am wholly unable to understand. What they are talking about is something which I am going to call Modernity in Art. I have always believed that an artist, whether he be poet, composer, painter, must be able to make his meaning clear to anybody of average cultural intelligence. Shakespeare and Milton and Wordsworth and Shelley made whatever they had to say perfectly clear. It is true that there have been poets—Donne and Browning, for instance—who were often highly, some have said needlessly, obscure. But in so far as they were not *trying* to be obscure, I hold that they failed in this part of their work to do their job perfectly. I doubt whether there was ever anything in Beethoven, with a few exceptions, which was not reasonably clear to the really intelligent and understanding listener of his day. Or in Wagner. Or in Berlioz or in Debussy. Or did not become so in the next generation. In the realm of painting I find comparatively little difficulty. You can always see what the old masters were getting at. You may not be enthralled by a painting of a side of beef. You may think as I do, that the Rokeby Venus shows a woman taking up an elaborate, unnecessary, and entirely unconvincing pose merely to look at herself in a mirror. Yet you have no difficulty in recognising that these two pictures represent (*a*) a side of beef, and (*b*) a woman lying on her side. Similarly, in the famous *Baptism of Christ*, by Piero della Francesca, the fifteenth-century Umbrian, you have no difficulty in recognising the figure in the background as that of a man pulling off his shirt prior to immersion, in exactly the same way that the modern footballer discards his jersey. Now there must be advancement in the arts as in everything else. We cannot stop it. And by advancement I mean not enhancement but complication, for I do not think that the world has improved one jot on the poetry of Shakespeare, the music of Bach, the painting of Michael Angelo. Young ladies, I said at the beginning of this talk that I was the last person who ought to address you. I repeat this. I live in Queen Alexandra Mansions, and should be quite content if Art had stopped short at the cultivated court of the Empress Alexandra.

To be perfectly frank, I haven't the slightest desire to read any novel later than Henry James, see any play later than Ibsen, hear a note of music after Richard Strauss, or look at any canvas after Renoir. I can only hope that the *Sunday Times* doesn't get to hear of this, since if it does it will sack me, and rightly.

Aug. 3 *Friday.* Picking up the telephone this morning, I overhear Leo on the extension talking to Norman Newman : " Really, doctor, you must prescribe for James something more than your boluses and bromides. That blasted *Ego*'s killing him. He thinks of nothing else, it robs him of his appetite, and drives him to drink. He has to take sleeping-draughts to forget it, and even then Arthur Bates tells me he hears him get up in the middle of the night and go into the study. Once he followed him and saw him fish the damn' thing out and start correcting it. He was at it for over an hour. I beg of you, doctor, make him send the stuff away, beyond reach. You will, doctor ? Thank you, thank you." There is a point at which fiddle becomes faddle. Balzac's painter, Frenhofer, dibbled and dabbled at the portrait of his mistress until nothing was left except a foot. How, since Bank Holiday looms, am I to prevent the orgy of " Frenhofering " that threatens me ? I don't forget that *Le Chef-d'œuvre inconnu* ends : " Le lendemain, Porbus, inquiet, revint voir Frenhofer, et apprit qu'il était mort dans la nuit, après avoir brûlé ses toiles." Or that Pope got himself into such a state over his translation of the *Iliad* that he wished himself hanged. J. A. hanging himself through too much *Ego* would be a charming irony.

Dine at the Savoy with André Bernheim and his wife. B. is a good-looking man in the forties, with white hair and a position in the French Ministry of Information. His pretty wife speaks French with an accent which intrigues me so much that finally I ask what it is. She says, " The purest Connemara ! " The other guest was Dorothy Dickson. She has the Victorian quality of *graciousness* which the modern beauty, pert and provocative, lacks. Reminded Dorothy how, years ago, Tibby Griffith had ranked her dancing with the frescoes of Michael Angelo, Milton's *Paradise Lost*, and Wagner's *Ring*. How I corrected Tibby, saying that the last word about D. D.'s dancing was Florizel's remark to Perdita about wishing she were " a wave o' the sea who might ever do nothing but that." Dorothy said, " Yours was the better criticism ; any woman would have preferred Tibby's." Later B. drove us to Paddington, where D. smiled her way through the crowds and somebody said, " She'll get a seat all right, even if it's in the cab with the engine-driver ! "

Photo Felix H. Man

Morning's at Three

Then to the Bernheims' flat in Charles Street, where we drank marc of extraordinary potency. A delightful evening, at the end of which my host presented me with a photograph of Irving as Vanderdecken in *The Flying Dutchman*.

Aug. 4 *Saturday.* Lunch with Hamlet, who says, " I would give all literature for one rare meal a day. I wouldn't swap the aural and visual arts, which I rate higher than the literary." Also : " The moderns are born great ; the romantics achieved greatness ; the classics have had greatness thrust upon them." And again : " My approach to the piano is to make it sound like the harpsichord." During lunch he asks for my opinion of

STONE AND FLESH

A Fragment

She-idol, plump and solemn, beetle-browed ;
Naked unendingly, awaiting Pan ;
An inhumanity of rock, unploughed
By casual engine or ungracious man ;
A bulging, lustless, super-fecund womb,
Swaying and sagging over tub-like thighs—
An acre of incarnate elbow-room—
As sexlessly insipid as pork pies.

And an amusing hour ends with the following dialogue :

HAMLET. May I introduce you to a friend who insists that the best art of the twentieth century has come out of the trumpet of a jazz-musician called Bix Beiderbecke ?

J. A. No.

Aug. 5 *Sunday.* Hamlet won't take no for an answer. Which finds me lunching at the Imperial Hotel with his three young friends. These turn out to be : Hugh Manning (twenty-five, and the Roger Livesey type), hoping to be an actor. Julian Holland (twenty, type of East in *Tom Brown's Schooldays*), admirer of Bix Beiderbecke, has a job at the B.B.C., and hopes to be a playwright. He and Hamlet at one time thought of a drama with Satan as the Creator and Christ as Fallen Angel, but dropped it. David Bench (a myopic, charming, Beetlesome child of seventeen) goes in for Yoga, spends the greater part of his time contemplating the tip of his nose which he can actually see, hopes to reduce life to a permanent blank, has written a book on *Civilisation without Activity*. Has never heard of " Palinurus," but when I quote " Others merely live ; I vegetate," is much impressed. Bring them round to Grape Street for coffee, and play them my " Strauss-Parodie " record, causing the Beiderbecke fan to say that this is white ecstasy and therefore inferior to the Negro article. They are immensely tickled by Leo, and he takes to them at once. In spite of their nonsense they are pleasant, well-mannered, engaging creatures, and not at all conventional Bloomsbury. Even when, at lunch, I produce a large sheet of paper headed "Bêtises," *and proceed to make notes*, they are in no way disconcerted. In view of their non-resentment at my treating them as precocious babies, am considering a little book to be called *L'Art d'être Grand-Oncle*.

Aug. 6 *Monday.* Letter from George Lyttelton:

Finndale House
Grundisburgh
Woodbridge
Suffolk
Aug. 5, 1945

DEAR JAMES AGATE,

It is many weeks since we have communicated, but what of that? You, I know, are in a perpetual state of overwork, and I hesitate to write, knowing that you will answer and give yourself so much less time for adding the final touch to what a host of readers is awaiting. When my old tutor, Arthur Benson, said something to Henry James in similar circumstances, H. J. instantly replied, "My dear Arthur, my mind is so constantly and continuously bent upon you in wonder and goodwill that any change in my attitude could only be the withholding of a perpetual and settled felicitation." What is that in Agatese? But the immediate occasion of my writing is your letter to *The Times* on Tom Richardson and your bold and welcome exaltation of artistic truth over factual. There are two very similar examples. George Hirst told me that he never said, "Wilfred, we'll get them by singles," when Rhodes joined him with 15 to get for the last wicket in the Oval Test Match 1902. And Rhodes told my nephew that Trumper never said, "For God's sake, Wilfred, give me a moment's peace," in the Sydney Test Match in 1903, though of course both these remarks *should* have been made. Must all the great "last words" go the way of Pitt's "My country," etc.!

I see Mr Clifford Bax has been in a high state of indignation with dramatic critics. Are there many who foam at the mouth when your name is mentioned? I expect it is all right when they meet you. "Having no good opinion of the fellow, I was resolved not to be pleased. . . . But the dog was so very comical that I was obliged to lay down my knife and fork, throw myself back upon my chair and fairly laugh it out." I won't insult you by saying where that comes from. I hope *that* was not touched up by James B.

The Election! Surely we haven't altered very much from Eatanswill, or is that the reaction of a mugwump? I don't think eighty years of education have done much for the sovereign people

—judging by the arguments that they seem to think good ones. My daughter is just back from Potsdam and has brought me a piece of Hitler's own table as a souvenir !

Yours ever,
GEORGE LYTTELTON

I reply :

Queen Alexandra Mansions, W.C.2
August 6th, 1945

DEAR GEORGE LYTTELTON,

I take my pen in a hand which, a few hours ago, touched that of Field-Marshal Montgomery, my admiration for whom is great, though less than that of the Southampton typist who, after being presented to Robert Taylor, vowed she would never wash her right hand again.

The encounter—alas, there was no photographer to record it—took place in the passage behind C. B. Fry's box at Lord's during the Victory match against Australia. I was one of a party which included Clifford Bax, Eric Gillett, Douglas Jerrold, R. C. Robertson-Glasgow, a witty poet called Denzil Batchelor, and other great and semi-great personages, including the Duchess of Malfi from the Haymarket Theatre. As I entered, Clifford put a finger to his lips, pointed to the Duchess, and raised his eyebrows as much as to say, " What about that *gaffe* now ? " I replied, also in pantomime, " I am James Agate still ! "

If there is one thing I enjoy more than anything else it is listening to experts talking shop, always provided the shop is not cats, postage-stamps, or motor-cars. Fry said about Whitington : " I'll tell you how that fellow will get out. Every stroke should be a piece of ' swing,' which means that the poise of the body must be *forward* in sequent sympathy with the swing. Every now and again this fellow plays a forward stroke with the body poised backwards. This means that he is bound to pop one up sooner or later." C. B. had hardly finished speaking when Whitington did exactly as he had predicted, and was caught at forward short-leg.

During a patch of dull play Fry told me this about the famous Ashes match of 1882. In the 1920 edition of the Badminton *Cricket*—the original of which was largely written by your family—" Plum " Warner writes, " The true story of this match has never yet been told." Two pages of magnificent reporting follow, though even here " Plum," out of the kindness of his heart, says nothing about the essential thing—the quarrel between Spofforth and Grace. W. G., as you know, was up to every trick of the game, including one or two of his own. In the second Australian innings Murdoch played a ball to leg and ran a single, the wicket-keeper, Lyttelton—your uncle ?—going after the ball and returning it to Grace moving to the stumps from point. Jones going out of his ground to pat the pitch, Grace promptly broke the wicket and Jones was given out. Later, in the pavilion, Spofforth said to

W. G., " By God, you deserve to lose the match for that. And, by God, you shall ! " Fry said he got the story from " Plum," who had it from Murdoch. In his, Fry's, view, the umpire ought not to have given Jones out—he was not attempting a run, and was justified in thinking that the ball, being landed in the wicket-keeper's hands, was dead. And that W. G., by going to the wicket, had constituted himself wicket-keeper within the spirit of the rules.

Had a few words with " Plum." D'you remember Motley on Thackeray ? " He has the appearance of a colossal infant, smooth, shiny, a roundish face, a sweet but rather piping voice, with something of the childish treble about it." This is a perfect description of " Plum " to-day. Told me that with ten hours of sleep, a tonic, and vast quantities of milk, he manages to keep going. Actually he looks very fit and well set for his century.

I went to Lord's partly in deference to the doctor, who has ordered me three weeks' rest. The labour we delight in physics brain-fag. Meaning that I am working only on *Ego*. I would invite myself down to see you if I thought you would like it and I could get there. The difficulties in the way of the latter are insuperable ; I will not stand in trains, and I cannot get petrol. And then there is a third difficulty. Britten's opera, *Peter Grimes*, the scene of which, as you probably know, is laid in Aldeburgh (or Aldeborough), has given me a phobia about Suffolk. So much so that in future if I can't go to Norfolk except via Suffolk I shan't go to Norfolk.

I entirely agree with you about the sovereign people. Coming back from Lord's, I heard one bedizened little baggage say to another, " I ses, not a lady wouldn't do it, I ses." And you will be amused to know that I interrupted this letter to ring up the Duty Officer at the B.B.C. to ask what the hell the Corporation meant by letting some ignorant female tell their ten million listeners that Oscar Straus was " yet another member of the Strauss family " ? Thus is history written and error perpetuated.

Ever,

JAMES AGATE

Aug. 8
Wednesday.

Again from George Lyttelton :

Finndale House
Grundisburgh
Woodbridge
Suffolk

Aug. 7, 1945

DEAR JAMES AGATE,

The worst (or best ?) of writing to you is that your reply always demands another, and so it goes on. You must often be in danger of being snowed under by your correspondents, though I find it hard to imagine any storm which you would not ride !

Thank you for the Spofforth incident, which I did not know,

though I often heard my Uncle Alfred talk of that match. The story is fairly fully told in Wisden, but not, of course, Spofforth's outburst; it adds that after a lot of angry talk, "a prominent member of the Australian XI admitted that he should have done the same thing, had he been in Grace's place." The old man had a good deal in him of an earlier champion, Lord F. Beauclerk: "My lord he comes next and will make you all stare With his odd little tricks a long way from fair." How did "It isn't cricket" become the most self-consciously high-minded of all verdicts? I never met Charles Fry till last year when "Plum" gave us lunch. He was very good company—made some very illuminating remarks on cricket, and a few strikingly wayward and heretical, though I fancy many of them were made to pull "Plum's" leg—*e.g.*, that Bardsley, Tip Foster, and Woolley were not among the twenty-five best bats of the last fifty years, that W. Gunn was better than Shrewsbury, that Tom Richardson's great bag of victims was largely composed of tail-enders (quite untrue), etc.

Thank you for Motley on "Plum." Excellent! "P.'s" great merit is that he has never become pompous or jealous or querulous as so many great games players do. Do you realise what a fine team could be made of cricketers who committed suicide? They don't on the whole grow old gracefully. In old days when my uncles talked of players they had known the reminiscences were always ending "died of drink."

I am sorry about your Suffolk complex, because we should much like to see you here, though like every one else we have no staff and roughish food. I suppose you think the county is entirely inhabited by "the lame, the blind, and—far the happier they!—the moping idiot and the madman gay." The original Peter Grimes was a much grimmer figure than I gather he is in the opera—a sort of male Mrs Brownrigg, who "wanted some obedient boy to stand, And bear the blows of his outrageous hand." We are about ten miles from Aldeburgh, in Fitzgerald's country rather than Crabbe's. I think I must soon take a hand in that stuffy little correspondence about the rose-tree on F.'s grave at Boulge.

Forgive all this rigmarole. Let me end with a bit of treasure trove which at any rate I know you will like if you have never seen it. Some one told it to the late John Bailey as the sort of specimen of Swinburne's humour which Gosse ought to have put in his Life and didn't—an invention of Swinburne's of Queen Victoria's confession to the Duchess of Kent of her one lapse from virtue, put for some Swinburnian reason into French: "Ce n'était pas un prince; ce n'était pas un milord, ni même Sir R. Peel. C'était un misérable du peuple, un nommé Wordsworth, qui m'a récité des vers de son *Excursion* d'une sensualité si chaleureuse qu'ils m'ont ébranlée—et je suis tombée." Perhaps it was a good thing he was not made Poet Laureate.

Yours ever,

George Lyttelton

And again from J. A.:

*Queen Alexandra Mansions, W.C.*2
August 8*th*, 1945

DEAR GEORGE LYTTELTON,

Your Queen Victoria nonsense is lovely.

I agree with Fry. Neville Cardus is responsible for most of the hocus-pocus about Woolley: "To add up the runs made by Woolley—why, it is as though you were to add up the crotchets and quavers written by Mozart." Perhaps I was unlucky with F. W., who, when I saw him, never did anything but get himself beautifully out, as Henry James would have said.

Nothing more of interest, except that at five minutes to twelve to-night I rang up the B.B.C.—this is becoming a habit—asked for the Duty Officer, and harangued him thus: "Sir, the fact that a Labour Government is in power is not a reason that your Corporation should muddy and defile the well of English language. Your announcer has just told us that 'The Government's no right' to do something or other. And 'It's only been told to-day that Mr Churchill. . . .' Sir, would you have Lady Macbeth say, 'The raven himself's hoarse,' or Macbeth, 'This supernatural soliciting can't be ill, can't be good'? Would you at your Morning Service say, 'Almighty and most merciful Father; We've erred, and strayed from thy ways like lost sheep. We've followed too much the devices and desires of our own hearts. We've offended against thy holy laws. We've left undone those things . . .'" And I slammed the receiver down without waiting to hear his excuses. Alan Dent tells me that the reason the B.B.C. won't employ me any more is that they think the miserable twopence-halfpenny they give for a talk should close the talker's mouth. Between you and me, I don't mind; they need me far more than I need them. Wait till the centenary of, say, Madge Kendal, when they will be on their knees to me—if I am still alive—to tell the public how she acted. And I shall say, "My dear Talks Department, ask young Footle and young Tootle. I will give you one tip, however. Tell F. and T. that Madge K. was not Harry Kendall's mother. For one thing, the spelling's different."

Ever,
JAMES AGATE

Aug. 9
Thursday.

Again from the Sudan:

2245367 *A.C. Zakon, C.B.*
28 *S.P.*, *c/o* 115 *Wing*
R.A.F., *M.E.F.*
1.8.45

MY DEAR MAN,

This particularly odious form of address is prompted wholly by your addressing me as your dear boy. I share the average distaste of the average male of twenty-one years (which, by the way, I attain this month—just a bit too late to do my duty for the Conservatives) at being called anyone's dear boy.

I must thank you for the expedition of your reply, a rare thing in these days, and inform you that I am suitably deflated by your completely opposite view of W. J. Locke. By the time I reach your venerable antiquity no doubt I shall have similar good taste. My chief reason for writing to you is to ask you to cast your magic over the vast public you variously entertain or annoy and ask a great favour of them. We have a painfully small library on the camp, consisting, unfortunately, mainly of detective stories. Oh yes, we also have a novel or two by the authoress Mrs Humphry Ward!

This state of affairs is not a dazzling outlook for the men on the station, and the situation is not enhanced by our long leisure hours. Owing to the intense heat most of the year round, we do not work after 1 P.M. This leaves us nine hours' spare time until lights out. We are lucky if we get one film during the week. Apart from a small native village, we are in the wide open spaces. As you will appreciate, such long periods with nothing to do are painfully boring. Imagine yourself in the situation; not more than five decent books, which one has read at least twice, within several hundred miles. "Desert Island Discs" has nothing on us.

My request is that you put an appeal to your readers to send us some books, specifically addressed. The normal result of a Books for the Services Fund is that the big stations take the best of them and leave the small stations with nothing but almost unadulterated tripe. Mr Agate, if you did this you would ensure a hundred happy airmen praying for you every night. Such cheap salvation must surely appeal to you.

I await, with some apprehension, your reply, and meanwhile remain,

Yours sincerely,
CHARLES B. ZAKON

I answer:

Queen Alexandra Mansions, W.C.2
August 9th, 1945

DEAR AIRCRAFTMAN ZAKON,

I feel for you, and think of a passage in Kipling's *Soldiers Three* which runs:

"There was the Canteen, of course, and there was the Temperance Room with the second-hand papers in it; but a man of any profession cannot read for eight hours a day in a temperature of 96 or 98 in the shade, running up sometimes to 103 at midnight. Very few men, even though they get a pannikin of flat, stale, muddy beer and hide it under their cots, can continue drinking for six hours a day. One man tried, but he died, and nearly the whole regiment went to his funeral because it gave them something to do. It was too early for the excitement of fever or cholera. The men could only wait and wait and wait, and watch the shadow of the barrack creeping across the blinding white dust. That was a gay life."

I imagine that to you 103 degrees represents the cool of the evening !

As you say, I am old ; indeed, half-way between second childishness and oblivion. This being so, infantile games are permitted me ; for example, one I have just played. Reading your appeal, it occurred to me that it would be fun to make you and your friends a present of a little library, each book corresponding to a letter of the alphabet. Leaping—perhaps " crumbling " would be the better phrase—out of bed, I first ransacked my own shelves, this resulting in some ten or fifteen volumes. I then hied me—" creaked my way " would be better—to the Charing Cross Road. I don't pretend that what I am sending you are the twenty-six best books in the English language. If they were I shouldn't send them. Let me remind you of an incident in Dumas's great novel. Fouquet, about to give a banquet and sending his major-domo to market, discovers him at the wine-merchant's placing an order for the cheapest *vin ordinaire*. Being reproached, the major-domo answers, " Sir, this wine is for your meaner guests, who would be offended by that to which they are unaccustomed." I quote from memory. So the books I am sending you will not all be the best. Some are masterpieces and some are not.

To change the note a little. When, at some future time, you hear people say what a selfish, curmudgeonly old boor I was, say that in Aleppo once. . . . You see how my mind wanders. What you might like to say is that once, on a day in August, I devoted some six hours to lightening the boredom of a band of unknown airmen, hoping that this might discharge, say, one millionth part of the debt I and all old fogeys and stay-at-homes owe to the youth of this country.

Yours sincerely,
JAMES AGATE

P.S. A bright idea glimmers in a corner of this benumbed brain. This is to use for packing of the parcels—there will be three or four—some score or more of Penguins.[1]

[1] Months later as *Ego* 8 was going through the press I received the following :

2245367 *A.C. Zakon, C.B.*
R.A.F. Unit, Malakal
M.E.F.

DEAR METHUSELAH AGATE,

I thank you for your letter of the 9th August. The personnel of this camp and myself are overwhelmed with gratitude for the trouble you have taken in order to send us some readable literature. The appearance of a venerable wraith, muffled to the ears and probably wearing red-flannel combinations, tottering unsteadily down the Charing Cross Road as it (the wraith) battled valiantly against the mild mid-August zephyrs, must have presented an unusual and alarming sight to the casual passer-by. Have no fear, Mr Agate ; whatever your other readers may say about you, I shall always think of you as a sort of Deus ex Queen Alexandra Mansions—somewhat dilapidated, but none-the-less a kindly god.

I remain, with all good wishes,
Yours gratefully incerely,
CHARLES B. ZAKON

Aug. 11 *Saturday.* Epigram from Clifford Bax:

> Thou hast conquered, O damn'd Galileo! Hiroshima is grey with thy breath.
> Now Science will atomise all things, and the arts are foredoomed to their death.

Aug. 12 *Sunday.* Taking the worst possible view of the atomic bomb, I still don't believe that it can "reduce the earth to a scorched orb circling the sun but with no one to distinguish night from day." There still remains the Law of Diminishing Returns. Which means that when the last bomb has been dropped—last because there are no more technicians left to make another—there will still be pockets of humanity in Greenland, Ecuador, Senegambia, Franz Josef Land, China, and the Australian Bush. The worst that could happen, then, would be the necessity to build civilisation all over again. And probably build it for the better. (I just don't believe that Eskimos, pigmies, and head-hunters could produce an eyesore as monstrous as the Odeon Cinema in Leicester Square.) It may be that Shakespeare's plays and Beethoven's symphonies will be lost. This would be a pity, though I think I might miss lesser things more. What was it that Elia resented that death should take from him? Not the major passions, but a trivial catalogue ending with "innocent vanities, and jests, and *irony itself*." I should hate to think that fun itself goes out with life. Somebody, somewhere, sometime, is going to re-discover that all the world's a stage, that the quality of mercy is not strained, and that the uses of adversity are sweet. Just as somebody, somewhere, sometime, is going to write a play to prove that ambition, jealousy, and tyranny don't pay in the long run. What I should hate to lose is the irrecoverable oddity. Say that passage in which Coventry Patmore describes his first sight of Leigh Hunt:

> I, being at seventeen or eighteen years of age, or perhaps younger, an admirer of the *Indicator* and *Rimini*, set off with a letter from my father, an old friend of the poet, informing him of my ambition to see him. Arriving at his house, a very small one in a small square somewhere in the extreme west, after a walk of some five or six miles, I was informed that the poet was at home, and asked me to sit down until he came to me. This he did after I had waited in the little parlour at least two hours, when the door was opened and a most picturesque gentleman, with hair flowing nearly or quite to his shoulders, a beautiful velvet coat and a Vandyck collar of lace about a foot deep, appeared, rubbing his hands and smiling ethereally, and saying without a word of

preface or notice of my having waited so long, " This is a beautiful world, Mr Patmore ! "

To cut it short, my attitude to the atomic bomb and the hurly-burly it is going to create is entirely Skimpolean ! " I am capable of looking on and of being interested. I *do* look on, and I *am* interested. What more can I do ? "

Aug. 13 *Monday.* Found this human document in Shaftesbury Avenue to-night :

Saturday 11*th August*

DEAR NELLIE,

I would like to thank you very much for your nice letter I was glad to see your handwriting once again. Well dear how is the world serving you these days alright I hope. Yes Nell I saw Bill but he did not mention any thing about going away. I had a letter from his mum she said that he might be home for a week end so I guess there was something going on may be Ted will meet him hope so for our sake yes Nell I do pray for them they are only kids yet I dont know what they feel like poor kids. Still Nell we will have to trust in the Lord to send them back to us. Well Nell I must tell you this there is a new lot of U.S. boys here now I am lucky I have pick up with a nice one I only wish you were here with me. This blokes name is Bob I have been out with him every night since he has been here I shall be sorry when he goes I have got to see him tonight I may be going to the dance and then I am going to the show on Tuesday so you can guess I am having a good time. Well Nell the news has just started I am waiting for them to tell us it is peace.

Cheerio,

GERT

Aug. 14 *Tuesday.* At twelve to-night it happens. To use Osbert Sitwell's phrase, " those clever, patriotic little apes of Japanese " have stopped " hurling themselves about." Japan has surrendered. And then the Prime Minister orates in a manner which drives home the *inartistry* of the Election. Where is the voice that launch'd a thousand ships and burnt the topless towers of Berlin, Hiroshima, and Nagasaki ? Where, in the new P.M.'s punctilious, careful accents, is the old leader's " swell of soul " ? Pathetic anti-climax—the curtain falling on a great actor, and the understudy taking the call ! One small glass of brandy, and since I find I can't sleep I go to my shelves and take down *The Return of Sherlock Holmes.*

It was, then, in a year, and even in a decade, that shall be nameless, that upon one Tuesday morning in autumn we found two visitors of European fame within the walls of our humble

> room in Baker Street. The one, austere, high-nosed, eagle-eyed, and dominant, was none other than the illustrious Lord Bellinger, twice Premier of Britain. The other, dark, clear-cut, and elegant, hardly yet of middle age, and endowed with every beauty of body and of mind, was the Right Honourable Trelawney Hope, Secretary for European Affairs, and the most rising statesman in the country.

And just as I am wondering whether Messrs Attlee and Bevin would recognise their honourable selves in the foregoing, the row starts. The plebs has got out of bed, and is on its way to Piccadilly Circus to celebrate.

PEACE

PEACE

1945

VJ Day. It is twenty minutes past eleven in the morning of the Greatest Day in History. H.M. the King has driven in procession to Westminster to open Parliament, and on the air nothing but antiquated musical comedies with the alternative of "X and his Apache Band" in "Fête Tzigane." Wonderful! Amazing! *Gigantesque!* Where, in God's name, are the L.P.O., the L.S.O., the Hallé Orchestra, the B.B.C. Orchestra? What has become of Beecham, Cameron, Barbirolli, Boult? Why weren't orchestras and conductors standing by? *Everybody, even Cabinet Ministers, knew it was about to happen.* Here, I suggest, is a programme the German wireless might have sent out if Germany had won:

DEUTSCHLAND ÜBER ALLES
DIE WACHT AM RHEIN
HITLERMARSCH
SIEGFRIED'S FUNERAL MARCH
(*In Memory of the Fallen*)
RIENZI : OVERTURE
EROICA SYMPHONY
EIN HELDENLEBEN
EIN FESTE BURG IST UNSER GOTT

The programme to begin at seven A.M. and continue till midnight, with relays of live orchestras and conductors and no nonsense about recording. People tell me the English win wars because they like musical comedy, and the Germans lose wars because they like music. I don't believe it. In the meantime my staff has the day off. I hate crowds, the Café is inaccessible, and it is raining. Nothing remains except to munch some stale bread and staler cheese, break my rule about the day-time non-consumption of alcohol, *and work*!

Aug. 21 *Tuesday.* At the revival to-night of *Lady Windermere's Fan* I asked Lady Alexander, exquisite as ever and looking like the lids of Juno's eyes, whether in the 'nineties peeresses at private dances wore tiaras. She said, "They wore them at the tea-table!"

Aug. 22 *Wednesday.* Lunch with Bertie van Thal at the Savoy, where a really extraordinary coincidence happens. (First let me say that Bertie's life at the Food Office is one unbroken sea of milk troubles. Either London is drowning in milk and there are no bottles to put it in, or there is an avalanche of bottles and no milk.) Now for the coincidence. At the next table is Kay Hammond with her little boy. Gathering that he is fond of cricket, I beckon him over and tell him how I once bowled out W. G. Grace. Whereupon John Clements leans across and says, " This is unbelievable. In the lounge before lunch I was telling John how at a public dinner my father heard W. G. say that on the sands at Blackpool he had been bowled first ball by a little boy of seven whose name he never knew ! "

Aug. 25 *Saturday.* Geoffrey Bennett rang up late to-night to say that at Wolverhampton Show this afternoon that old gentleman, Ego, came out of his retirement and, exercising all his old charm, romped home in a class for private turn-outs.

Aug. 28 *Tuesday.* Clifford Bax's dinner to C. B. Fry. Last night at the Ivy. Seating : Fry, Ernest Short, Guy Butler (holder of the world's 300 yards record for nine years), R. H. Howe, Clifford, Arnold Bax, Denzil Batchelor, J. A. Fry was in great form and as difficult as ever to tell anything to. He is like R. L. S.'s Cockshot in the essay " Talk and Talkers "— " Let me see. Give me a moment, I *should* have some theory for that." C. B. doesn't need to see and he doesn't want a moment. I told the table about my conjuring tricks, and he at once explained them. I gathered that they have something to do with the Ivy's electric wiring system. Said he had no regrets on retiring from first-class cricket. " The big matches were fun, but I never want to see Leicester and Derby again as long as I live." Went on to tell us how he was thinking of a new career. Racing. " I shall go to a racing stables for a year, after which I shall be an immense success." Denzil Batchelor said quickly, " What as, Commander ? Owner, trainer, jockey, or *horse* ? " D. B. also said, " What a treat it would be to hear some B.B.C. announcer say, ' Ladies and gentlemen, it is now 7.55 P.M. As we have nothing worth putting on the air we shall close down till to-morrow morning. Good night, everybody. Good night.' "

During dinner the question arose as to the world's funniest book.

" Most humorous " were, I think, the exact words. The voting went as follows, each diner being allowed two votes.

Alice in Wonderland	4 votes
The Diary of a Nobody	2 ,,
Vice Versa (Anstey)	1 vote
Eliza (Barry Pain)	1 ,,
Eliza's Husband (Barry Pain)	1 ,,
Don Quixote	1 ,,
Pride and Prejudice	1 ,,
Experiences of an Irish R. M.	1 ,,
Candide	1 ,,
Tartarin de Tarascon	1 ,,
Tartarin sur les Alpes	1 ,,
Berry and Co. (Dornford Yates)	1 ,,

No mention of Amanda Ros, Anita Loos, or Damon Runyon. And not a word for *Pickwick.*

Later somebody carried me off to a night-club—my first venture in this kind. From the fact that one had to go burrowing in the ground under a garage to deposit one's hat, and climb three flights of stairs, I gathered that the place was extremely smart. Lighting a deep heliotrope, reminding me of the little café in Harlem called Moon-Glow. Instead of goings-on to shock Heliogabalus a frigid propriety. Numberless and immaculate waiters. And, of course, too much band. Boring. Or would have been if a clever and rising young actor had not expounded to me, at length, his plans for starting a repertory theatre.

Aug. 30 *Thursday.* Twelve jeweller's shops failing to produce what Old Eccles called " a jewelled gaud," I have arranged with the *Daily Telegraph* to insert the following in its Personal Column :

Elderly dramatic critic requires baby's rattle.

Sept. 1 *Saturday.* In a letter from Neville Cardus :

I am sick of Australia ; compared with Sydney or Melbourne, as far as culture or common sense go, Rochdale is as Athens under Pericles. I have not heard ONE witty remark from an Australian in five and a half years. *Dein bin ich, Vater !—rette mich !*

Ever,

NEVILLE

Sept. 2 *Sunday.* Letter to Jock:

*Queen Alexandra Mansions, W.C.*2

September 2*nd*, 1945

DEAR JOCK,

If I had not passed a self-denying ordinance in the matter of work I should now be setting about a formal essay entitled " A Gossip on a Novel of Charles Dickens." However, I compromise with a letter. And naturally a letter to you, who awakened my too-long-dormant interest in *Dombey and Son.* I have read this in bed every night since your letter to me in the earlier part of this summer. What a masterpiece! Twenty times have I had to put it down through sheer excess of admiration.

Were you at any time struck by the resemblance of Edith Granger to Hedda Gabler? This first occurred to me when Cleopatra says, " The sword wears out the what's-its-name." And Edith says coldly, " The scabbard, perhaps." On the next page is Cleopatra's superb remark about Henry VIII: " Such a picture, too, he makes, with his dear little peepy eyes and his benevolent chin!" You remember that Chesterton singles this out? It is, I think, the best thing in the book, with the possible exception of Cousin Feenix's remark on the occasion of his call to apologise to Dombey for his " lovely and accomplished relative's " behaviour: " I have been in a devilish state of depression ever since; and said indeed to Long Saxby last night—man of six foot ten, with whom my friend Dombey is probably acquainted—that it had upset me in a confounded way, and made me bilious." Do you remember G. K. C. on Cousin Feenix?—" As consistent and as homogeneous as wood; he is as invincible as the ancestral darkness." But I won't quarrel if you prefer the reply of Mr Toots on being told by Susan Nipper that Florence will never love him: " Thank'ee! It's of no consequence. Good night. It's of no consequence, thank'ee!" One of the most moving things to me in the book is the fact that Dickens does not forget the dog, Diogenes. " Autumn days are shining, and on the sea-beach there are often a young lady and a white-haired gentleman. With them, or near them, are two children—boy and girl. And an old dog is generally in their company."

The last page suggests something which will infuriate you—that there are too many pages. Arthur Bates, who looks after me, said the other evening on seeing me immersed in *D and S*, " Should I like that book?" I at once asked him what kind of books he liked. He said any kind. Could he tell me the names of some of their authors? After thinking for a few minutes he said—and I give you my word I'm not inventing or improving—" Shakespeare, Byron, Keats, Tennyson, Damon Runyon, Sherlock Holmes, Alan Dent." When I had recovered I read a page of *D and S* at my topmost reviewing speed and found it took me two minutes. (Nobody can beat me at reading quickly when I want to.)

Allowing Arthur three minutes—it would be nearer four—the result must be thirty-four solid hours of reading. As I don't suppose he gets more than half an hour to read each day, which includes newspapers, it follows that it would take him between three and four months to get through *D and S*. And that is too long. Do you realise that in thirty-four hours he could read a dozen crime stories ?

The point is how to get young people to read Dickens, and I suggest by cutting him. The characters I should leave out of any shorter *Dombey* would be Sol Gills, Capt. Cuttle (who is desperately unfunny), good Mrs Brown, Alice Marwood, the Toodle family (in part), John and Harriet Carker. I should reduce Walter Gay to a minimum, and cut at least half of Florence, whose value largely disappears with the death of Paul. I feel too that those interminable colloquies when Dombey, Edith, and Carker go into conference might be shortened.

Look again at chapter XX—" Mr Dombey goes upon a Journey "—and tell me whether it should not end at " He had seen upon the man's rough cap a piece of new crape, and he had assured himself, from his manner and his answers, that he wore it for his son." This is superb, worthy of Balzac at his most transcendent. Why go on ? Isn't it better to shorten masterpieces—written in an age when there was more time on hand—with a view to getting the present age to read them, than to leave them in their integrity and the certainty that they will not be read ? (There is always the full text for whoever wants it.) I know all about Tennyson and his " I wish there were a great novel in hundreds of volumes that I might go on and on." Our young bank-clerks are not Tennysons. Why, out of a too-nice regard for punctilio, should the next generation—or this—be deprived of all knowledge of Miss Tox, Mr Toots, Cleopatra, and Joey B. ?

Of course, shortening needs to be done not only with care but with a touch of genius. There would be no re-writing, and the plot would be kept together by italicised résumés. Why don't *you* do it ? You could do all the novels in something under three years. Please don't send me a MacStingerish reply. They've already cut Shakespeare's *Hamlet*, Boswell's *Johnson*, and Handel's *Messiah*. And I've just cut Agate's *Ego* !

Ever,

JAMIE

P.S. My favourite minor characters in this great book ? The Native and Mr Towlinson. The first is an enchanting combination of Man Friday and Queequeg. The second is all the devoted people who have looked after me from Freddie Webster onwards. If I am a trifle inconsequent please know that I am writing this at 3 A.M., half in and half out of bed.

P.P.S. Did you see that G. W. Stonier recently expressed his willingness to give all Dickens for three pages of Proust ?

P.P.P.S. Two remarks I came across recently. One about C. D. by that ass Emerson: "He has no insight into character." The other by Emily Eden anent *Pickwick*: "The only bit of fun in India."

P.P.P.P.S. Good night!

Sept. 9 Letter to George Lyttelton:
Sunday.

*Queen Alexandra Mansions, W.C.*2
September 9th, 1945

DEAR GEORGE LYTTELTON,

I am sixty-eight to-day. I propose to celebrate it by *writing* a birthday letter of which you shall be the recipient.

By the time you get this you should have received *Ego* 7. I think you'll agree that Harrap's have produced this beautifully. NO misprints that I can detect, though there are one or two small over-lookings on my part. For instance, on October 9, when I went to Brighton, I appear to have spent the evening both at the films and at the theatre. Actually I went to the pictures in the afternoon. On page 218, entry for October 16, the grammar is a little wonky, and on page 293 the little besom's backside doesn't want a comma after it. But there's nothing I am really worried about except the entry for July 25 on pages 156 and 157. When this left my hands Heredia had no accents, as you know he mustn't have. Authorities: the compilers of *Les Cent Meilleurs Poèmes* (*Lyriques*) *de la Langue Française*, Larousse, who even gives a picture of him without the accents, Dent's *Short Biographical Dictionary of Foreign Literature*, the *Encyclopædia Britannica*, and my brother Edward at the age of fourteen. I have spent a great part of my life keeping Heredia clear of accents. There were none in the original passage which occurs in *Their Hour upon the Stage*. There were none in the page-proofs I passed immediately before printing. And now some well-intentioned person makes me write "Hérédia" twice! I feel exactly as though somebody had made me talk about "out-Héroding Hérod."

Have done pretty well for birthday presents. Cables from Charlie Rogers, my ex-houseboy, and Neville Cardus. From John Barrington a beautiful walking-stick in snake-wood with tortoise-shell handle and gold mounting. From Gwen Chenhalls one pair of socks, one handkerchief, and half a pound of sausages. From Coral Browne, pretty woman and good actress, a bottle of whiskey. From Leo Pavia, Adelaide Ristori's *Études et Souvenirs*. From George Harrap a pipe, and from Jock two tickets for a Beecham Concert. On the whole I think that isn't a bad lot. Anyhow, I'm satisfied. As it is my birthday I shall give myself the pleasure of copying out for you something you will recognise, but in the form in which Ristori spoke it:

" Le Thane de Fife avait une femme. Et maintenant où est-elle? Ne pourrai-je jamais rendre ces mains propres ? Assez, Seigneur, assez, avec tes terreurs tu gâtes tout. Toujours cette odeur de sang ? Hélas ! tous les parfums de l'Arabie ne pourront jamais désinfecter cette petite main ! Oh ! oh ! oh ! Lave tes mains, va mettre ton vêtement de nuit, ne sois pas si pâle ! Je te le répète. Banco est enseveli et il ne peut sortir de sa tombe ! Au lit ! au lit ! On frappe à la porte, viens ! viens ! viens ici ! donne-moi la main. Ce qui est fait est fait. Au lit ! au lit ! . . ."

This gives me an idea. I think I shall translate the whole play into this sort of lingo and then send it to the French Benjamin Britten to turn into an opera.

Yours ever,
JAMES AGATE

From Jock :

Spooncreel
Maybole
Ayrshire
September 7th, 1945

DEAR JAMIE,

A Very Happy Birthday!

And I'm beginning to believe at last that you *do* grow old, because you begin to use *understatement* after years of abusing the other thing. You say, " Don't be offended if I say that there is beginning to be a shade of fainéantisme about you ! " *Beginning*, indeed ! And *a shade*, forsooth ! I know all about myself——

And yes ! I *will/shall* write for Home and van Thal a " Letter to a Godson on Serendipity—its Meaning, Use, and Abuse." My self-knowledge, my Macbethian " strange and self abuse," will stand me in good stead and help me to't. And I shall drive myself —nay, flog myself—into sending them 12,000 relevant words on or before the 7th March, 1946. That is an undertaking, a promise.

And now about this not-easily-defensible notion of your abridging Dickens—or my abridging Dickens—or anybody's abridging Dickens. It *could* be done—I might even permit myself to go so far even as to say it *should* be done—for schoolchildren between twelve and sixteen (who read drastically abridged Swift and Defoe anyhow). Even there I would insist on its being done (if it must be done), not by any one person, but by a committee of six highly sensible Dickensians. For a random suggestion :

(1) J. B. Priestley
(2) W. H. Salmon (editor of the *Times* weekly, with whom I had a wondrous Dickens pow-wow at the Press Club the other night)
(3) Robert Lynd
(4) Rebecca West
(5) James Bone, and
(6) either You or Me.

For adults I would not give the scheme any sanction. Any adult worth a hoot tries Dickens once and, if he finds him palatable at all, re-reads his own favourite sections *à son gré.* Here are we, Jamie, you and I, two adults; both presumably worth several hoots in some respects, and we don't begin to agree in detail about a novel which finds us both madly enthusiastic—*Dombey and Son.*

You want to cut Captain Cuttle (who is " desperately unfunny " to you and G. K. Chesterton, but delightful in all he says and does to the rest of the world); the Toodle family in part (and I wholly adore it); half of Florence (who is to me the most tolerable and touching of all of Dickens's maidens); and (more understandably) good Mrs Brown and one or two minor characters.

But, look you! some of your likes are my aversions. What do you, or we, or our committee, do about that? I have always found Joey Bagstock exceedingly tiresome, and I skip (when I re-read) the innumerable descriptions of his incipient apoplexy—just as most people probably skip the nauseating references to James Carker's teeth. *No, no, no!* And no again—the more I think of it! He would be a very brave man who should abridge a Dickens novel for adult readers. You try it, if you dare. It would be like trying to kidnap Master Alexander MacStinger! (And *did* you observe, by the way, how Mrs MacS. quietened that masterful mite during her wedding to Captain Bunsby?)

Ever thy

JOCK

P.S. Boswell's *Johnson*, Handel's *Messiah*, and *Ego* are beside the point. They are not fiction. Or are they?

*Queen Alexandra Mansions, W.C.*2

September 10*th*, 1945

DEAR JOCK,

Ye'll dae a fine Letter, and Rubicon will be proud of his Gemel. Erudite allusion for the use of German editors later on.

Yes and no about your Dickens suggestions. I would trust Rebecca West with an abridgment of Shakespeare but not Dickens. No woman has ever laughed at C. D., and the sex is not going to start now. On the whole I think I am against a committee. My plan would be one novel, one abridger. As follows:

Pickwick	J. A.?
David Copperfield	J. B. Priestley
Bleak House	Bernard Darwin
Great Expectations	Neville Cardus
Dombey and Son	Alan Dent
Martin Chuzzlewit	George Lyttelton
Nicholas Nickleby	Robert Lynd
Little Dorrit	Hugh Kingsmill
Our Mutual Friend	D. B. Wyndham Lewis

There was an enchanting little scene in the Café Royal last night. This was when John Barrington, the irresponsible young man about whom you will read in *Ego* 7, approached my table bearing a tray on which was a cake of his own baking with sixty-eight matches stuck in it. Which were then lit while a small choir of his friends sang "Happy Birthday to You." The C. R. has known some extraordinary scenes, but nothing, I take it, pleasanter than this. There was champagne, and I wish you had been there.

Ever,

JAMIE

Sept. 12 *Wednesday.* I am perfectly well aware that one should not lose one's temper over trifles. I lose mine *when they interfere with my work.* Wrote to the Telephone Manager in Gerrard Street yesterday to inform him that the war is now over and I am tired of wasting one hour a day owing to his blasted telephone not working. Threaten a letter to *The Times* giving an hour-by-hour account of one day's attempts to avail myself of a service for which I pay a half-yearly bill of over twenty pounds. End with the polite assurance that I don't want to make a fuss, but can something be done please? Result, the 'phone to-day has been completely dead—at any rate up to five o'clock, while all messages to engineers from outside telephone boxes have proved unavailing. If this continues I shall go over the road, dial 999, and demand the immediate presence of police, fire-engines, and ambulance.

I cannot understand why the little Carlton Theatre in the Tottenham Court Road is not full to overflowing. The custom there is to have one French film and one British one; by telephoning beforehand one can always find out when the British rubbish has exhausted itself. The French films are invariably entrancing. At least they are entrancing to me. I saw to-night a model little film called *Les Yeux Noirs*, with an exquisite performance by Simone Simon and a most moving one by Harry Baur, in my opinion as good an actor as Jannings at his best. When is the British film industry going to wake up to the fact that it hasn't got an actor who can play men of a certain age? Always with the exception of Frederick Leister, whom it doesn't use, and Alfred Drayton, whom it won't use except for farce. There is a delicious performance, too, by Jules Berry, who seduces like a gentleman, and not, as a British director would insist, like a counter-jumper in sports jacket and size eleven in tennis shoes.

Sept. 15 *Saturday.* Letter from Ivor Brown :

> *In the Chilterns, pretty, little, odious country—odious, that is, if you find big country and moorland amorous. This leads to cogitation on why odious should be a passive adjective and amorous active. There is no answer, as in most queries concerning English usage.*

Sept. 14*th*

DEAR JAMES,

Thank you very much for *Ego* 7, which you ought to have called The Seven Against Ego or Septem Contra Me, the Seven being Jock, Leo, Lyttelton, Van Thal, Cardus, Shakespeare, and Amalgamated Anons. You are getting lazy—incredible—and relying too much on the stooges. Of course, you can write them (bar Shakespeare) out of the field, but the man that pays his fifteen bob merits more of you and less of other people. When *you* are writing the book it is better 'Ego' than ever : when not, not.

Yours,

IVOR

Sept. 16 *Sunday.* Went to Birmingham yesterday to judge the Harness Classes at the Show given by the Sutton Coldfield Equitation Club. Had a look at my foal, which is coming on nicely and gives every sign of living up to her name, "My Pretty."

Sept. 18 *Tuesday.* It is the firm conviction of all newspapers with what Montague called "the largest circulation in the solar system" that their readers are interested only in headlines. There is a magnificent example of this in the paper to-day. Soberly the article sets forth that

> The whaling season opened yesterday with the departure for the Antarctic of two of the world's biggest factory ships, the British-built *Sir James Clark Ross* and the *Empire Venture*—each manned by 300 Norwegians—and 16 whale-catchers and trawlers.

And the sub-editor says to himself rightly : Who cares ? He then remembers that increased whaling means increase of oil for all sorts of things, including cosmetics. Which gives him his headline :

IT MAY MEAN LIPSTICKS

Whereupon half the female population of these islands apprises itself of the departure for the Antarctic of, etc., etc. *C'est gigantesque!* Indeed, it's almost as gigantic as the whales. Or as Leo's typing, whereby " new era of prosperity " becomes " new ear of prosperity," " Jock " turns into " Kock," and Pinero writes a play called *His House in Cider*.

Sept. 19 *Wednesday.* In the *Daily Telegraph*'s Personal Column:

Elderly critic's godson, fourteen weeks, thanks *Daily Telegraph* reader for beautiful rattle.

Sept. 21 *Friday.* I am no transmogrifier. I do *not* want to see *Gerontius* danced, hear the *Eroica* arranged for string quartet, or *Das Lied von der Erde* transcribed for piano-accordion. I do *not* want to read *Tartuffe* as a novel, or see *Die Welt als Wille und Vorstellung* filmed. I just don't believe in the artistic impulse behind the transmogrification. Let's take X's best-selling novel, *Peepshow for Cyclops*. I just don't believe that one morning X's agent goes to him and says, " Say, boss, d'you reckon print's your book's best vehicle ? I see it as a play, and so do Messitup's. You'll have to change the setting from Biarritz to Blackpool. As a matter of fact, I mentioned this to Stanley Blockhead. He set to work and got it into three acts that'll amaze you." Or that a couple of years later the agent goes again to X and says, using the grammar of his kind, " Look here, between you and I, that play notion didn't quite work out. I see *Peepshow* as a film. In fact, so does Morris Dummkopf, who wants to produce it with Franz Esel as director. You'll have to turn it round. Make your British soldier an American marine, and substitute Bataan for Blackpool." I shouldn't mind these well-intentioned worsifications. But I just don't believe they happen. I believe the agent goes to X and says, " Say, Big Boy, just cut that artistic bunk, willya ? Jeezers, are you nuts ? Turn the darned thing into a play somebody can make a film of afterwards ! What, you won't ? Well, then, let Hymie Greenstuff do it. I got him to dramatise Lysol's *Fresh Woods*. *New Pastures* he called it. We sold it to Niagara Films for a packet. They made it for Harry Twitch and called it *Blue Mantle*. It cleaned up everywhere." Every moment of to-night's *A Bell for Adano* proclaimed that it was not conceived as a play. And why call the hero Joppolo ? " Melancholy trisyllable of sound, unison to Nincompoop and every name vituperative under heaven." I tried all the variations. Proppolo and Coppolo, Doppolo, Floppolo, Moppolo—fond spouse would be Mrs Moppolo—Sloppolo, Woppolo. The bell ? This merely shows the author of the original story believing that money-grubbing Sicilian peasants drool like sentimental American novelists.

DEATH OF LEO

Sept. 26
Wednesday.

A woman friend of Leo's, who was to have taken him to hospital this morning for a rest cure, telephoned me at eleven o'clock that he had passed away. " I couldn't have wished a better end for him. It seems he went to bed very happy, grumbling at the best of landladies, and died in his sleep." He had cried wolf so often that it was not until last week that I thought about a doctor, who insisted upon a long rest. To occupy his mind I made him spend yesterday reading and reviewing a book about music. He produced an admirable, concise, logical, and faultlessly typed notice ending: " The usual misprints are happily absent. Perhaps this is because the book has been produced in America, where proof-readers seem to take more trouble than they do in this dear, slap-dash land." Dear, muddle-headed Leo! I had asked him whether one should spell Austen with an 'e' as a *first* name. Whereupon he threw up his hands and said, " Jane did! " Just as I was remonstrating about this the door-bell rang, and a soldier announced a car for Greenford; I had forgotten all about a lecture engagement made some months ago. I said, " Well, Leo, this means no silly nonsense about good-byes." I did, however, manage to get out something about his unending devotion. But he cut this short, and waved me out of the room. Even so, I had no notion that anything serious was impending. His courage in sticking to his job deceived us all.

Sept. 27
Thursday.

At the theatre to-night Jock handed me this:

33 *King Street*
Covent Garden
*W.C.*2

26*th September*, 1945

DEAR JAMIE,

I am genuinely sorry—but rather more for you than for Leo, who is already in his Jewish heaven and fussing in the library of that dubious paradise, I've no doubt!

It is all very odd this death-and-dying business. You may remember me telling you something about my queer " psychic " (I suppose it needs the inverted commas) experience at the death of our dear kind Hugh Walpole. Well, as soon as I put the telephone down this morning I found myself at my piano and playing without choice—if you know what I mean—the first and last movements of Schumann's *Waldscenen* suite—the *Eintritt* and the *Abschied.* My hands just picked out this particular suite, I don't know why, and put it up to be played. I have never heard Leo play it, though he has in his time played me lots of out-of-the-way Schumann. It sounded wonderfully appropriate—the questing romantic entry into the forest, and the resigned and not over-sad leaving of it. And I found myself playing with far more than my usual expressiveness—with an expressiveness I can't usually command. It was, I know (though you may think me mad to say so), just dear old Leo saying Hail and Farewell to me—with a good deal of his own superb musicianship especially *telepathed* for the occasion.

He was the queerest, most exasperating, most endearing mixture of Lamb's George Dyer, and Proust's Bloch, and a wondrous spluttering, splenetic, benign character in Turgenev's *Rudin* called—as I remember—Pigasov. I am unable to imagine your Grape Street flat without him, and I shall very much miss his shuffle, his drawl, his screech, his snuffle, his laugh, his complaints, his compliments, his Viennese courtesies, *and* his brains, whenever I call on you again.

Sympathetically,

JOCK

Sept. 28 *Friday.* *The Times* prints this :

MR I. L. PAVIA

Mr James Agate writes :

" Leo," as he was generally called, was immensely proud of having studied under Leschetizky, and even more proud of that notice which a famous musical critic gave him when he appeared as a juvenile prodigy at the St James's Hall some sixty years ago. " He went at the *Waldstein* sonata like a young avalanche, *fortissimo sempre crescendo e prestissimo sempre accelerando*, keeping his feet cleverly over the straightforward bits, staggering gamely through the syncopated passages, going head-over-heels up and down the flights of octaves, and finishing, flushed but unbeaten, after a record-breaking neck-or-nothing ' reading ' that would have made Rubinstein gasp and Mme Schumann faint." The boy was destined to be a failure in a wider field than piano-playing, but also to prove in his own person—to the everlasting credit of the law of compensation—that the lady in the Henry James story was not talking entire nonsense when she reflected that " There was something a failure was, a failure in the market, that a success somehow wasn't."

Leo Pavia had a measure of genius, and all of it strictly unmarketable. He was a walking literary as well as musical reference library, and knew most of whatever there is to be known about Restoration comedy, Johnson, Jane Austen, Dickens, Thackeray, Goethe, Schiller, Ibsen. He could quote Richardson ! He translated Wilde's plays into German, wrote a great deal of music that was half Johann and half Richard Strauss, and was for many years a player of professional bridge in which he combined maximum skill with fantastically poor cards. No man ever enjoyed bad luck more ! He was schizophrenic long before the thing became fashionable, half of him being entirely rational, the other half living in a world in which it was taken for granted that pigs have wings and cows jump over the moon. His piano-playing was marked by an exquisite cantabile, but he could not pick up one object without knocking over two others. He was a combination of Lamb's friend George Dyer, Tchehov's Ephikhódof, and half a dozen characters in *Alice in Wonderland*. He was a superb talker who never listened, or, listening, got whatever was said the wrong way round. He had the best sense of pure fun, plus the finest wit, of any man I have been privileged to know, with a gift for making conversational *gaffes* both natural and cultivated. Vulgarity of mind died in his presence. His death creates a void which his friends will not attempt to fill.

By preposterous coincidence the only other obituary notice in *The Times* to-day is one of the composer Leo most hated—Béla Bartók.

Sept. 29 *Saturday.* Two pews were more than enough to hold the little gathering at the Crematorium. Helen Roeder ; Betty Ricketts ; George Mathew ; my houseboy, Arthur Bates, breaking his holiday and bringing a posy ; and J. A. The door of the chapel had been left open, letting in a flood of autumn sunshine and the twittering of a few late birds. From the organ the Adagio from the Sonata Pathétique, then Helen, George, and I took it in turns to read " Fear no more the heat o' the sun," after which the slow movement from the *Emperor*. Leo had always said he wanted Shakespeare and Beethoven.

Oct. 3 *Wednesday.* " Surtout, pas de génie ! " wrote Villiers de l'Isle-Adam at the head of one of his *Contes Cruels*. All about an aspiring journalist who, being asked his price, replied, " Three francs a line." The editor observing that not even Hugo or du Terrail made such extravagant demands, the young man coldly remarked, " I see that M. le Directeur fails to realise that I am *totally* unknown ! " He goes on to swear that he is possessed of an unbeatable *niaiserie* of ideas and an incomparable banality of style.

With Leo Pavia

To which the editor replies, "O Youth! O springtime of life! Let me tell you, young man, that to be utterly without talent is to be an outstanding figure. That I have spent twenty years and half a million francs in pursuit of this unique phenomenon. That my office-boy is the author of four magnificent dramatic works which have been crowned by four academies! Convince me, young man, of your perfect nullity, show me a manuscript full of faulty spelling, of which the French is not even approximately French, and all of it written in a handwriting that nobody can read, satisfy me that your claim to be a complete imbecile is valid, and I will pay you *six* francs a line!"

Interviewing several aspiring secretaries, I ask each what his ruling passion is. The first says reciting Gertrude Stein. The second elects for reading Edith Sitwell in bed. The third, when asked whether he has read *Pickwick*, replies superiorly, "Yes. But in French, of course!" I finally settle on a young man whose passion is writing essays on *Carlyle considered as Humorist*, and *Dickens as Social Reformer*. But there is this in his favour—*he is as ignorant as one can reasonably expect*, having read no line of Scott, Thackeray, or George Eliot. (It goes without saying that he can spout Gerard Manley Hopkins, D. H. Lawrence, and T. S. Eliot by the yard.) Obviously very willing, types quickly, efficiently, and intelligently, has no notion of spelling, and helps me with my English! For example, I am told that I must not call Falstaff "the old toper, sorner, fribble." The first two words are permissible, it seems, but not fribble. And then it starts. Patiently I explain that fribble was the word used by Henry James to describe Balzac's Baron Hulot. Which means that I must then tell him who Hulot was, and throw in a kindly word about Balzac and James. In the middle of which it occurs to me that fribble was not H. J.'s word but George Moore's—which entails a lecture on G. M.! By which time I have forgotten what I was going to say about the old toper, sorner, and whatever third appellation John Booth-Palmer would approve. However, one cannot have everything, and I have always thought that the editor in the French story demanded too much!

Oct. 6 *Saturday.* Brother Mycroft sends me a cutting from the *Manchester Evening News* for October 4, '45.

THE BOY WITH HORSE-MANIA

Magistrates at Manchester County Court to-day heard a novel complaint. The father of a 16-year-old Stretford boy, charged with stealing a cycle, said: "I have a motor mechanic business in which I want him to help me, but he has horse-mania.

> "He leaves me to go sleeping in stables, and associates with any characters so long as they have something to do with horses. He is so horse-mad that I don't know what to do with him."

The boy was remanded for a medical report. Why? Shallow, and even Silence, would have had enough wit to tell the father to put the lad among horses.

During the war the Savage Club dinners became luncheons. To-night the dinners were resumed; I attended and presented the Club with the marble bust carved by Sarah. (See *Ego* 6, p. 195.)

Oct. 7 *Sunday.* Cancelled my engagement at Birmingham next Sunday. The train journey, two lectures at 3 and 6 P.M., the wait on New Street station for a train which is bound to be late, to arrive at Euston and queue up for non-existent taxis, and then walk home, without a meal since breakfast—no, it isn't good enough. Have offered to go if I am motored from and to Grape Street. Doctor concurs.

Wrote 150 words for an advertisement for second-hand machinery. Also 1200 words telling Moscow why I think Edith Evans is a good actress.

Our film critics:

> Shakespeare has provided Ida Lupino with the title of her book on four generations of Lupinos. She calls it *The Dusty Way,* taken from her late father Stanley's favourite quotation from *Macbeth,* "All our yesterdays have lighted fools the dusty way to death."
>
> *Sunday paper*

Oct. 8 *Monday.* In a letter from a young highbrow:

> But what we can hardly learn, except with great difficulty and a sublime thick-skinedness [*sic*] and patience, is that other people who evince the same wrong-headedness as we ourselves did in our own time of madcap wool-gathering and flaunting egoism of youth have just as much right to despise us for having passed to that measure of understanding which is, to their minds, something near the border of indistinction and extinction as we have to despise them for being, as we think, arrested morons of the thinest [*sic*] water.

Ends by comparing me unfavourably, *very* unfavourably, with "Palinurus." "There you have a writer full of wise sores [*sic*] and really modern instances."

Oct. 9 *Tuesday.* So, fifty years after Edmond de Goncourt's death—he stipulated twenty—we are to have the full text of the *Journal. The Times* is lukewarm about this, and there is opposition in France. I quote from the seventeenth issue of the new and admirable French weekly, *Spectateur*, principally devoted to theatre and films.

> Edmond de Goncourt collectionnait les racontars scandaleux qui, même refroidis par le temps, gardent une odeur nauséabonde. Évidemment les gens dont il est question là-dedans sont disparus depuis belle lurette, et beaucoup de ces histoires sont déjà très éventées. . . . Victor Hugo, à l'extrémité de son âge, gardait un goût puissant pour les jeunes personnes. . . . Zola, qui avait épousé l'amie de son impécunieuse jeunesse, fit, devenu célèbre, deux enfants à sa femme de chambre. . . . Alphonse Daudet est mort d'une maladie très pénible, dont périrent plusieurs rois de France. . . . Maupassant, avant de finir chez le docteur Blanche, dormit avec pas mal de dames grandes ou petites . . . les belles révélations, en vérité! Et tout à fait de nature à rehausser le prestige littéraire de la France. Paul Bourget, lorsqu'il était étudiant, a fait ses farces. Catulle Mendès a aimé Augusta Holmès qui . . . Mirbeau a épousé Alice Regnault qui . . . Léon Daudet a divorcé d'avec Jeanne Hugo qui . . . Qu'est-ce-que tous ces commérages apportent de neuf dans l'histoire de la "vie littéraire," pour employer la pompeuse expression de Goncourt? Cet homme consignait religieusement de pareilles misères, sans omettre les détails les plus crus, les particularités les moins ragoûtantes, reniflant avec délice les sécrétions les plus faisandées de la nature humaine. Loin d'en réduire l'importance, il en aurait volontiers ajouté. Il y a en lui du Restif de La Bretonne, du Maxime du Camp, et de l'Horace de Vieil-Castel. Si on publie toute sa friperie intégralement,—qu'est-ce-qu'on dira? On dira que les grands hommes ont leurs faiblesses et que l'humanité ne sent pas toujours bon. Mais on dira surtout qu'Edmond de Goncourt était un vieux cochon, doublé d'un hypocrite, qui faisait des mamours aux confrères dont il volait les secrets pour les déshonorer devant la postérité. Est-ce un tel résultat que cherchent les membres de l'Académie Goncourt, chatouillés par le démon de la curiosité, et ne vaudrait-il pas mieux
>
> . . . qu'en un profond oubli
> Cet horrible secret demeure enseveli?

I disagree with the writer in the *Spectateur*. I want to know everything that can be known about considerable artists. The point —though Goncourt may not have intended it—is not that Victor Hugo ran after little girls, but that the runner after little girls should write imperishable masterpieces.

Oct. 10 *Wednesday.* Letter from Leo's and my little Irish friend :

18 *Park View Avenue*
Harold's Cross
Dublin
6*th October*, 1945

DEAR JAMES,

I am desperately sorry.

Like Harold Skimpole I am a " mere child " and my emotions are usually false. But I am genuinely sorry. Leo was always very kind to me in his letters, and I don't think I ever fully realised that he was seventy and ill. It seems incredible that a sick man could write with such unfailing cheerfulness, but I might have known from passages such as this :

" I grow serious. And if you had had a heat-wave and then a week of freezing cold, rain, snow, sleet, *and* a cold in the head so violent that when you sneeze the houses on the other side of the road commence to wobble . . . you would be in a grave state of mind. I was so grave I thought for a whole day of nothing *but* the grave. And about the Sting. Sting, do I say ? Not at all ; at the worst, only a mighty clout on the head."

Again :

" I was a cynical child, bitter-tongued and ruthless. That I have grown so sweet and benevolent in later years, is just the mellowing of a vintage wine. Oh, John, pray that the dust and the cobwebs may not cover the bottle all too soon ! "

I've nothing more to say. I can't be flippant in the realisation that Leo won't answer me. But this is awful ! I shall shed tears in a moment. You are very lucky to have had a brother like Edward Agate and a friend like Isidore Leo Pavia.

Sincerely,
J. E. JORDAN

Oct. 11 *Thursday.* From Raymond Mortimer :

As from the Reform Club
*S.W.*1
October 6, 1945

DEAR JAMES AGATE,

I recommend no one to read *Ego* 7, or for that matter any of the *Ego's*, in bed at night, as I have been doing, for one can't put the bloody book away and get to sleep. I am flattered, gratified, amused by your references to me. I hoped my style, like my person, was at least as spare as yours, and now am wondering how to amend it so that the gentle reader won't think me fat.

I want to argue with you about some words, no, not argue, you don't like argument—I want to insinuate some doubts into your blissfully assured mind.

P. 26. *Minoperative. Vive le néologisme,* but this particular example is unplausible. *Minus* isn't an adjective like *magnus,* and wouldn't usage demand *minoroperative* ? I agree that would be a vile word. But isn't yours rather vile too ? I saw a pin-table saloon the other day in the prettiest town in England—it was called The Playdium.

P. 41. " The allusion, of course, is . . ." Why " of course " ? I suspect that Quin was talking to a lady at her tea-table, with a *négrillon* in attendance. Nothing surprising about this—why drag in Hogarth ?

P. 152. I am scribbling this in the country, far from a Dumas, but are you sure that " des amis, des amis comme Prudence " shouldn't be " amies " ? They appear as " elles " in the next sentence.

P. 156. What authority have you for embellishing Heredia with acute accents ? The answer to this, I suspect, may be " Barrès." But Heredia himself never, as far as I know, used the accents. Of course, the pronunciation is as if they were there, but the name is Spanish.

P. 177. *Haphazardly.* Admissible, but is it worthy of so discriminating a word-fancier ? *Haphazard* makes a very pretty adverb with nothing added to it.

P. 251. *de Musset.* You can quote a thousand instances to support you, but is it not better usage to say either *Alfred de Musset* or just *Musset* ? Proust was once hauled over the coals by a friend for the same habit, and answered that he supposed in future he must call the painter Dyck, *tout court.* I'd like to quote Sainte-Beuve to support my view, but I can't find the reference.

P. 255. I doubt if the Duchess of Sermoneta, who is an Italian, would write *Ceracolo,* since there is no such word. But the misprint may be her printer's, not yours.

P. 258. *She looks like I do in a spoon.* I suspect that Mrs Campbell would have said " *as* I do " ?

P. 271. *Bon viveur.* I just don't believe it, though there's a club in a coign of Mayfair with this name. A *bon vivant* is an epicurean like yourself ; a *viveur* is a rake, whether or not like yourself the reader cannot easily discover from your otherwise so strip-teasing volumes. I wouldn't deny the possibility of a *viveur* being *bon,* but don't you mean *bon vivant* ?

I've not forgotten your inconceivable fireworks at the Churchill Club. You were what I once saw advertised in Liguria, a *Professore pirotecnico.* Nor have I forgotten your hospitality. I hope to persuade you soon to eat *chez moi.*

Yours ever,
RAYMOND MORTIMER

P.S. I was interested in the figures you give of the words written by Balzac and Dickens. Can you tell me where to find these? I have long wanted to know how the great novelists compare in mere productivity. Your own record leaves me flabbergasted. . . .

> . . . and still the wonder grew
> That one small hand could set down all he knew.

I have replied:

Queen Alexandra Mansions, W.C.2
October 11*th*, 1945

DEAR RAYMOND MORTIMER,

How nice in a world of atom bombs, strikes, and a shortage of everything except stupidity, to discuss something that really matters.

P. 26. *Minoperative* is a poor thing, but I've created it and I'll stick to it.

P. 41. Because the book of theatre anecdotes from which I got this story went to the trouble of a footnote to make the point about the Hogarth print.

P. 152. Have looked it up and am relieved to find that " amis " is right.

P. 156. When I saw this I could have drunk hot blood! I enclose a sheet of the page-proof finally passed by me showing the unembellished " e's." And then some clever fellow altered it behind my back.

P. 177. This only shows the danger of using English when French will do. I ought, of course, to have written " armed *à l'improviste.*"

P. 251. Isn't this rather according to the taste and fancy of the individual? I would go to the stake rather than talk of de Balzac or de Maupassant or de Goncourt. In speaking I generally say Musset, but the balance of the sentence—" Merle Oberon is as much like George Sand as I am like de Musset "—seemed to my ear to require the " de." I'm very likely wrong.[1]

[1] I *am* wrong. As *Ego* 8 was going through the press I received a letter from Belgium containing this paragraph:

" Une seule erreur que je relève dans *Ego* 7: l'emploi du 'de' quand vous citez Alfred de Musset sans citer son prénom. On dit 'Alfred de Musset, Alfred de Vigny, Henry de Montherlant, le duc de Saint-Simon,' mais d'autre part 'Vigny, Musset, Montherlant, Saint-Simon,' sans la particule."

P. 255. I am quoting at two removes—Dicky Helme and the Duchess. And possibly Viardot-Garcia got it wrong. I suspect the word to be *Cenacolo.* I have no Italian dictionary and am not an authority on da Vinci.

P. 258. No, I think that's what Mrs Campbell said. I should certainly say, " He stammers like I do," though I should write, " He stammers as I do." After all, which of us, waiting on a railway platform and seeing a train draw in, has not said, " This is us " ? Do you suggest, " This is we ! " ?

P. 271. Don't think I can plead guilty ! What I mean to imply is a *bon vivant* with a dash of the *viveur*, and that is why I created *bon viveur*, knowing that it isn't French. I suppose that when one plays about with words one ought to make it clear that one is playing about.

Re Balzac and Dickens. I have no authority for the figures, which are my own assessment. But what, after all, are seven, eight, or even ten million words ? I read in to-day's *Evening News* that a Mr Charles Hamilton, the creator, under the pen-name of Frank Richards, of Billy Bunter, that perpetual schoolboy whose adventures filled the pages of *The Magnet* for years and years and years—I read that this genius estimates his total output at 60,000,000 words !

I want to thank you for taking so much trouble. This question of accuracy has become an obsession with me. In the seven volumes of *Ego* I have found fifty-three definite errors which have crept in despite a vigilance fantastic to the point of brain-sickliness. My diary may be forgotten with me, but there's a possibility that it may be reprinted, and I hate to think of error being perpetuated. I am doing all I can to prevent this. The errata are carefully copied into each volume of my specially bound set. My publishers, my literary executors, and my lawyers have copies. Thus have I tried to make assurance doubly, trebly, quadruply sure. All the same, I shouldn't be in the least surprised to find you appearing in 2045 A.D. as Mortimer Raymond ! Anyhow, bless you for the letter.

Ever,

JAMES AGATE

Oct. 12 *Friday.* Our intellectuals again ! The new outbreak is called *Focus One*. I cull from a poem entitled *Broadjump* by Don Roscher :

> Day's first urine
> Finds me desperately embracing
> The anonymity that is To-morrow.

To me this is not poetry. But then, I should not consider

> Brushing with hasty steps the *dung* away

to be poetry.

Next I try the prose : *Nine Men Upsidedown* by Reginald Drake. I read :

> Outside the clangour's clash a butcher trips, gripped in the shark-maw hulk of mutton falls, head in sheep's carcase nipped at neck, his leather legs and blue-white apron sprawls.

One has only to re-set this to see that it is verse of some kind :

> Outside the clangour's clash a butcher trips,
> Gripped in the shark-maw hulk of mutton falls,
> Head in sheep's carcase nipped at neck,
> His leather legs and blue-white apron sprawls.

Again :

> Awhile the clammering rookblack gossips crane,
> And flowerstall chalkface stares with redlip pout. . . .

And so it goes on. I can see the point of microbes and black-beetles ; the highbrow defeats me. It would be interesting, by the way, to know at what date the highbrow first came into being. There were none when I was a boy ; we did not dream of calling intellectual giants like Browning highbrows. The term was not used about any of the contributors to *The Yellow Book*. I still think the best thing ever said about the genre is Basil Macdonald Hastings's " There's nothing like consulting a highbrow if you want to hear something that is funny as well as daft."

Oct. 13 *Saturday.* Watching Alec Clunes's Hamlet at the Arts Theatre last night I remembered the postscript to Hazlitt's essay entitled " The Fight " : " Toms called upon me the next day, to ask me if I did not think the fight a complete thing ? I said I thought it was." It was only when I turned up the essay this morning that I realised that Hazlitt used as motto :

> . . . The *fight*, the *fight's* the thing,
> Wherein I'll catch the conscience of the king.

And remembered that the Gas-man, showing his tremendous right hand, would say, " This is *the grave-digger*." Odd ! Decided that Alec's Hamlet was complete in itself, which means that to-morrow I shall not be comparing it with any other Hamlet. I liked it very much and went round to Alec's dressing-room afterwards. For two reasons. First, to tell him how good he had been, and second, to blow him up for leaving out the jingle about " Imperious Cæsar." That Shakespeare could, wittingly or unwittingly, at this juncture, contrive something that is less than great poetry and more than doggerel, something with a hint of the nursery rhyme that *in its place* is better than grandiosity's tumbling seas—this is sheer miracle.

Oct. 17 *Wednesday.* In *Ego* 4, page 147, I wrote, " How long was Robinson Crusoe on his island before he saw Man Friday's footstep ? Answer : Ten years." Where, if you please, is the flaw in that ? In the length of time ? No. Where I went wrong, and where, I suppose, ninety-nine people out of a hundred would go wrong, is in taking the footstep to be Man Friday's. It wasn't, as an unknown friend has been to a great deal of pains to point out. Here is the evidence, the pages being taken from the edition published by S. W. Partridge and Co. :

" Being now in the eleventh year of my residence, and, as I have said, my ammunition growing low, I set myself to study some art to trap and snare the goats, to see whether I could not catch some of them alive ; and particularly, I wanted a she-goat great with young. . . . It happened one day, about noon, going towards my boat, I was exceedingly surprised with the print of a man's naked foot on the shore, which was very plain to be seen on the sand " (p. 110).

R. C. reflects : " That I had lived there fifteen years now and had not met with the least shadow or figure of any people yet " (p. 122).

He sees his first trace of savages : " It was now the month of December, as I said above, in my twenty-third year ; and this, being the southern solstice (for winter I cannot call it), was the particular time of my harvests, and required me to be pretty much abroad in the fields, when, going out early in the morning, even before it was thorough daylight, I was surprised with seeing a light of some fire upon the shore, at a distance from me of about two miles, toward that part of the island where I had observed some savages had been, as before, and not on the other side—but, to my great affliction, it was on my side of the island " (p. 137).

He cannot sleep : " It was one of the nights in the rainy season in March, the four-and-twentieth year of my first setting foot in this island of solitude, I was lying in my bed or hammock, awake, very well in health, had no pain, no distemper, no uneasiness of body, nor any uneasiness of mind more than ordinary, but could by no means close my eyes, that is, so as to sleep. . . . In my reflections upon the state of my case since I came on shore on this island, I was comparing the happy posture of my affairs in the first years of my habitation here, with the life of anxiety, fear, and care which I had lived in ever since I had seen the print of a foot in the sand " (p. 148).

He meets Friday : " About a year and a half after I entertained these notions (and by long musing had, as it were, resolved them all into nothing, for want of an occasion to put them into execution) I was surprised one morning by seeing no less than five canoes all on shore together on my side of the island, and the people who belonged to them all landed and out of my sight." Then follows the famous account of Crusoe's rescue of the savage (p. 152).

And here is the K. O.: "I was now entered on the seven-and-twentieth year of my captivity in this place; though the three last years that I had this creature with me ought rather to be left out of the account" (p. 174).

My correspondent ends this letter: "From this it will appear that the footprint was not Man Friday's at all, but was seen some eleven years after Crusoe's shipwreck and thirteen years before Friday came into the picture. I trust that in some future *Ego* you will see fit to put this serious matter to rights."

Oct. 18 *Thursday.* 'Sblood, but is there no more "to" a Greek tragedy than to a musical comedy? (I am writing this immediately after the Old Vic's production of *Œdipus* at the New Theatre.) It is proper that after *Pass Down the Car, Please!* the producer should be haled out of the wings to praise the wardrobe mistress and tell us who arranged the dances. Proper because musical comedy has no effect on the mind. But the whole point of Greek tragedy was to stir the Greek mind profoundly, and send it home reflecting that no man is to be counted happy until he is dead. The Greek audience was not depressed? Like Mrs Gummidge, it revelled in depression? I am using a non-Greek mentality to look into a Greek one? All this is not the point. *The old tragedy is profoundly moving even if you don't believe a word of it.* And then Michel Saint-Denis ruined it with a speech about how nice it was to be producing plays again, and even nicer to be associated with Dame Sybil. After which he meticulously and categorically thanked everybody. In the world of opera, where the sublime and the ridiculous are one, this nonsense is just not tolerated. At the end of *Tristan* no producer comes forward to thank Messrs Squills for the love-philtre, or Messrs Cordage and Wain for the new rigging. Nor do they follow *Elektra* with *The Pirates of Penzance*! Who wants to see *The Critic* after *Œdipus*? I didn't and wouldn't. And so left, declining to entertain an Œdipuff complex.

Oct. 24 *Wednesday.* *Ego* 7 published.
Letter from Clifford Bax:

*D2 Albany, W.*1
23 *October*, 1945

MY DEAR JAMES,

Only twenty-four hours ago I was writing to thank you for *Gemel*, a gift which was totally unexpected: and now here I am writing once more to Grape Street and to thank you for *Ego* 7. But, if in one sense only, I am a confirmed Egoist, and therefore

Photo John Vickers

Laurence Olivier in "Œdipus Rex"

had already snapped up a copy at Prince's Bookshop. I have sent it to Meum Stewart.

I thoroughly agree with myself—that we are not quite good enough for *Ego*. Crabb Robinson had all the luck. Goethe really was a considerable mind. Hazlitt we agree about. And then there was Coleridge who presumably was NOT a bore; Keats, Shelley, Byron, and Wordsworth, the old prig, and delightful Lamb. What you could have made of them. . . . Still, although you are not nearly selective enough, *Ego* is, I believe, more readable than Bennett's companionable Journals. I suspect you would be wise to let humour run in and out like an April breeze in a copse, and not to search for it quite so diligently. Nevertheless, I have not ceased telling myself that the ants have no navy.

Gemel is extremely clever—so far as I have read in it: but it doesn't progress, and you made the ruinous error of buttonholing your reader. Surely you realise that the object of a novelist or story-teller is to draw the listener into the story? But you cannot do this if you make your book in some degree a dialogue—no, monologue—between Author and Reader. It is as though the actors in a play were every now and then to say, like Bully Bottom, "I'm not really a ferocious lion. Just imagine me with my feet on the mantelpiece," and so on. You destroy your own spell.

Going back to Dryden, do you know his exquisite lyric "When Alexis lay pressed . . ."? I would have put it in my anthology with pride, only it would not "do" for schools.

Thank you for the books and for the spirit which sped them hither.

Yours ever,

CLIFFORD BAX

I have replied:

MY DEAR C. B.,

It is possible that the characters in *Ego* with the exception of Charles Burgess are small Fry. But one must do as one can, as Dr Johnson remarked.

I accept your criticism about the too-diligent search for comic relief and have crossed out yesterday's entry about the October gale doing its strip-trees act.

Ever,

J. A.

Oct. 30 *Tuesday.* From my little Irish friend:

18 *Park View Avenue*
Harold's Cross
Dublin
27. 10. 1945

DEAR JAMES,

Many, many thanks for *Ego* 7, in which I am engrossed. You really can't realise what a pleasure it is to be able to have at least one of your books in my possession. Of the twenty-seven books of yours which I have read, *Ego* 7 is the first I have owned. The book seems to me a great deal less vulgar than *Ego's* 1 to 5 (I haven't read 6).

Page 15. I believe *Ego* will become, after some preliminary ups-and-downs, a classic. A few years after your death, people will cease to read *Ego*. Then, after a century or so, some clever young man will "discover" you. Whereupon, people will read the *Ego's*, and then write books about them. Then, essays will be written about your "circle," and enquiries will be made. . . .

Pages 160–162. I'm very interested in what you say about Oscar's plays. I myself can only bear *The Importance* and *Salome*. The others creak, and are exceedingly dull. Recently in this God-forsaken city Mr Edwards produced *An Ideal Husband*. As soon as I heard it was to be done I started a campaign against it. I besieged Mr Edwards (who, by the way, has grown tired of me; the novelty of being told your business by a child wears off) with complaints. But it was produced, I was bored to death, and everything was a great success. Not that I object to artificiality. I adore Congreve and Sheridan. But two hundred years have not yet tarnished the gold of the characters of *The Way of the World* and *The School for Scandal*. Fifty years have sadly chipped the gilt-paint of Oscar's creations.

Page 280. George Moore. Once, when I was more priggish than I am now, I thought G. M. an odious character. Careful reading and re-reading of *Ave*, *Salve*, and *Vale* taught me how wrong I was. He had, I think, a singularly fresh and unspoiled mind. I, a schoolboy, take myself very seriously. I take my views on sex, religion, and politics, all very seriously. George Moore was another schoolboy who did much the same. A proof of his eager, schoolboy-eager mind is the perfect gravity with which he related his expedition with Æ on bicycles, in search of the ancient Irish gods. He was always credulous and always absurd in a manner startlingly like mine. The "sinning" of G. M. can be taken just as seriously as the "sinning" of a schoolboy. Susan Mitchell, in her very good book on George, wrote, "Mr Moore is no Rabelais, his Irish nature forbids it." And again, "Perhaps the Latins can sin gracefully, the Irish cannot." Which hits the nail on the head. G. M. was a very great literary craftsman, but he never grew out of his callowness.

In case you're interested, Dublin is getting crazier and crazier, vulgarer and vulgarer. If things continue as they are, Dublin will become the stronghold of Philistinism. The latest UNFORGIVABLE eccentricity has been to present *A Midsummer Night's Dream* in Persian settings and costumes. Everybody (except Sybil Thorndike's son, Christopher Casson, who played Oberon) seemed to have his mouth full of half-masticated buns.

I beg and implore you for a picture of Leo! He himself promised me one "when I get back all the things I have given to various people to take care of."

My very best wishes, dear James,

J. E. Jordan

Nov. 1
Thursday.

Paul Howard, Leo's old friend, sends me by air-mail from Australia Leo's last letter to him. I cull:

We have a high opinion of 7, full of me as usual. He's busy with 8 now. No one ever plays Godowsky nowadays here. The pianists are always sniffy about the poor old darling, say he is too overladen and what not. Then you simply can't get a copy of any of his works either new or second-hand. I have toured London in vain. And most difficult to get in New York, I'm told. Why don't you have your copies photographed and distribute them, as Leopold used to do with his MSS.? My admiration is as great as ever, but I have nothing to feed it on except memory. And when we moved from Swiss Cottage the Symphonic Metamorphoses were lost in the transit. I hear an old gentleman in Shropshire possesses a copy of the Albeniz Tango-transcription and sits on it all day lest it gets stolen. The only copy in England, so they say. The British Museum has two pages of the Triakontameron, but it's still closed. Do ask your Governor-General whether he can't do something about it—I hear he plays the Sonata marvellously. You don't deserve this nice witty letter because yr last letter to me was a Stinker. But I'm nothing if not forgiving. You must be getting on, too, Paul. I'm turned seventy with twenty-five diseases but still do a seven-hour day seven days a week. And my piano-playing is still exquisite, and I am still the best Chopin player in Europe.

Looking through Cerfberr and Christophe to-night, I came across something which is pretty close to Leo. It occurs in the article on Schmucke (*Le Cousin Pons*):

Allemand catholique, homme d'un grand sens musical, naïf, distrait, bon, candide, simple de mœurs, doux et probe de caractère.

Add wit, and there would be the essential Leo.

Nov. 2
Friday.

From Vivien Leigh:

As from 4 *Christchurch St.*
Chelsea
October 30*th*, '45

My dear James Agate,

I am absolutely delighted to have your *Ego* 7. Whether you thought of me in my enforced purdah or whether you had quite forgotten that—for me—unhappy circumstance, it was extremely kind of you to think of it and I know it will cheer and entertain me exceedingly. Thank you so very much.

I have only glimpsed so far, but one of my glimpses tells me you are to abandon the Glohwurms. *Please* don't, they have become a greatly looked forward to family and I don't think we can do without them.

I wanted to write to you when I read the news of Leo Pavia's death but Jock said "Don't," so I didn't, but I do now send you my sincere sympathy along with my good wishes and hopes that we shall meet in the spring, when I hope to be allowed to work again.

Yours ever,

VIVIEN LEIGH

To which I replied:

Queen Alexandra Mansions, W.C.2
November 1st, 1945

MY DEAR VIVIEN LEIGH,

Thank you very much for your letter. Hurry up and get well or people will think Larry thrives in your absence. *He is becoming a great actor*, and I was preparing to say so when Saint-Denis upset me with his speech-making.

Alas, poor Katzengebiss, Gänsebrust, and Glohwurm. Leo Pavia was their father; I was only their godfather. No, there can't be any more. They are perfect and imperishable, and I shall leave them in their perfection and imperishability.

Roll on, spring! If winter comes can Vivien be far behind?

Ever,

JAMES AGATE

Nov. 11 *Sunday.* The *Illustrated London News* has a photograph of the recent gale, with a wave dashing against a breakwater forming a magnificent picture of Ralph Richardson as I see him in the rôle of Lear. Cut this out, mounted it and sent it to Ralph, and received a charming reply.

Nov. 12 *Monday.* Letter from the Isle of Wight:

Sometime ago, my husband read an article, written by you which said that whilst reading a book called *The Turn of the Screw* by Henry James, it was so thrilling that you had to stop reading it for a while, even though you were sitting on the Leas at Folkestone and surrounded by hundreds of people. This intrigued my husband, who has since tried to obtain a copy, but has never succeeded. Would you please tell me who the publishers are, or better still, where I could get a copy?

The reply:

Queen Alexandra Mansions, W.C.2
November 12, 1945

DEAR MADAM,

Your letter being opened, Mr Agate's eyeballs turned back to front, he frothed slightly at the mouth, and fell into a fit from which, I regret to inform you, he has not yet recovered.

Yours faithfully,

JOHN BOOTH-PALMER
Secretary

Photo "Illustrated London News"

Ralph Richardson as Lear

Later : My employer showing signs of consciousness, and his lips moving, I bent down and caught the words, "Out of print."

Later still : I am glad to say that Mr Agate's consciousness is now restored. His first words on coming round were, "Damn the woman! I'd forgotten all about the book, and now she's brought it up again."

J. B.-P.

Nov. 13 *Tuesday.* Attended the memorial service for Henry Ainley at St Martin-in-the-Fields.

About H. A.'s personal "tragedy" I have nothing to say. And can have nothing. "I am myself indifferent honest." Nor can *Ego* be concerned with his private virtues. His humility. His fortitude. His will to continue the struggle. His gentleness. His kindness. His readiness to help others. God rest him! But in so far as *Ego* is and has been concerned with the theatre, to say nothing might be deemed a slight. Very well, then. I blame Nature for having given this near-great actor too much and not enough. For having lavished on him a combination and a form which automatically brought up Hamlet's description of his father, to which was added a voice like a cathedral organ. For having drawn back her hand and given a man physically endowed to play tragedy the instincts of the comedian. H. A. was almost the worst Hamlet, and quite the worst Macbeth I have ever seen. I dealt faithfully with both these performances at the time; the curious will find the notices in *Brief Chronicles.* About Ainley the comedian I did not see enough to make up my mind. I never saw the play called *Quinney's.* In *The Great Adventure* he seemed to me to be admirable in the first act but too big for the rest of the play. Of his Strickland in *The Moon and Sixpence* I find that I wrote: "Let it be said that Mr Ainley always acted up to the height of his author's intentions, and sometimes soared a good deal beyond them." And again of his performance in *Iris*: "The essence of Maldonado is repellence, of Mr Ainley, attraction." Of his Hassan:

> Mr Ainley did, perhaps, less than was possible with Hassan, and he was bound by his part to remain, let us say, in the middle distance. And I think his ghazal, beginning "How splendid in the morning glows the lily," was too full-throated. The lines did not hang in the air as they should. The thing is a cadenza to be caressed, and Mr Ainley proclaimed it something after the manner of battalion orders.

I missed, alas, his Benedick. Of his Prince Fazil I wrote: "Mr Ainley eludes absurdity with skill." In *The Anatomist* the play let the actor down:

> Mr Ainley prepared the way magnificently for a truly terrible picture of the a-moral scientist in action, only to find that there was no battle to be fought.

These are all of the actor's performances that I remember except two. He returned to the stage in St John Ervine's *The First Mrs Fraser*, and I wrote:

> Mr Henry Ainley received a tremendous ovation on his return after his long and serious illness. I should have welcomed him if he had appeared as Caliban, in which rôle he would, I venture to think, have been happier than in the part of the Scotch financier. For there are the beginnings of nobility in Caliban, and Mr Ainley has always been the embodiment of that commodity. His mien is still, and must ever be, noble, and his gait majestic. His voice continues to be that which an American writer has described as "the Bells of Bredon voice." On this actor the paltriest morning-coat takes on the aspect of a wedding garment. In plain English Mr Ainley is more the antique Roman than the modern Scotch man of business. Of course he acted well, but it was only in the way in which kings travelling incognito may be said to act well. Mr Ainley is cut on the grand scale and suggests less of the little scale than anybody living. I can only offer him this consolation for a failure in verisimilitude: that though Henry Irving was a great actor he could not have played pawnbroker, linen-draper, or milkman. Majesty is majesty, and there's an end on't.

The last play in which I saw him was Bridie's *Tobias and the Angel*. I wrote:

> Mr Ainley acts superbly throughout. His assumption of common humanity is very well done, and he is not afraid of diminishing his Angel by the use of irony and even fun. He looks magnificent whether in rags, golden mail, or ultimate white. When in the last scene he stands pedestalled and remote from the reunited family he seems more than life-size, in the way in which Michael Angelo could create a figure more than Man and less than God.

Ainley's tragedy as actor consisted in this, that his tragic figures were less than tragic size. "The greatest artist is he who is greatest in the highest reaches of his art." Only in the lower reaches did Ainley achieve anything that could be called greatness.

Nov. 14 *Wednesday.* Letter from Vernon Rendall:

43 Black Lion Lane
*Hammersmith, London, W.*6
November 13*th*, 1945

Dear Agate,

I was very glad to see in the *Sunday Times* last Sunday your decided view about this modern-dress mania applied to tragedy of the past. It simply won't do. It does not modernise; it only emphasises the gulf when players are " masked in our modern small-souled garb." The phrase is Heine's, and he has, to my thinking, hit on the real trouble. When I went years ago to two of King Edward's Garden Parties, the Orientals in their gowns were more effective to view than all the expensive fantasies of feminine fashion.

I did not see Andromache in evening dress when I was at the Lyric. She was ill, and the other woman who took her part was more reasonably attired. But I noticed her small boy in flannels as a blot on the scene. The translator, who happened to be next to me, agreed that a purple robe would have been much more suitable for a son of Hector and grandson of King Priam. As for the wrestling act which precipitates him into the arms of a soldier, it is pure farce. And Helen, pleading for her life, talks like a flippant fish-wife. However, the fine and hard-worked Hecuba makes the play worth while.

These moderns, it seems, must guy or debunk somehow any tragedy of classic repute. I don't so much object to soldiers in a bright uniform strange to us, but the Herald should have been differentiated from them—at least by a special head-dress. In the Greek drama he is a real sacrosanct swell, under the special protection of Hermes, and even Kings are shy of interfering with him when he takes to violent action. I could not see *Œdipus*. He was guilty of killing a Herald, a shocking crime, and this being so, I don't see how any scholar can regard him as innocent from the Greek point of view. As Sophocles has arranged the story, the Herald could not be the one man to escape, as he would have proclaimed the affray abroad as an outrageous wholesale murder of a sacred mission to Delphi. Euripides in his account avoids the herald-killing, which must have struck the Athenian audience as beyond any possible justification. Perhaps this flaw in the plot of Sophocles kept his play out of the first prize. Who on earth told you that the style of Sophocles was bald ? I should like to examine the gentleman's bumps. I have read thousands of books in five languages, and to my mind Sophocles has the most accomplished style the world has seen. I ought to know, as I have been studying him steadily for fifty years, and was taught by one of the great authorities on him. He can use common words and adapt common phrases with magical effect. So could Shakespeare, but he had a way of not keeping it up for more than ten lines or so. So could

Virgil with his " Sunt lacrimæ rerum," but his rhetorical variations grow tedious now and then. In the second Æneid there are four different words for Troy and the Trojans in little over a line.

I must apologise for writing so much.

Yours sincerely,

V. Rendall

My old friend makes one mistake. I have never said that Sophocles' style was bald. Having no Greek, how could I ?

Nov. 16 *Friday.* I had a great fright to-day. Having treated myself to Szigeti's recording of the Mendelssohn Violin Concerto, I sat down after lunch with coffee and a cigar and had it played to me on my E.M.G. gramophone. The first three sides were admirable. Lovely tone; Szigeti, the L.P.O., and Beecham all in great form. Settling down to the Andante, I heard the most appalling, unaccompanied rubbish. " You've changed the record ! " I shouted. " No, I haven't," said the houseboy. " Start it again ! " I said. The same vile muck. And I thought that at last " it " had come, " it " being the madness that my occasional brain-storms make me aware and afraid of. I thought of Johnson's fears. Of Lear's prayers. Of that poem in which Dowson, I think it is, claims that the insane are to be envied. I remembered that the other day, as I was sitting in the cinema, the screen faded out and all my old nightmares enacted themselves all over again. Alcohol, my doctor had said succinctly. Then I thought of Maupassant coming home one night to see himself sitting in his own arm-chair. Could there be aural as well as visual hallucination ? Why not ? Why shouldn't I be mad ? Haven't I worked hard enough to expect madness ? I had been drinking rather less than usual lately. But then my unexpected conjuring feats had been turning up more often ; yesterday a collar-stud thrown on to the piano-lid stood on its head. On Monday I had dreamed of an actor for the first time in my life, and on Tuesday morning that actor was the first person I met. Yes, I was certainly mad. And then I realised that I must take hold of myself. And did. Began by examining the record, and found on the fourth side Paganini's—it would be that devil—Caprice No. 9, *La Chasse*, with the concerto resuming on the *fifth* side, after which it remained uninterrupted. Since it runs to seven sides why didn't the makers put the Paganini stuff at the end ? Better still. Why not leave the side blank ?

Nov. 18 *Sunday.* Scott Goddard, deputising for Ernest Newman, who is on holiday, writes at length about Michael Tippett's " Symphony 1945." The audience, he says, were cool. But at the beginning of the article he incautiously lets out that he heard two rehearsals, an "illuminating lecture" by the composer, and the performance before he "felt the flesh growing over the bones." Suppose that before I could enjoy a play I had to attend two rehearsals and listen to a chat by Mr Shakespeare or Mr Ibsen ! In the next column Eric Newton says of Epstein's "Lucifer" that "for all its emotional tensity, *it isn't quite the right shape.*" Italics mine. Why didn't Scott Goddard say of Tippett's symphony that for all its emotional tensity it doesn't make quite the right sort of sound ?

Nov. 20 *Tuesday.* Letter to the Editor of the *Daily Express* :

SIR,

Here is a list, for which I vouch, of my attempts to communicate with you by telephone this morning :

11.00 Get "Telegrams."
11.02 "Telegrams" again.
11.04 Still "Telegrams."
11.06 Cleaners at a night-club.
11.08 Butt into private conversation.
11.10 P.C. continued.
11.12 "Toll."
11.14 "Telegrams."
11.16 Dialling tone, but no answer from anybody.
11.18 'Phone goes dead.
11.20 "Telegrams."
11.22 Another private conversation.
11.24 Dialling tone, but no answer from Operator, Engineers, "Trunks," "Toll," or "Tim."
11.26 "Telegrams."
11.28 "Engaged" signal before completion of dialling.
11.30 Ear-splitting noise.

Having wasted exactly thirty minutes I then send my houseboy out to some near-by telephone boxes to ask you to telephone me. Three are out of order, but he is lucky with the fourth.

11.35 You ring me up.

This has been going on for weeks. I manage somehow to contact the engineers twice a day. I hope they are well. I enquire after their families. Our relations are of the friendliest. Once a smooth-spoken young gentleman came round, fiddled about, and assured me that my telephone was in perfect order. "Better," he said, "than many others in the neighbourhood."

May I suggest that the Government would do well to stop concocting plans for an ideal world in the future and set about some for making what world we have work now ?

Yours, etc.,
JAMES AGATE

At a party in Chelsea a few nights ago the guests played a new form of the old game of Consequences, each writing down what seemed to him or her the most idiotic line that could get itself printed in a magazine devoted to modern verse. The host was so much impressed with the imbecile sequence that he made a fair copy and sent it as a serious contribution to our highest-browed Bloomsbury editor. In due course he received a letter which talked of " unusual promise," and would the young poet care to submit something of greater length ?

Nov. 21 *Wednesday.* Stevenson has something in " A Gossip on Romance " which I think is extremely apt to the cinema :

> There is a vast deal in life and letters both which is not immoral, but simply non-moral ; which either does not regard the human will at all, or deals with it in obvious and healthy relations ; where the interest turns, not upon what a man shall choose to do, but on how he manages to do it ; not on the passionate slips and hesitations of the conscience, but on the problems of the body and of the practical intelligence, in clean, open-air adventure, the shock of arms or the diplomacy of life. With such material as this it is impossible to build a play, for the serious theatre exists solely on moral grounds, and is a standing proof of the dissemination of the human conscience. But it is possible to build, upon this ground, the most joyous of verses, and the most lively, beautiful, and buoyant tales.

To which I would add films. Can it be doubted that if R. L. S. had written for the screen his pictures would have dealt with ships and shipwrecks, bullyings and mutinies, skulls, cross-bones, and the ends of planks and ropes ? Or that his dialogue would have teemed with allusions to long-boats and jolly-boats ? I feel that he would have wanted all films to be boys' films. Certainly, *Captain Kidd*, at the London Pavilion last night, is a first-rate boys' film, full of the hurly-burly of the pirate seas in the days of William and Mary. Laughton is grand throughout, with a good deal of sly humour. (Why doesn't Hollywood go to the nearest bookshop—are there bookshops in Hollywood ?—dig up a copy of *Jonathan Wild* by that good scenario writer, Fielding, and present our Charles as that Truly Great Man ?) There was nothing for fourteen-year-olds in Noel Coward's *Brief Encounter*, at the New Gallery this morning. The story concerns a married woman who has the misfortune to fall in love with a married doctor. " What happens to Laura and Alec might so easily happen to you or me," says Synopsis. But what I want in the cinema is something that can't possibly happen to me.

Synopsis goes on to remark that this "makes screen entertainment which is unusually arresting and full of drama and suspense." I wonder! Alec persuades Laura to meet him in a flat borrowed from a friend, and then—I am still quoting Synopsis—"the unexpected return of the friend prevents anything worse than a humiliating flight for Laura." Worse? *Worse?* But surely this postulates the world of what a man or woman should choose to do. The world of passionate slips and the hesitating conscience. The world in which some things are moral and others immoral. It was for and by this world that Stevenson held the theatre to exist. I believe that if R. L. S. had been present at the New Gallery to-day he would have protested that what he was seeing was theatre rather than film, and psychological novel rather than theatre.

Nov. 22 *Thursday.* Emrys Jones, reviewing *Ego* 7, writes:

> Mr Agate gives the impression that he is always coming from Somewhere and going Somewhere. . . . Of the private Mr Agate we know little from these journals. One feels that when he gets down to writing about himself he is very much reviewing the public character that he is. Such reticence, admirable in most parts, is not the stuff of which great diaries are made.

But of course I'm always going to and from places when I can get the transport. Yesterday, for example, I had a luncheon that I couldn't get out of, a matinée that finished at five o'clock, and a play that started at half-past six. In addition, I should have attended an amusing publisher's cocktail party had it not been that in that hour-and-a-half I had to get to and from Grape Street and review five books for the *Express*. After the evening show, and out of sheer courtesy, I looked in at a stage party to celebrate the thousandth night of something or other. What time does this Mr Jones think that I have left for a private life? And what does he want to know about how I spend the private hours that are left? Am I to tell him that at midnight I covet my neighbour's ox, at 1 A.M. his ass, at 2 A.M. his wife, and from then till breakfast-time his sisters and his cousins and his aunts? Hamlet could accuse himself of such things that it were better his mother had not borne him. But he did not tell Ophelia what those things were, and I doubt very much whether he confided them to his "tables." What is good enough for Hamlet is good enough for me.

My letter to the *D.E. re* the telephone service appeared yesterday morning. From which moment my 'phone has been dead.

Nov. 23 *Friday.* I am always delighted when anybody sends me an old book. To-day arrives *The Gentleman's Magazine* for the year 1768. Enchanting articles on The Identity of King Charles's Executioner, Arguments against the Inoculation of Children in early Infancy, A New Improvement in Fire Engines. A review of an Essay on the Future Life of Brute Creatures contains this :

> All who have hitherto attempted to reconcile moral and natural evil with a first cause infinite in power, wisdom, and goodness, have been driven into absurdities that might well warn others, like a beacon, and prevent their shipwreck.

Good eighteenth-century Unitarianism ! The number for March has a poem entitled " On hearing the Rev. Mr Dodd Preach." (Presumably one of those sermons " addressed to the passions.") This begins :

> Heard but the libertine thy pulpit lore
> Pathetic Dodd ! the wretch would sin no more ;
> No more with vice his ebbing life disgrace,
> With riot mark, or infamy debase !

And ends :

> Go on, judicious Pastor, awe the bold,
> Still, still improve the Young, reclaim the Old,
> With pleasing energy thy Saviour preach
> And virtue animate, and candour teach,
> Still make fair chastity thy darling theme,
> While Magdalens support and prize its fame ;
> Then nor till late, may Heaven reward thy care,
> And make thee angel in a brighter sphere.

Underneath is written in ink : " Since Hang'd."

Lastly, this item from the Historical Chronicle for February :

> A most horrid murder was committed at Wotton-Underidge, in Gloucestershire, by one Wallington, a shearman, who, about ten in the morning left his work, and in a cruel manner murdered his own father. It has since appeared that the murderer was out of his mind : for upon examination he said he had seen a vision, and that the devil had commanded him to do the murder exactly at ten o'clock ; and it was observed that he went out several times to look at the clock, and that he kept his time precisely. He then went to a neighbour and with seeming satisfaction told him *he had done it* ; and being asked what, his answer was, *he had killed his father.*

Nov. 25 *Sunday.* It was to be expected that the musical critics would make a field-day of Purcell's bi-and-a-half centenary. I think Martin Raymond in to-day's *Observer* provides the best fun. At the Wigmore Hall jamboree

> the two chief figures among the performers, Benjamin Britten and Michael Tippet, did not merely perform music : they were evidently

> out to put a case: the case for the rediscovery of a great composer of the highest importance for present-day music, still grievously crushed under "the bulwarks of music in 19th-century England."

There is, it seems, in Purcell's music,

> a kind of unsentimental, impersonal objectivity, a determination, while stating all kinds of emotion in precise and sometimes extreme terms, never to be overwhelmed by any of them, a modesty of statement which, after the emotional excesses of Tschaikowsky or the late Viennese, satisfies a deep need to-day.

And then what Stalky would have called the Martiniferous Raymond begins to have his doubts.

> It seems somehow impossible to build up a night's programme of Purcell's works that is not jumbled or monotonous or both. . . . The stuff doesn't add up. It never allows the mysterious and complicated atmosphere of concentrated festivity which is the secret of a concert to arise.

(Then why throw stones at Tschaikowsky and Strauss who have this "concentrated festivity" at their finger-ends?) The article concludes:

> The simple truth seems to me that Purcell cannot be fully revived so long as our musical culture remains, in the main, bound up with concert-giving and concert-going. Of course, if the great cities should disappear, and the concert-halls and the concert audiences with them, and music should again become a mainly home-made affair, a matter of families and circles of friends singing and playing together for their own enjoyment—then, I think, Purcell's day will come again. But not till then.

Which gives me the following little musical scene:

SETTING: *A drawing-room in Glossop.*

FIRST MUSIC-LOVER. Rather a pity about that bomb destroying Manchester, don't you think? Not the city, of course, but the Hallé. They were in the middle of *Heldenleben.* I must say I think it's rather a shame.

SECOND MUSIC-LOVER. In some ways, yes. What about trying out a new Purcell I've discovered? Sonata for dulcimer and stromento di porco?

Jay Pomeroy invited me to his box at the Cambridge Theatre this afternoon. Myra Hess in Mozart's B flat Piano Concerto (K. 595). The shallowest water by which this melodious bird ever madrigalised. Then Tschaikowsky No. 5. Drenched with self-pity. But I like listening to it just as I like looking at a fuchsia drenched with rain.

Nov. 26 In a letter from Jock :
Monday.

I had a singular experience last week. I went to the National Gallery and heard an excellent String Quartet—the Zorian—play Beethoven in C minor (in the Op. 18 set) and Béla Bartók No. 4, said to be the toughest of the six. Wasn't that plucky of me ? The Beethoven begins divinely, continues agreeably, and concludes in a Haydnish, busybody way. But the Bartók, the Bartók ! It's no good saying you've never heard such noises, for *I have* heard such noises. It's evocative music all right. The opening *Allegro* took me straight back to childhood and gave me in turn the rusty windlass of a well, the interlinking noises of a goods train that is being shunted, then the belly-rumblings of a little boy acutely ill after a raid on an orchard, and finally the singular alarmed noise of poultry being worried to death by a Scotch terrier. The second movement, *Prestissimo con sordino*, gave me continuously and throughout its short length the noise of a November wind in telegraph-wires on a lonely country road. The third, *Non troppo lento*, began with a dog howling at midnight, proceeded to imitate the regurgitations of the less-refined or lower-middle-class type of water-closet cistern, modulating thence into the mass snoring and wheezing and body-sounding of a Naval dormitory around the dawn —and concluded inconsequently with the 'cello reproducing the screech of an ungreased wheelbarrow. The fourth movement, *Allegretto Pizzicato*, took me straight back to the noises I made myself, on wet days indoors, at the age of six, by stretching and plucking a piece of elastic. And the fifth, *Allegro molto*, reminded me immediately and persistently and vividly of something I have never thought of since the only time I heard it : the noise of a Zulu village in the Glasgow Exhibition in the year 1911 when I was six —a hubbub all the more singular because it had a background of skirling Highland bagpipes. *Both* noises emerged in this final movement of this Fourth Quartet of Béla Bartók.

These are not worked-up impressions invented to amuse you. I set them down on the back of my programme while listening to this music. There was a big audience, and an enthusiastic one. They all seemed to me to have the frozen, perfunctory smiles of the crowd that watched the Emperor walking through the streets in his wonderful New Clothes—just before the small child piped up : " But the Emperor has nothing on ! " The queer thing is that I have a conviction (all the stronger after hearing this amazing work) that the Emperor Béla *has* something on. And I'm furious at being unable to see quite what it is !

Nov. 27 To err is human, etc., etc. But what would Pope have
Tuesday. thought if he had known that the *Oxford Dictionary of Quotations* would give his dates as " 1786 ?–1872 " ! Perhaps that interrogation mark was never happier ! In view of this

I shall not lose much sleep over a Scotch lady's rebuke that Jock should not have written, and I should not have printed, ' stravaging ' when, actually, the Scots word is ' stravaiging.'

Nov. 28 *Wednesday.* Lectured to the Royal Society of Arts. Title: " A Moment in the History of the Theatre." Went off all right, I think. C. B. Cochran in the chair. House full, but nobody from the commercial managements though they all had special invitations sent them.

Nov. 29 *Thursday.* In a letter from a lady:

I saw Henry Irving twice only. The first time was in *The Bells* at Swansea. The only picture remaining in my memory of that performance is that of Irving taking off his gaiters. Before the play began, the crowd of people in the gallery, mostly young Welsh men, whiled away the waiting time by singing. Irving sent out a message from his dressing-room to say that he was sorry he could not hear well enough from that distance to appreciate the music fully, but he would be honoured if the audience in the gallery would remain after the performance and sing again for him. They did. Irving came before the curtain and listened for twenty minutes to the harmonies of *Aberystwyth*, *Cwm Rhondda*, and *Dafydd y gareg wen.* You know them. Irving then spoke his thanks and said that the evening would always live in the storehouse of his memory. " I wish you all a very good night." That was Irving, the man. The second time I saw him was not long before his death. I was walking along the sea-front at Minehead, when I became conscious that the people ahead were parting to stand at the sides of the pavement. Strolling along between them, bowing slightly to right and left, came Irving. It was a royal procession of one. That was Irving, the actor.

Nov. 30 *Friday.* Telephone put right and letter of thanks despatched.

Dec. 8 *Saturday.* In Kipling's poem about the old three-volume novel occurs the line:

We never talked obstetrics when the Little Stranger came.

But Kipling is demoded, as all Bloomsbury knows; there isn't a pair of unwashed, uncombed, long-haired corduroy trousers pretending to be a poet that hasn't complete contempt for the author of *The Seven Seas.* To-day when we sit down to write verse we are midwives to a man. I open *Voices on the Green*, a collection of New Writing about Childhood, and discover that modern genius talks obstetrics *before* the Little Stranger comes.

> "You dream," he said, "because of the child
> Asleep in the nest of your entrails. . . ."

And I think of a line from *David Copperfield*:

> "Ba-a-ah!" said my aunt, with a perfect shake on the contemptuous interjection. And corked herself, as before.

Dec. 11 *Tuesday.* Took Jock to the Press view of *Cæsar and Cleopatra.* So bored that I didn't know where to look! Cæsar like an elderly Peter Pan, and Cleopatra just out of Roedean. Apollodorus the apple of every shopgirl's eye, and so on. Poor use of the camera which prompted Jock to whisper, "This is the first time I've thought of Alexandria as a rose-red city half as old as Denham." Lunched with Donald Wolfit, after which I came back to the flat, and read in Winifred Graham's autobiography how Father Ignatius, who had preached about Marie Corelli's *Sorrows of Satan* at the Portman Rooms, took for his theme the authoress's "*The Vision at the Savoy*, a story of Christ passing through the fashionable supper crowd in that well-known hotel off the Strand." How the preacher had patted her and said, "Go on, my dear child, like this." Shall ask *Express* readers whether Ignatius could have been loyaller.

Dec. 14 *Friday.* Sibelius is reported to have said on his eightieth birthday last week, "If you want to discuss art you must talk to men of business. Artists only discuss money." This is something the public refuses to understand. I started my day's work at 9 A.M., corrected the proof of my first *Tatler* article on the *Cæsar and Cleopatra* film, and having done this set about a second article on the same theme, the *Tatler* requiring a double dose in view of Christmas. Titivated to-morrow's *Express* article and revised Sunday's stuff, by which time it was 9 P.M. Grabbed a bit of food and took ten minutes to climb five flights of stairs somewhere in Covent Garden to keep a long-standing, flat-warming engagement. Had just enough breath left to say I like plenty of soda when some earnest ass wanted to know what I thought of the Shaw film. Put into use my special technique, which means that when total strangers come up to me and say, "Do you mind my talking to you?" I reply, "Not at all, so long as you don't mention any play, film, book, or piece of music." "But that's what I want to talk about," said a young man two evenings ago. I asked him to excuse me, saying that I had been working since breakfast-time and that I made it a rule not to take part in any intelligent conversation after ten o'clock. He said,

" I am deeply sorry for you." I said, " You impertinent young hound. Go and be sorry in some other part of the Café ! " Thus is a reputation for rudeness thrust upon one ! I gently explained to to-night's bore that I had spent the day trying to do justice to a great writer, that I couldn't put ten hours' work into a sentence, and that I was too tired to try. He said, " Sorry ! I ought to have known you would have had enough of the pictures. Very tactless of me ! What do you think about a National Theatre on the other side of the river ? "

Dec. 16 *Sunday.* Writing in 1908 about a little book which somebody had put together about Sarah Bernhardt, Montague had this noble thing:

Like many of us the author saw the paragon in her prime, and as long as any two such persons live and can communicate, the world retains some sort of corporate sense of the nature of her greatness: after that, her death, now unfinished, will become complete—as complete as that of a Dürer might be if the paper had mouldered away under the last of all the surviving impressions and reproductions of his prints and nothing remained but the stuff written about them in books.

And now Maurice Baring has gone, Maurice who wrote about Sarah better than Montague, or Symons, or anybody.

When I have seen the parts that Sarah Bernhardt made her own performed by lesser artists I have wondered what has happened to the play. If it was classical, *Phèdre*, for instance, one wondered where all the glory that was Greece, and all the grandeur that was Versailles, and all the music that was Racine had gone to: one longed in vain for those haunting, thirsty eyes that sent an electric current through the whole theatre, for that voice that made you think the words were being spoken for the first time; for those gestures which were too swift to analyse, for that harmony and rhythm in utterance, movement, speech and silence, crescendo and diminuendo, speed and pause and delay, that combined to produce and build something as concrete as a beautiful frieze or statue, as logical and ordered and disciplined as a great fugue, and as intangible as the gleam of sunshine on a wave or the reflection of a rainbow in the clouds.

The date of this, as far as I can gather, is 1923. Twenty years later the writer, an old man verging on seventy, semi-paralysed, was painfully, at the expense of many hours of labour, putting on to paper in his own hand letters from his retreat in Scotland to a dramatic critic whom he hardly knew. Letters about their common recollection of performances fifty years ago. Montague is dead. And now too is Maurice Baring. I must believe that a little more of that " strange russet leaf " which was Sarah Bernhardt has died with him.

Dec. 18 *Tuesday.* Speech delivered at the Gaumont-British Annual Press Luncheon, J. Arthur Rank in the chair :

Mr Chairman, Ladies and Gentlemen :

There is a scene in Pinero's *Sweet Lavender* in which Mr Bulger, a hairdresser, is about to blunder into a married lady's bedroom. Deterred, he says, " I dare say I could have passed it off with a pleasantry." I dare say I could pass off to-day's occasion with a French quotation and a joke or two. Rightly or wrongly I feel that something more serious is called for, and my defence for taking up this attitude is based on a longer professional interest in film criticism than anybody in this room. The article on Charlie Chaplin entitled *Hey, but He's Doleful!* published in the *Saturday Review* in 1921 with the sanction and encouragement of Filson Young, and being one of my earliest contributions to that paper, was the first criticism of the film as a serious art and the film actor as a serious artist to appear in the Press of this country. That fact establishes my *bona fides* to-day.

Critics are always being told that their criticism should be constructive. Very well, then. I have been graciously accorded six minutes, and I intend to employ those minutes constructively. Whatever may be feasible in the domain of Lewis Carroll, in the world as we know it constructiveness is possible only *before* an event. To say of a cathedral that it is hideous, and to say no more, is destructive criticism ; constructive criticism will say, " That cathedral's damned ugly. Pull it down, build it differently, and in this different way." But why not run up the building in the mind's eye, as it were ? Why not visualise the deed before the attempt ? Lady Macbeth is very sound on this subject. "Things without all remedy should be without regard." " What's done cannot be undone." This applies not only to cathedrals but to cinemas, and to the films exhibited in cinemas.

Mr Rank has just spent an enormous amount of time and money and enterprise and courage. With what result ? One critic is bored. Another critic would hate to sit through *Cæsar and Cleopatra* again. A third talks of " a cold triumph." A fourth holds the picture to be " hollow at heart." I can well believe that Mr Rank is dismayed and hurt by this. (Let me tell him that he will be much more dismayed and hurt to-morrow when the *Tatler* appears and some whey-faced fellow tells him of an article which he wanted, but was not allowed, to call *Cheops and Tomato Sauce.*) If Mr Rank is disappointed in the critics it can only be because they have failed to give him that help which he feels should be the reward of time, money, enterprise, courage. But, I repeat, help, constructive help, can be given only before the event. There is nothing to be done now about this film. But how about *St Joan* ?

Let me use my mind's eye to pierce the future and say now what will inevitably be held later about any film made from this great play. Théodore de Banville, practising as a dramatic critic nearly a century ago, laid it down that "the eye grows swiftly weary of all stationary spectacle, however spectacular, and demands motion." From which one could almost think that he foresaw the cinema, where the shots change every forty seconds. Now might not Théodore, were he living to-day, have gone on to ask how an essentially peripatetic medium can hope to interpret an essentially static play? Maurice Baring, whose death we all deplore, asked "whether it was a greater thing for a poet to have soared high into the heavens of passion, or to have dived deep into the grey seas of reason. 'Into those seas,' he said, 'Victor Hugo never dived, and into those heavens Goethe never soared.'" Taking my cue from Baring, I say that into the ocean of knees-under-the-table, hammer-and-tongs, Shavian argle-bargle Mr Pascal dives something constrainedly, while into the swift-moving firmament of the cinema's archangel Gabriel Mr Shaw never soars at all.

Not once in *St Joan* does this master-playwright "let himself go" cinematically speaking. He refuses to show us the coronation, obviously any film director's *bonne bouche*. He refuses to give us the defence of Compiègne and that unsuccessful sortie in which the Maid was taken prisoner, surely another cinematic tit-bit. He insists upon talk, magnificent talk, but still talk. Words, words, words. He proceeds from the argument in the English tent to the pow-wow in the ambulatory of the cathedral, and thence to the trial scene. For the better part of two hours nobody crosses the stage, and hardly his legs. In his preface Shaw says, "To see Joan in her proper perspective you must understand Christendom and the Catholic Church, the Holy Roman Empire and the Feudal System, as they existed and were understood in the Middle Ages." In what perspective, then, does the screen propose to show us this great figure? As a girl dressed in men's clothes and so rude that the soldiers take her for one of themselves? As a young woman in blue armour adorned with silver stars, brandishing a gold sword, and prancing about on a white charger? Shall we be given a coronation scene with specially built organ and specially trained choristers? A pitched battle between the Maid and the Duke of Burgundy? And a slap-up bonfire at the end? Since Joan talks like blazes, blazes are her appropriate end. But in the play the blazes happen off-stage. To build a picture on what Shaw deliberately left out may be a film director's idea of fun, but it will not be Shaw's play, whereas to re-create the talk word by word and syllable by syllable to the exclusion of everything extraneous may be Shaw but will not be the film public's idea of fun. The essence of cinema is to cut the cackle and come to the 'osses. Shaw in *St Joan* deliberately cuts the 'osses and sticks to the cackle.

One word more. If any picture I, as a film magnate, am to make must be a Shaw picture I should choose *Androcles and the Lion*, in which Rome could flaunt her decadence *ad lib.*, and the sound recorders be given a free hand with the clash of chariots, the groans of gladiators, the plaints of martyrs, the impatient snarls of wild beasts. On the other hand, if I were not bound to Shaw I should go to some great English novel, say Thackeray's *Esmond*, where the author's intention is not impeded but swept on by the duels, the great battles, the crowd and court scenes, the press of famous men, the onrush and array of history. I should consider Kingsley's *Westward Ho!*, or Reade's *The Cloister and the Hearth*. On one of these I should spend my million, and if I had a few pounds left over I should take a *little* studio and make a *little* picture out of Shaw's masterpiece.

Lastly, I should give a luncheon to the Press and say, "Ladies and Gentlemen. Such and such are my plans. Tell me what is wrong before I start to work on them. Tell me now." I have ventured to tell Mr Rank what must, even with genius at the helm, be wrong about *St Joan*. I hope he does not make this picture. I hope that, if he does, it will gross twenty million pounds. For that will be his only reward.

Dec. 20 Thursday. Lying in bed at 4 A.M. and reading *Little Dorrit* to cheat myself of feeling ill, I came across this :

> Bar said, there was a certain point of mental strain beyond which no man could go; that the point varied with various textures of brain and peculiarities of constitution, as he had had occasion to notice in several of his learned brothers; but the point of endurance passed by a line's breadth, depression and dyspepsia ensued. Not to intrude on the sacred mysteries of medicine, he took it, now (with the Jury droop and persuasive eye-glass), that this was Merdle's case?

Was this, I wondered, J. A.'s case? Bicarbonate of soda, hot water, and half a teaspoonful of sal volatile answered Yes.

Christmas Day. Jolly luncheon party at Louis Sterling's. A lieutenant in the R.N.V.R. told me that when he was in command of a patrol yacht on the Thames he had as mate a surrealist painter whose masterpieces fascinated the engineer, a pure Cockney. "Blimey," the latter said, "I'll have a go." And proceeded to depict a pint pot, giving it half a face with one eye situated in the chin and a couple of cogwheels for ears. And proudly submitted it for criticism. "Y-e-s," said the surrealist, putting his head on one side. "It has *balance*, of course!"

In the evening to supper with Gwen Chenhalls, the only other guest being Anthony Asquith, who, knowing he was going to meet me, brought and gave me a volume of Morley's *Miscellanies*, inscribed to Margot Asquith by the author. After which we had a hammer-and-tongs argument about the ultra-moderns. Surrealists and Atonalists. Since Puffin doesn't read Dylan Thomas and I won't listen to Bartók the fight was along Tweedledum and Tweedledee lines. For me the whole matter is summed up in Malcolm Sargent's story of how he stopped a rehearsal and asked the composer whether he meant B or B flat. And received the answer, "I knew when I wrote it, but I don't now. Play which you like!"

Boxing Day. Worked in the morning and took Ralph Baker to lunch, after which I relaxed. Smoked Louis Sterling's Christmas cigar, drank some of Lady Hardwicke's bottle of whiskey, read Morley on Machiavelli, noting how Margot had underlined the noblest passages, and turned loose among my gramophone records Joseph Azzopardi, a young Gibraltar evacuee and friend of my houseboy in bed with toothache. Nobody rang up, and the whole a perfect afternoon except that towards the end the gramophone decided to play everything presto and couldn't be dissuaded.

Dec. 27 *Thursday.* Wrestle for half an hour with an article by Rayner Heppenstall in the new highbrow miscellany, *Orion*, on that super-boshite Georges Bernanos, to whom, I understand, infant Bloomsbury turns as soon as it has got through *Reading without Tears.* I cull:

> The night a new priest arrives in the village, a man is murdered. The new priest, sensitive, pale and mysteriously ill, turns out in the end to be a girl. The murdered man was the expected priest. The girl commits suicide after a confession. Lesbian practices lay at the root of her disorder. In other words, she had broken a very serious *tabu*. The priest paid the price of her guilt and unhappiness. After masquerading as a priest and thus taking his function to herself, she also must die. That is the plot of *Un Crime.*

Give it up and, deciding that I like my eroticism neat, without bogus psychological trimmings, turn to the Marquis's *Juliette,* which some kind soul has sent me as a New Year's gift.

> Le calme rétabli, les deux cadavres furent jetés dans un trou à dessein préparé au fond d'un petit jardin attenant au cabinet où cette scène venait de se passer, et l'on se rhabilla.

I would give all the Bernanos bunk for those three words "Le calme rétabli."

Dec. 29 *Saturday.* Attended the *M.G.* dinner to James Bone, retiring after forty-odd years on the staff and as a director. The greatest London editor the paper has ever had. Highly distinguished gathering of sixty, and lots of people present whom one had thought dead long ago, all of them spryer than me! The speakers, without exception, read their bits. I had prepared and got by heart an elevated composition modelled on Hazlitt's Farewell to Mrs Siddons: "The stateliest ornament of the public mind . . . a voice to open the chambers of the human heart . . . a trumpet to awaken the sleeping and the dead." Vastly fine! But I am very small beer at the *M.G.* nowadays and was not called on. Or at least not until some fourteen or fifteen other speakers had had their say—after which the Chairman looked at his watch and said, "Well, I think that's all, unless Mr Agate would care to say a few words." Now I hope I know when is the time for oratory and when not. So I jettisoned my speech and said a few words out of hand.

Dec. 31 *Monday.* From Chesterton's *Criticisms and Appreciations of the Works of Charles Dickens*:

> All this was what Dickens stood for; that the very people who are most irritating in small business circumstances are often the people who are most delightful in long stretches of experiences of life. It is just the man who is maddening when he is ordering a cutlet or arranging an appointment who is probably the man in whose company it is worth while to journey steadily towards the grave.

Why did I not think of this when Leo was alive?

INDEX OF PERSONS